Gordon Sinclair

A LIFE ... AND THEN SOME

Gordon Sinclair

A LIFE ... AND THEN SOME

SCOTT YOUNG

BALLANTINE BOOKS
TORONTO

ISBN 0-345-35958-5

This edition published by arrangement with Macmillan of Canada.

COVER PHOTOGRAPH: courtesy of Pat Morse
COVER DESIGN: Brant Cowie / ArtPlus Limited

Printed in Canada
First Ballantine Books Edition: October 1988

ACKNOWLEDGEMENTS

For purposes of researching Gordon Sinclair's time on earth and his sometimes devastating effect on those who shared his life from near or far, I had a few head starts. I was a reporter, just turned twenty-three, at the *Toronto Star* in 1941 when he was being treated more like a faded beauty than a shining star: remembered for his past triumphs but given no chance to add to them by being sent to help cover the war. I knew him and many of his closest colleagues in newspapers, radio, and television from then on.

Still, there was an immediate hitch. I thought, like many others, that Gordon Sinclair's life was an open book. It wasn't. He had a surprising private side to his life, and it is in this respect that I must be most grateful for the help given me. The key was turned very early. I was interviewing a woman who said, "There are some things I'd like to tell you but I really should check with the family first." She called Sinclair's son Gord in Montreal and asked how frank she should be. Gord Sinclair, to his eternal credit, answered: "If you are going to err, err on the side of truth." Blessed be the biographer who hears that line and becomes its beneficiary, as I was, from those closest to him both inside and outside the family.

My list of people to thank, if I gave it in full, would be something over fifty. Instead, I hope they will bear with me if I approach them in groups, except to thank Shirley Wilson for transcribing taped interviews, Joan Taylor for library research, Millie Moriak and Pat Morse for knowing where some of the bodies were buried, Linda Larsen as the

Star's liaison, and Patricia Kennedy for her creative comments in the manuscript's margins. Carol Lindsay, chief of the *Star*'s closely guarded library, gave me all the viewing and copying facilities I required. The management and staff, present and past, of CFRB gave me interview time, boxes of archival material, and use of an office for as long as I needed it. Everyone I spoke to at *Front Page Challenge*, stars and staff, present and past, was generous in sharing with me the suspense which they, like the show's audiences, always felt while awaiting, as one put it, "what the old son of a bitch was going to say next."

If there are errors, they are mine.

Scott Young
Cavan, Ont.
July 1987

CONTENTS

HOW DID HE GET THAT WAY?

"Everything was a pain or a joy to Mother."
—Gordon Sinclair in 1966, explaining his main childhood influence.

Gordon Sinclair was generally considered to be the most loved, hated, coarse, stubborn, unafraid, and irreverent Canadian of his time. He earned this reputation not all at once, but by a lifetime of calculated outrageousness and gradually increasing confidence in his ability to get away with it. His bag of tricks included a strong sense of the ridiculous in matters of common religious beliefs, and he treated sex, at least when he was not personally involved, mainly as a vehicle for comedy.

He was a short and stocky man, five feet six and about 160 pounds, with nothing in his physical presence to make heads turn. But he arranged to make them turn anyway, even to gape, by the garish outfits he wore, or, during one period, by the Rolls-Royce he drove. His walk was the strut of a bantam rooster. He was a true Canadian celebrity.

But it is equally true that, celebrity being no bulwark against mortality, a short time before Gordon Sinclair died in May of 1984 a few weeks prior to his eighty-fourth birthday, he was home in bed, sick and depressed. He had been there for almost three weeks. His absences from radio station CFRB had become more frequent as his long life went on and were always a cause for concern in the station's management. One reason was that in his periods of depression, his gloom often fuelled by a good deal of Scotch, he was apt to sink into the conviction that his career was over and that he should quit and leave the station bereft of its most dependable meal ticket. When executives from the station called, or when he made such an assurance-seeking call himself, he would inquire plaintively, "Who wants to listen to an old man?" Then, sometimes in tears, "Are you sure you still want me around?"

Foolish question. For many years the sharp upward swings in the station's listenership at certain hours, sometimes to almost fifty per cent of the potential audience in 'RB's large metropolitan listening area, precisely matched the times of Sinclair's regular shows. It was accepted by friend and foe alike that, without Sinclair, CFRB would have difficulty maintaining its position as the strongest station in the nation's richest radio market. So when he was absent for more than a few days, word would go around CFRB that something had to done. Someone should cajole, flatter, reinforce—whatever it took to persuade him to get up-and-at-'em again.

Betty Kennedy did the job best. She had been his colleague at CFRB for twenty-five years, and for the last twenty-four of those had been the attractive female presence on the panel of *Front Page Challenge*, the weekly television show that had made Sinclair a national figure. More than that, Betty and Gordon liked one another. She thought he was kind beneath that rambunctious exterior. He spared her the raw jokes he served up to some women, and though he rarely used endearments for anyone, including his wife, he sometimes called her "darlin'." When he had been away from work for a few days she would sometimes drop in to see him on her way home, bringing flowers, a small gift, supportive talk. They were an interesting combination: the shrewdly combative but often depressed old, and old-looking, curmudgeon and the coolly self-possessed woman who thought, and looked, younger than her years. So, in April 1984, Sinclair missing, management anxious,

Betty Kennedy once again became the emissary.

The Sinclair home on Burnhamthorpe Park Boulevard didn't stand out from its neighbours. Despite minor architectural differences, these homes all represent an era and a sense of affluent, middle-class values. It was the second home that Gordon and his wife, Gladys, had owned. Their first had been a small and drafty place on nearby Burnhamthorpe Road, built on the cheap with borrowed money. But in the early 1930s, when Sinclair's first bestselling book, *Footloose in India*, had produced several thousand dollars in U.S. royalties that he hadn't been expecting, he shook the cheque in the face of a friend and said, "This is my new house."

They built at the edge of a fairway on the Islington Golf and Country Club, and when Betty Kennedy parked her car near by on that evening in April 1984, they had been in it a few months short of fifty years. In that time the house had not been changed a great deal. Inside was a lot of dark wood. Behind the leaded windows it was comfortably roomy, rather than spacious. Many houses basically like it, built at about the same time, are found in affluent Toronto districts such as the Kingsway and Moore Park and Forest Hill. Gordon and Gladys had brought up their children there in an often acrimonious marriage and eventually, their offspring gone to their own careers, had grown old along with the house.

When the children were young, Gladys had had live-in housekeepers, but by the 1980s the only regular daily help was Gladys Chamberlain, who was from Jamaica and had been with the Sinclairs for many years. She usually was referred to by Gordon as "Black Gladys" to distinguish her from his wife, who by then was in her eighties, sometimes forgetful, her eyesight severely damaged by cataracts. She also was hampered by obesity and the effects of two broken hips, and could move around only with the help of a device called a walker.

"When I went to the door, Black Gladys opened it," Betty Kennedy recalled. "When I said I'd come to see Gordon, she said, 'He's not seeing anybody, he's in his bedroom and he doesn't want to see anybody.' But the other Gladys was behind her. Many people thought she was not really very with it by then, and sometimes she wasn't, but sometimes it was because she couldn't see. Maybe this time she heard my voice. Anyway, she came to the door in her walker and said, 'Who is it?' "

"I said, 'Gladys, it's Betty Kennedy, how are you? I just came to see Gordon, I'm concerned about him.' And she said, 'You go upstairs, he'll want to see you.' "

Betty walked through past the two Gladyses. She knew the house well. The archway to the dining-room was at her left, to her right the open door to a downstairs washroom and Gordon's study with its neat files, bookshelves, and old typewriter. She walked upstairs alone, knowing the way, and stopped in the doorway to his bedroom. The window drapes were drawn. Although it was still daylight outside, the room was dark.

She could dimly see him in bed and spoke from the doorway. "Gordon, I won't stay long, I know you're not feeling well."

"Come and sit down," he welcomed her.

Betty sat beside him near the head of the bed and asked how he was feeling. He sighed, half a groan. "I don't know what's the matter with me, Betty. I was going to go to work this morning, dammit! I only got as far as the bathroom. I started to shave and my legs started to shake, just wouldn't hold me. I had to come back to bed. What do you think's the matter?"

Betty was a little surprised at being asked for her medical opinion. She said she had no idea but she hoped it was going to pass and he'd be all right. They talked further about how he felt. Then he said, "Well, you know, I'm going to be eighty-four in a few weeks and maybe that's it."

"Oh, come on, Gordon, that's not like you," Betty admonished. "That just doesn't sound like you at all." But she also wondered herself if he really was near the end.

A few days later, after being off from April 5 to April 24, he did go back to work. He worked his usual broadcasts for three more weeks. Then, on May 15, 1984, he took a driving test, required annually because of his age. He passed in fine shape and broadcast on his long-running five-minute *Let's Be Personal* program an upbeat piece about the test, the courtesy of the inspectors, and how even civil servants can be pretty good if you give them a chance. He was back to business as usual, as far as anyone could see. Betty Kennedy dropped into his office after his 11:50 a.m. newscast that day to say, "Do you remember that we've got two shows to do tomorrow?" They were scheduled for two *Front Page Challenge* tapings.

He looked up from his desk. "No, I didn't. Okay, darlin', fine," he said. "I'll see you there." Betty left thinking that he was very chipper that day, his old best self.

Within a few hours he had his last-ever moment of consciousness.

Throughout his life he had spent hundreds of hours of air time infuriating the righteous with his scoffing at all religions, from Christianity up, down, and sideways. He would ridicule those people who believed in a personal God and implored Him to save the Queen, heal their boils, sink their putts, or give the nod to their side in a war against fellow-religionists of some other nationality who no doubt were sending up their own earnest petitions to God at the same time. Sinclair also liked to declaim that if there was such a Being as God, He should be utterly ashamed of Himself. "Folks, just think of all the cruel and heartless things He's done, or allowed to happen—if He's so all-powerful. Then tell me why you throw good money into the collection plate and go to church and sing hymns!"

That was the line, with infinite variations. He also said from time to time that if there did turn out to be a life after death, he would be the most surprised guy in heaven, or hell, wherever he happened to wind up.

There is no certain way to describe anyone's childhood except in terms of how the child seemed to others and how

5

he seemed to himself, placing both opinions against the time, place, and circumstances of his being young. The aim of all this is to attempt some kind of judgment on the permanent influences of the early years, or clear tendencies that obviously could be related to what kind of a man the subject turned out to be—in short, the extent to which the child was father of the man.

For instance, as a child, did he feel that a day without shocking somebody, preferably a churchman or a woman, was a day without sunshine? Not that is on the record anywhere.

Was he obsessed with money? Only to the extent that any child whose parents have to scrape and save may develop a feeling that it is easier on the nerves to have money.

When a boy, did he favour outlandish clothes of the sort that once led a stranger at CFRB to inquire, "Who's the guy who's dressed like a Number Seventeen pizza?" or in other ways do what he could to make himself noticeable? No evidence, Your Worship.

Did he scoff at religion and the very idea of a God up there somewhere pulling levers and pushing buttons to make everything work? On the contrary, he was brought up as a devout Methodist, each Sunday attending church twice and Sunday school once, teaching Sunday school and a Bible class until he was in his early twenties, going to midweek prayer meetings, and in summer often to be found frequenting the tents of barnstorming evangelists—becoming, by his own account, converted more times than he can remember.

Because Gordon outlived his childhood contemporaries, he becomes for purposes of biography the principal witness, and not a very trustworthy one when he was engaged, as he often was, in creating myths about himself. As an example, his own account of his birth, given from time to time in speeches or broadcasts, usually started out something like, "The wolves were howling across the road on the night when I was born. . . ."

Or, as it appears in his book *Will the Real Gordon Sinclair*

Please Stand Up (McClelland and Stewart, Toronto, 1966), "In the manner of a town-crier describing the visit of a banshee or monster, Mother often told me that when I was born and she was lying on a bed of indescribable pain, the wolves howled."

If he had happened to stop there, it would have created the impression that he'd been born at a blizzardy outpost somewhere in the Canadian wilderness. Some of his readers and listeners still believe that to this day. Chances are that he omitted, or they missed, his usual next few sentences in which he typically explained that he was born in his grandfather's rented house near Toronto's Riverdale Zoo. The wolves were howling because it was their feeding-time.

At the time of Gordon's birth in 1900 his parents, Alexander (Sandy) Sinclair, a furniture finisher, and Bessie Eesley Sinclair, who worked at various jobs including picking biscuits out of the oven at Christie's Bread, were living with Bessie's father, Albert Robert Eesley. Sandy was a quiet man, Bessie a woman of hair-trigger judgments and a notoriously sharp tongue, habits which on the evidence she seemed to have passed on intact to her first-born. Possibly some financial setback made them dependent, which could have been what Gordon referred to when, recalling his childhood, he wrote without further explanation, "Mother was never tossed into the street after I was born, but it had happened before my birth."

Whatever the circumstances of that old eviction, buying a house became Bessie's obsession. According to Gordon, it took six years, two years before his birth and four after, and "all Mother's doing", for his parents to get together the down payment on the home they eventually bought. Their scraping and saving during that early time, and precarious finances thereafter, no doubt laid the foundation for Gordon's own obsession with money.

Gordon acknowledged later that some of what he'd always believed were his own memories—mainly things that happened while the Sinclairs were still in the Eesley house on Carlton—might be items of family folklore repeated so often that a small boy could convince himself he had been an eyewitness. One such gray-area event, exciting on any level of authenticity and one that would be welcomed by the beneficiary even today, happened when he was parked in a go-cart outside a butcher shop on Parliament Street just south of Carlton.

This was probably in 1902 or 1903. While Bessie was scouting the piles of unrefrigerated meat on big white platters in the shop, a friendly spaniel trotting along the sidewalk jumped up and licked Gordon's face. This caused the dog to lose his grip on a damp piece of paper he had in his mouth. When it fell, Gordon, in the very first wise financial move of his life, seized it—a ten-dollar bill!

Immediately passersby swarmed around. "There was much talking, partly congratulation, partly wonder about who had lost the bill, what should be done now, and where do you suppose this came from?" Bessie, charging out and pushing her way through to find out what the fuss was about, didn't wait for a recorded vote. She took the money, grabbed the go-cart, and pushed Gordon off at high speed for home, exercising "that classic strategy known as getting the hell out of here." Ten dollars was a week's pay for many a workingman of the time.

Gordon was certain he remembered that incident first-hand. But he couldn't unequivocally account for being so young that he had to travel by go-cart, yet old enough to remember every detail so clearly.

All the same he had other memories that by actual dates happened before he was four years old. He didn't think that all of them could have been in the category of family yarns repeated so often that he'd made them his own. He remembered seeing rats in the house where he was born, and his mother's complaints about them, and remembered a bitterly cold day when his mother pushed him in his go-cart far west in the city nearly to High Park, sometimes sheltering in doorways, to collect a few dollars from a building-and-loan association that was in shaky condition financially, meaning that her savings might not be there if she delayed even one day.

He also had a vivid memory of his Grandfather Eesley's body being brought home one Saturday night.

The story that he "was fed as a boy" went something like this: Grandpa Eesley, coming from his work as a millwright on a Saturday with his week's pay in his pocket, had stopped with some fellow-workers at a tavern on Yonge Street. After a few rounds of drinks he stumbled and fell on the floor, whereupon with much laughter and kidding by his drinking friends he was pulled to his feet and helped outside for a little fresh air.

Outside the tavern (where years later the Northgate Hotel and still later the Ports of Call did business in drinks and food) was a big water-trough for the horses that filled the streets then, before the age of the automobile. Grandpa Eesley's companions proceeded to duck his head in the horse trough, but in their drunken enthusiasm for the task of bringing their pal around they drowned him.

For many years Gordon fully believed that version, told it and retold it. You might imagine the way he would deliver this amazing tale by radio—"Just think, folks, a man drowns in a horse trough right on Yonge Street! How about that? And it's true! My own grandfather! Would I kid you about how my own grandfather died? You could look it up!"

As it happened, Gordon eventually looked it up himself. Many years later, when as a reporter he had access to records in the coroner's office, he decided to check how his grandfather's death had been described in officialese. He found out. It was true that Albert Eesley had fallen in the pub; eyewitnesses said so. It was also true that he had been ducked in the horse trough in an attempt to bring him around; eyewitnesses agreed on that, too. But according to the official story he still hadn't regained his senses, so was taken back inside to a rear room where he died, the record said, of a heart attack, a coronary. The coroner's report said so, right there in black and white.

Still, it was rather uncharacteristic of Gordon that he

never publicly questioned that official account. Think of the tale that he could have spun on his *Let's Be Personal* program many years later on CFRB: a rerun of the good old drowning-in-a-horse-trough yarn, always a favourite, and then his reading of the official version, delivered with rising intonation until he's got you with . . .

> So this story that our whole family believed from that first night, when sad, crying people brought Grandpa Eesley's body home and told us about it, the story that our family believed for thirty years, is now said to be wrong! But is it wrong? You know and I know, and it shows up in the papers every week or so, sometimes the official cause of death given on those papers is not what really happened, or so people will claim. I've been a reporter all my life, folks, and I'd say from my experience that there's at least a fifty-fifty chance that the first story, the one we heard that night, might well have been correct, but had been glossed over so that a drunken escapade wouldn't wind up with charges of murder or manslaughter. Covered up! And maybe in a good cause, who knows?

The little family lived at the Eesley house until, "in the mud of early spring" of 1904, with Gordon not quite four years old, Bessie twenty-nine, and Sandy in his early thirties, they moved into their own home at 9 Howland Street just north of Gerrard Street and east of the Don Jail.

Later in life Gordon described the district as "a new area of small houses". Either his later affluence changed his perspective or he was anxious to protect his reputation for humble beginnings, because the house wasn't especially small by today's standards.

It was semi-detached, sharing a wall with one neighbour, and had three storeys. In common with all but upper-class homes of the time, 9 Howland had no electricity, using gas for cooking and lighting and a coal furnace for heating—but it did have six rooms. That was more than enough to make room for a boarder or two to help with the $1,800 mortgage that was left after Sandy and Bessie had paid down their hard-won six years of savings, $400, against the $2,200 purchase price.

A little more than a year after the move, in September of 1905, Gordon's brother Murray was born. It was to be nearly eleven years before Gordon's youngest brother, George, was born on Valentine's Day in 1916.

One boarder was remembered by Gordon as a catalyst of sorts in sending Bessie into one of her monumental snits about the evils of drink. This boarder, a "stately white-haired widow", had travelled a good deal, including a visit to Rome. Once she spoke a few words of Italian to a pushcart peddler named Pete who frequented the street. Delighted, Pete brought the widow a bottle of his home-made wine. Bessie, one of those so-called temperance workers of the time who were about as temperate as a typhoon, flew into a rage. Despite Pete's hand-wringing apologies, Bessie slapped a ban on ever dealing with Pete again, and made it stick.

Gordon's father, Sandy, didn't share Bessie's views on a lot of things, including the evils of drink. He never debated drink with her, wouldn't dare, but other differences led to frequent loud declamations by Bessie and long and respectful silences by Sandy.

Bessie, wrote Gordon once, "didn't like to think things over. If she got a notion in her head she wanted to say it instantly, get it out." Gordon's critics, and even his friends, were to see this as obviously a trait Gordon shared all his life.

Sandy was the opposite. "On the face of it he was a very mild man and the weak person of the two of them," said their son George in a 1986 interview, "but that was a misleading first impression. He was a lot more thoughtful than Bessie and had a pretty good mind." Neither was he totally dominated by his explosive wife. When Sandy felt the need, he'd slip in the side door of a saloon at Broadview and Queen—well away from their own neighbourhood, where someone might tell Bessie—and pass his flask, accompanied by twenty-five cents, across the counter. That amount would buy several ounces. At home he would have to sneak to the cellar for the odd snort because he simply didn't want to risk the kind of encounter with Bessie that she always won by sheer lung-power. Gordon didn't remember making a judgment at the time, but he later wrote, "It did seem a dreadful thing that a man could not honestly indulge his own taste in his own house but had to sneak into the cellar." Along with his money obsession and inheriting his mother's cutting tongue, there might have been a reaction to that part of his childhood in Gordon's own life. As a husband and father he drank at home when and in whatever quantity he wished.

As far back as he could remember, he was always small for his age, trying to stay out of fights on that account, but he was inquisitive, curious, and exceptionally observant of what went on around him. He would stand in Elias Medd's grocery store at the corner of Howland and Gerrard, waiting to be served, and unconsciously absorb the sight and smell of the place so thoroughly that seventy years later he could make a radio listener feel right there beside the cocky little boy. The aroma from the coffee-grinder, as Mr. Medd cranked it by hand, blended with all the other smells—of loose tea in lead-lined boxes, bacon, honey, cheese, soap. In spare moments Mr. Medd weighed out into plain paper bags pounds and half-pounds of such staples as sugar, flour, soap chips, tea, rice, or white beans. This was the only pre-packaging common at the time, and it helped speed things up when the regular customers came in. Even at that age, he had a writer's eye.

As people with sharp eyes and fond memories do, Gordon seemed to remember everything. Recreating these times and places in anecdotes years later, he was to bring his boyhood Toronto vividly to life: his chats with friendly prisoners from the Don Jail who were cutting grass and cleaning up Riverdale park; his impression that when the paddy-wagon unloaded a clutch of prostitutes they all seemed jolly and cheerful; his reports of the crows cawing in the nearby wilderness of the Don Valley at the first hint of spring; his reactions to the horrors of sulphur and molasses, commonly fed to small boys as a spring tonic.

The many small streams that then flowed through Toronto into the Don River or Lake Ontario were filled every spring with the coarse, bone-filled fish called suckers. At the height of the sucker run street-hawkers would sell them three for a nickel. Quiet Sandy Sinclair would sometimes take his two small sons, Gordon at seven or eight and Murray a mere toddler, to where they could scoop up suckers with their bare hands. When they had a burlap bag filled, they would take it home. Gordon was later to meet many people to whom the suckers were a staple food, for when they were cleaned and put down in barrels full of heavy brine, the bones would disintegrate, making the whole fish edible as a base for chowder and other meat substitutes. But in his childhood, "poor as we were, Mother would never try to cook them," called them "slave food . . . not meant for humans."

The earliest recorded case of Gordon Sinclair stubbornly resisting what he believed was misguided authority occurred during his first year at school. When that great day in spring came, the first one warm enough that he could shed his shoes and go in his bare feet, he didn't realize that the school authorities might not approve. The first day he arrived at school in bare feet, a kindly teacher sent him home for his shoes. He obeyed. The next day, when he appeared bare-footed again, another teacher, a stern and grim redhead named Miss Wynn, sent him to the principal, who also sent him home. On the third day, once more implacably bare-footed, he was sent home and told to bring his mother back with him.

When they duly presented themselves, the principal told Bessie that Gordon was not really a bad boy but did have an excess of animal spirits "and might one day grow up to earn $5,000 a year, because animal spirits were good, especially in boys." In the meantime he would still have to wear shoes.

Years later, when Gordon was forty-five, he happened to meet Miss Wynn again—the redhead he had thought was very stern and grim—to discover "to my amazement that she seemed much my own age. I could even have fallen for her. She must have been a very young teacher."

One summer pastime was swimming in the Don River, which was clean then "and fairly fast, with pleasant groves of willows on some of the banks and golden sands at the bends. . . . Nobody had a bathing suit. But we were modest. When a train would go by . . . we would either kneel in the water or cover ourselves with our hands. . . .

"Once a group of girls about our own age or even younger came swimming as we were, in the raw. This caused a measure of interest but not really a stir, until their parents came to take them away. Then there was a lot of face-slapping and abuse and the girls were told that they should be ashamed of themselves. But nobody told the girls *why* they should be ashamed of themselves." Although Gordon in his later years had an aptitude for embarrassing both women he met and the people in his radio and television audience with crude remarks about females, at this time he was obviously simply observing.

In summer there were Wild West shows. Once when Gordon had a job carrying water to a show's horses, he saw the real Buffalo Bill, "and was let down to find him enormously fat, and apparently drunk all the time." The repertoires of travelling tent shows which came every year usually included the famous slave-time story called *Uncle Tom's Cabin*, which he found scary because of the bloodhounds and the villainous Simon Legree. When evangelists came to town preaching "the fieriest of all hells and the most tranquil of all heavens", the aim of all such foes of the devil was a good count of converts. Gordon usually played along—"The evangelists had one of their most frequent converts in me. Being converted never seemed to do me any real harm."

But it's apparent in reading Gordon's recollections of childhood that the most important and lasting impact on his life was his mother, Bessie. When he first began his autobiographical *Will the Real Gordon Sinclair Please Stand Up*, the working title was *Life with Bessie*, and the book's focus was on intimate family matters. His brother Murray, by then a first-rate newspaperman and editor whose asthma had caused him to move from the *Toronto Star* to Arizona to work nearly twenty years earlier, was allowed to read it. He had always been opposed to Gordon's using family recollections, even in brief broadcast reminiscences, and he raised hell. That must be the only explanation why, when it was published, that book's first chapter was focussed mainly on Aimee Semple McPherson, the shapeliest evangelist of her time. His account of life with Bessie is held off until his second chapter, which begins:

> Bessie Eesley . . . influenced my life more than anyone else. Her influence covered a span of 61 years and three months—my age when Ma died. . . .
> She had sparse chestnut-colored hair which grew scarcer as she burned it with hand-curlers heated over a naked gas burner or coal fire. She had an abundance of spirit, a capacity to exaggerate almost everything, and [at the time Gordon first remembers] . . . her fingers were burned from packing Christie's soda biscuits, hot from the ovens, and usually without gloves, for $3.50 a week. . . . Mother was of Scotch-English blood but American born, "a bundle of red, raw nerves," as she put it. . . . Everything was a pain or a joy to Mother. . . .
> I've often wondered how people could possibly consider the Scots a dour race when I think of my Mother. She and all her kinfolk were talkative, argumentative, easy to take offence or delight, opinionated and happy. Mother was a great one to laugh and sometimes to mimic people who refused to laugh. . . . She often laughed uproariously at her own barbs and gags, but they had to have a measure of wit, and a dirty joke had to be funny, not just dirty. In

retelling such yarns, Bessie always cleaned them up, and a woman's sexual area, in Mother's specialized language, was always her "Mary Ann," while that of a male was his "John Thomas," except in the case of small boys. Then it was the "wee Peter."

In part of one chapter about his mother, Gordon related a time when he found out about menstruation, the hard way.

One day . . . I found, in the cellar, what looked like a bucket of blood, and since Mother was nowhere to be found I felt sure she'd been murdered and buried under the coal pile or out in the yard.

It turned out, however, that this was merely the cotton bindings that she had used in the normal menstrual flow, this being long before there were any packaged aids to be picked up at the drugstore. Women had to make their own, to wash them and reuse them, and boys could be astonished and dismayed.

Gordon always thought it was sort of funny, later in life when he was taking a prurient interest in sex and female functioning, and also began investing, that one of the first stocks he bought was in a company making sanitary napkins—which paid, as he had expected, steady and excellent dividends.

One of his early influences led directly to the fact that Gordon always was sympathetic to the plight of working men and women. When the American Newspaper Guild tried to organize the *Star*, and later CFRB, Gordon signed up both times and wore his Guild button openly when some others either didn't join or were wary about admitting they had. This attitude stemmed originally from one of the bad times in the Sinclair family when his father had been working from seven each morning until five in the afternoon for Nordheimer's, a German company, polishing pianos for 50 cents an hour, or $25 a week.

Dad thought this was too low a rate. Not just for himself but for everybody. Dad had little schooling, no competence with sums or words, but he had a stubborn way of arguing. . . . He persisted in trying to get more money for all of the men. After a series of warnings that this sort of radical and ungrateful behavior would get him fired, he *was* fired.

Hard times hit quickly [there was no public welfare, unemployment insurance, or mother's allowance], and Mother, who could panic at the loss of a nickel in actual cash, set her young but toothless face [her teeth had all been extracted in some dentist's over-reaction to a much lesser dental problem] in a hard line and said we would lick these grasping foreigners.

So we had meagre meals and a cold house and hand-me-down clothes for a few months. Then the piano moguls let Dad know he could come back again. He was to get an actual piece of cash in hand— $20, I think—and a raise for himself, but he was to abandon all that talk about a general raise for everybody. Dad went back but his spirits were low and he was unusually quiet and depressed. He tried to organize a small committee aimed at a union, and there were meetings in our house. . . .

But that was the beginning of another end. Only one other man really supported Sandy Sinclair, a Jew named Morris who used to exclaim, "We lick them, Sandy! No man alive can beat the combination of Scotchman and Jew already! No man. Not ever."

But when word got around about the union meetings, Sandy Sinclair was not only fired again, but blacklisted. No other factory making pianos or refinishing furniture would hire him. This was the toughest time ever for the Sinclair family. Gordon's memories were of his father bouncing unsuccessfully from one job to another, including once selling second-hand furniture. Finally he was offered

17

steady work as a school janitor. But Bessie, finding that the job would include cleaning washrooms, flamed, "You'll work in no washroom till after we've starved to death, and not even then!"

Obviously those times left permanent scars on Gordon, in at least two respects. His father finally had to leave home and work at an Ohio mill for one of Bessie's brothers, managing to send home $10 a week. This kept soup on the table, but bills went unpaid and there was nothing left over. Then Gordon was troubled by something he remembered as being a constantly pounding heart; perhaps from a fever. The family doctor refused to see him because a previous bill, from an illness of Murray's, had not been paid. The doctor suggested Bessie take Gordon to the free outpatient clinic at the Hospital for Sick Children.

He was about nine years old at the time. They walked the two miles or so. It was winter and Bessie was wearing a fur coat, a present from one of her well-to-do brothers. At the hospital she was scolded by a clerk for coming in a fine fur coat to try to get charity medicine, and they were turned away. Bessie didn't try to explain that her husband was away and they had no money and this was the only coat she had. Gordon was not examined at the time, and he believed that the heart difficulties he had for life stemmed from that early untreated illness.

So the years from when he was eight until he was ten or so, including the only Christmas he ever had where there were no gifts, stamped him with certain prejudices forever: he always took the side of the workingman in a labour dispute, and he never spoke a good word for the Hospital for Sick Children—another event later in his life solidifying that bitterness.

But finally the young Sinclair family's hardest time came to a happy end. Gordon woke one morning to hear the unmistakable sound of a thaw: snow dripping from the roof. He ran down the hall to spread the great news, to find "there was a man in bed with my mother!" Then he realized that the man was his father. Murray ran in behind him and picked up Sandy's bowler hat and put it on, and "when we all broke into laughter Dad woke up, the picture of contentment."

CHAPTER TWO

GROWING UP

"For a boy who wanted to dally with a girl, there was always a handy location and usually one or several willing lassies."
—Sinclair, remembering his teen years.

If Gordon Sinclair were growing up today in exactly the same circumstances, with the same curiosity about life, the same energy, and the same schooling, he wouldn't have the slightest chance of landing a writing job on even a minor newspaper. "Look, son," the college-bred editor of paper after paper would say, perhaps even kindly (it would be hard not to feel sympathy for this skinny young man—fully grown, he was five feet six inches and weighed about 120 pounds—with his ridiculous Grade 8 education and an ambition to be a reporter), "I've got twenty applications here from people with journalism degrees. Have you tried circulation? Or maybe maintenance?"

Yet even as a child he was a story-teller. He would come home with lurid stories that provided the dinner-time entertainment in those days before radio or television. A barn had burned; he had blow-by-blow details of frantic horses, some escaping and others dying in the flames. They'd scoff and he'd insist and the next day it would be in the papers. He'd go happily with his father and Harry Passmore, a neighbour who was a newspaper reporter, to a fire or a hold-up, and at home he, not his father, would be the one telling the tale. A runaway team of horses crashed through a plate-glass window; he had the gory details of

20

how one, badly injured, had to be shot by a policeman. He held his audiences, even if it meant out-shouting Bessie and getting a clip on the ear for doing so.

If there were dull details, he left them out; almost as if, like the journalist he was to become, he knew that what interested people was the essence, not a clutter of facts that would lose his listeners.

The Sinclairs got their first family telephone when he was ten, their first electric lights a couple of years later when they moved to Bowden Street near the Danforth (and kept chickens in the back yard to supply the family's eggs). At the time he'd done a few typical small-boy jobs, the only connection with newspapers being that for a short time he delivered the *Sunday World*, but he didn't like the job so he quit. ("The old story about newsboy to star reporter was never part of my act," he remarked later.) His home influences didn't encourage any thought of newspaper work. Bessie tended to deride Harry Passmore's job as a reporter—always prying into other people's affairs, she called it. When Sandy did discuss with Gordon what he should do in life, his advice was to become an accountant, or at any rate never to work in a factory for hourly wages.

But the early signs of a gift for reporting were evident. When he was fourteen and still in public school, a few weeks before the first shots were fired in the First World War, he went by train and lake steamer to visit his mother's brothers and their families in Ohio and Indiana. Bessie thought enough of his vivid way of story-telling that she suggested he keep an account of his summer's experiences so he could tell the family all about them when he got home. That began a diary habit that persisted, although not all can be found now, for nearly seventy years.

That first year his diary showed a lively sense of what was going on around him. Among his American aunts were the first women in his experience who swore and drank whisky. He listened to heated arguments about the U.S. Civil War from men who had fought on both sides. He learned to drive an automobile—a Reo owned by an uncle. His diary

21

notes stayed away from any sense of traditional travelogue, but were enough to set him off on the stories when he got home.

Still, apparently nobody suggested this sort of thing as a career. If anyone had listened with fascination and opined that he had the makings of a writer, Sinclair would have made sure later in song and story that such prescience was recognized. Anyone who ever gave him a leg up got credit loud and clear.

When he returned that September he went back to school in Grade 8, where he usually stood first in a few subjects and sometimes first in all. There is some no doubt unintentional ambiguity in Gordon's later accounts of his next few years, including his few fleeting references to girls. Once he came home from school on a hot summer afternoon to find all the blinds drawn and the nubile fifteen-year-old daughter of a boarder stark naked in the Sinclair dining-room. His solution to this shocking situation was to walk, not so rapidly that he couldn't take a good look, past the open doorway and into the kitchen. This is one event he reported to no one in the family, but every afternoon as long as the heat wave lasted he steadfastly took the same route to the kitchen and she steadfastly wore no clothes, until Gordon's Grandmother Eesley happened along one day and raised hell.

No doubt this was a consciousness-raising exercise, but where it led in his awareness of females is not documented. Neither is the exact chronology of his working experience for the next few years. One summer he enlisted in what was called the Soldiers of the Soil (or sos) plan. Because so many young men were joining the armed forces, farm help was very scarce. Under sos, city boys too young to enlist were sent out to work for farmers who paid $22 a month, plus bed and meals. Gordon was probably in this work force in 1915, although once he wrote that first he had a job, then served with sos. He might have been referring to his part-time work on Saturdays helping delivery drivers from Simpson's department store, or helping a man with a fruit stall in the St. Lawrence Market.

His sos summer started with forty boys setting out from Toronto by train to be dropped off along the way at stations where their employers would be waiting. Gordon's destination was a 200-acre farm owned by Alexander Campbell in Peel County, not more than a couple of dozen miles from Toronto. When he got there the farmer "was visibly shaken by my runt size." Gordon was then a couple of inches short of his full adult height. After half a day of shovelling manure (he promptly had changed the sos initials to mean Shovelling of Shit), he was exhausted. On the face of it, Campbell wasn't getting what he'd bargained for. He had a car and he could have driven Gordon home and made a deal for a bigger boy.

Instead, for the next three months Campbell found lighter work for him—papering in the house, white-washing the barn—and "an increasing bond of affection" sprang up between them. Gordon ate heartily, put on weight and strength, and at the end Campbell paid him $75 instead of the $66 he had contracted for. Gordon had had his bicycle shipped up from Toronto during the summer. With the $75 in his pocket, he pedalled happily away down the dirt road. "By the time I got home, I was broke, having bought a suit, a gun-metal watch, and several gifts for Mother, who took this unexpected extravagance in stride and said she was glad to have me home."

That autumn of 1915 he went back to school, his first year of high school. Early in 1916 he had an experience that later in life he often used as a prime example of the almost incredible inhibitions of the time. He got home from school one evening "to discover a lot of fussing and bustling and strange people." Among those present was a former boarder, a Mrs. Knight, who took Gordon into a bedroom and showed him a new baby, his brother George.

Bessie was small enough that one would think her pregnancy would be easily apparent (and Gordon by then *did* know where babies came from), but "I had not even suspected his coming. No mention had been made . . . and Dad seemed sheepish and embarrassed," seeming to feel he had to explain "how surprised he was".

Gordon's stay in Grade 9 did not last until the end of the school year. In those days banks were permitted to send recruiters into the schools. When one of these made a pitch to Gordon—$25 a month and a free hot meal daily—he went home excited to talk it over with his parents. He never did say what his dad thought. Perhaps he had not been able to get the floor. But, "decision was instantaneous so far as Mother was concerned. 'Take the job. . . . You've already got more education than your Dad or any of his brothers.'" He took the job.

When he reported in the spring of 1916 for his first day at the main branch of the Bank of Nova Scotia on King Street West, across from the *Toronto Star*, which was to shape his future, he wore below his high stiff collar and carefully knotted tartan necktie the short pants that were common among boys of his age at the time. This caused a reprise of that week in childhood when he'd kept going to school in bare feet.

When he presented himself for work, he got a long look from his supervisor, and then was told that short pants were okay for today, but tomorrow he had to wear longs. He owned no longs, and for some reason he did not ask help from his parents with this serious problem which threatened his future as a financier. The next day he reported again in short pants. Sent home to put on long pants, he wandered the streets instead. The next morning once again he reported for work in short pants. The bank knew when it was licked. A friendly male clerk was detailed to take Gordon out and buy him some long pants. This was done, and paid for out of petty cash, but the saga wasn't over yet.

As skinny as Gordon was, the new pants were quite tight on him. What might be termed (in more ways than one) the outcome was pure Sinclair. Years later, many matters of sex or other natural functions were to be treated regularly on his broadcasts as being funnier than they were shocking, usually causing the CFRB switchboard to light up—but occasional outrageousness was definitely part of his appeal. Such stories as his tale about the fate of his first pair of long pants never did anything to hurt his listener ratings.

"One day when I was mailing out dividend cheques to shareholders, a bundle of them slid . . . to the floor. When I bent to pick them up, the seam in those bank-bought pants gave way, and my testicles popped out. I was busily picking up the cheques when one of the sombre ladies reminded me that I really should be feeling a draft."

He found the situation "more amusing than horrendous", but it had caused a stir that spread through the branch like wildfire. Apparently it was felt that, as some images spring to mind unbidden, as long as Gordon was in daily view the memory of that ripping sound and the amazing sight that followed would interfere with the smooth functioning of the branch. Accordingly, he was sent to a smaller branch a few blocks away at Queen and McCaul streets.

His work there provided the "most enjoyable work I ever did in the bank", partly because of some warm, kidding friendships with young women fellow-employees. Also, most of the customers were Jewish merchants or owners of small factories and he liked their good spirits and hustle. He was out among them every day delivering bank drafts. They sent presents home to his mother, invited him to their homes, and "kept telling me I should quit the bank—a smart boy like me working for wages!"

Another customer on his route was the University of Toronto. One day, crossing the campus, he dropped in to a building to see what the inside of a university classroom looked like, and stayed to listen to Professor James Mavor (the grandfather of Canadian-culture guru Mavor Moore). That day Professor Mavor was "telling the most fantastic stories about Peking, which he branded as the most beautiful city in all the earth." Gordon stayed to the end of the lecture and from then on attended Professor Mavor's lectures every time he could, estimating that he had heard forty in all. Sometimes he and the professor chatted after a lecture, but no one ever asked for his credentials. "Years later, during a winter-time month in Peking, I could see

Professor Mavor in every street and park and gateway." He thought that if he'd ever had a chance to sit for examination in the professor's courses, he would have stood at the head of the class.

His absences on those days might have contributed to his being fired a few months later, but the specific cause of his dismissal was that he threw a sopping-wet sponge at one of the tellers and hit the branch accountant instead. At any rate, his bank experience had launched him in the business world and helped him get several jobs later, the first being in the office of Eaton's department store, where he started early in 1917.

Official biographical information on publishers' questionnaires or in bibliographical guides always notes that Gordon was in the Canadian army from 1917 to 1919, serving only in Canada. He was actually a part-time soldier in a militia unit (a sort of Home Guard) of the 48th Highlanders, whose active components had been fighting in France since early in the war. The militiamen lived at home rather than in barracks and worked normal hours at their factory or office jobs or professions, but on certain nights of the week they would turn out in full uniform (Gordon's first kilt) for training.

Gordon sometimes kidded later about having a war wound, showing a scar on his leg. On one of his training nights he was clinging to the outside of one of the open streetcars of the time when a cavalryman running alongside swung himself aboard. As he did so, "his spur ripped across the bare knee below my kilt and blood spurted. It looked worse than it was," but after a rather funny debate on whether a militiaman should go to a military or a civilian hospital, he was taken to Toronto General to be patched up.

His experiences with girls at around this time of his life he later recalled with circumspection. Once he said on CFRB, "Stories that modern girls and boys are delinquents far coarser and more sexually flagrant than the delinquents of my day are simply not true in terms of my own experience. For a boy who wanted to dally with a girl, there was always a handy location and usually one or several willing lassies, but the idea didn't have the slightest interest for me. Sometimes word would get around that there was going to be a big girl party at a certain barn, usually on a Saturday afternoon. . . . I sometimes went to these affairs to watch and would be invited to take my turn, but the idea simply had no appeal. One girl I remembered was quite insistent and when I went away she called me names. . . ."

This disinclination to get sexually involved was not out of character. If his story may be taken at face value, his libido at the time was not overpowering. Also, his lively imagination of how Bessie would react if she heard about it must be taken into account, given the mores of strictly-brought-up young people of the times. The pulpits rang with the hell and damnation that attended unsanctified sex, but a much more powerful deterrent for a responsible young man was fear of getting a girl pregnant, having to face her family and his family, then to marry in haste and shame.

There were no birth-control pills. The word condom was rarely heard, "French safe" or simply "rubber" being the common usage. He knew what they were, and what they were for. For him and other young bucks, getting them was the hard part. They were always kept under the drugstore counter, and the trauma of facing the friendly neighbourhood druggist and stammering, "What I'd like is, uh . . . ", kept many a young man lingering in front of a drugstore rehearsing his approaches and then, often as not, deciding to treat his love to an ice-cream soda instead.

He was nearly nineteen, and "still a frightened male virgin", when he

> eventually did obey the normal calls of the body. It happened in Kew Beach Park [in Toronto's eastern Beaches area] and the girl of the case immediately raced off to pour out to her father her pent-up guilty feelings. He had her call me to make another date and

when I got to her house on a Sunday afternoon, the father beat me unconscious. He blackened both my eyes so that I could hardly see to ride my bicycle home. [On his way home he collided with an automobile whose female driver berated him.] . . . The girl called me many times after that. She sent me notes and pictures of herself, which I still have, and she knitted me a long cocoa-colored scarf at Christmas, but I never saw her again.

It seems obvious from his "I never saw her again" that this first sexual experience was not with the girl who seemed to be his "steady" all through 1919 and into 1920. Her name was Ann and she was a co-worker at Eaton's. In the earlier part of the year, before his defloration, they had seemed to be warm friends, but not lovers; going to many movies, generally getting along. But then, in his daily diaries, the mood changes. One might guess that Sinclair, having had one experience, was urgently campaigning for more. Their relationship was not explained straight out, except in the sense that it was pointedly *not* explained, while her name occurred several times a week in his diaries.

Ann lived on Crawford Street, north of College in west-central Toronto. Sometimes her parents were out for the evening. When they weren't, Sinclair as a footnote to the evening might remark, "We could not use the house." Sometimes Ann came to the Sinclair home when his parents were out. The conclusion that they likely slept together must be reached more by inference than by stated facts. He and Ann went to three or four movies a week; after one of them he noted that he took Ann home and didn't get to bed until 2 a.m., adding: "I sure made a hash of things tonight." Another: "In evening went up to see Ann but things did not go quite as nice as possible." They went to a movie and Ann did not feel well and "treated me rather shabbily." Or another night, "treated me very well."

That June he and four friends, including one named Sam,

bought a tent and set it up on the eastern Beaches, south of the Kingston Road in Scarborough. They often stayed overnight, sometimes with girls—including Ann—as company. Sinclair was still living at home and sometimes went there in the morning for a bath "and a good sleep". But one Sunday, June 29, a cheerful group of the young tenters, friends, and girls were in Sam's truck when it tried to beat a fast-moving streetcar at Stop 19 on the Kingston Road, and didn't make it.

Sinclair had seen the crash coming. He and some others riding in the bed of the truck leaped off just in time. Those in the truck's cab were not as fortunate. One girl was killed on the spot, Sam was seriously injured (he recovered), and Ann's sister died two days later. Sinclair's diary shows no emotion in recording these facts. He went to see the dead girl's body at the funeral home and to the hospital to see his friend Sam, "who nearly died on Tuesday night". He testified at the inquest, which returned a verdict of accidental death.

That summer, also, Sinclair was making his first attempts at writing for publication. A clipping pasted into his diary relates that in a basketball game at the Broadview Y, McMurray's team had beaten Sinclair's team 21-16. One hazy report from the period has it that Sinclair got tired of playing in games that never were reported in the papers, so took his complaints to the major sports editors of the time—W. A. Hewitt of the *Daily Star*, J. P. Fitzgerald of the *Telegram*, and others at the *Globe* and the *Mail and Empire*. They said if he would bring the game results in, they'd print them. So he wrote out brief reports in longhand and delivered them on his bicycle or by streetcar. In one of his biographical summaries many years later, he stated that his first publication had been in 1919 in the *Star Weekly*, probably a short and unsigned sports result.

After that the months rolled on, with Sinclair's diary mainly recording the weather, crises at the office, and the ups and downs of his relationship with Ann. She cried when he went on a holiday. They saw a good movie but the night "was spoiled later." The tendency among guilt-ridden lovers of that era was to spend periods between love-making telling each other that they must stop, it's wrong, what if we have a baby, etc. There was an echo of such palaver in Sinclair's diary for January 1, 1920, when he said that he and Ann "made some resolutions." In pencil underneath, not in his writing, and dated January 17, was: "Gord did not keep said resolutions."

Before this time, however, Eaton's had fired him. His own official account, repeated many times on the air and elsewhere, was that an Eaton's supplier was urgently in need of money and that good-guy Sinclair, taking pity, had been dismissed because he okayed paying the bill before it was due.

His diary tells a totally different story: that a supplier, "a Jew", had come into the office and "got very saucy, demanding a cheque. I refused to give it to him." The supplier threatened to get Sinclair fired, and went to see a higher-up. The next day Gordon was fired. In concocting his official story later, he might have been ashamed that he had singled out the man's religion when writing in his diary; he rarely at any other time showed racial or religious bigotry.

The relationship with Ann seems to have been side-tracked a few months later, by which time Sinclair was working for a firm that made calendars, Rolph-Clark-Stone Limited. Out with some of his new female co-workers, he had "the wildest night of my career, wine (the hard stuff), women and song," followed by a ferocious hangover. Still, one more diary entry mentions going home with Ann and "we had a *very* enjoyable evening," with the "very" underlined.

From then on he saw a lot of a girl named Frances, a co-worker in his new job. Diary entry from late March: "Got a letter from Ann returning all the junk I had given her."

That month Sinclair had been hoping for a raise. When he didn't get it, he started answering job advertisements and going for interviews. He didn't apply at any newspapers.

Family pressure at home was still in favour of his wearing three-piece suits and becoming a wheel in the business world, and that's where he concentrated his job hunt. Northern Electric offered him $20 a week as assistant credit manager, but Gutta Percha and Rubber Limited, and Woods Manufacturing Limited both offered $23, more than he'd ever made before. Some time in April of 1920 he started work as a junior bookkeeper in the purchasing department of Gutta Percha, whose offices were at 47 Yonge Street.

He celebrated the warming spring weather and his new $23-a-week affluence by buying a canoe. In those days a canoe ranked a close second to a car in terms of getting girls, and he started to play the field again.

One day he and France, as he had begun to call Frances, paddled from the reactivated beach tent to the original Woodbine racetrack (later renamed Greenwood), left the canoe on the beach, went in for one race, then left. Later the same day he took Ann paddling. Some days he'd have a double bill: "France and I paddled in afternoon and Ann and I at night." Other flirtations and pickups happened from time to time. He was also pitching two or three times a week in a baseball league made up of Gutta Percha workers. He had fun that summer and fall.

Gladys Prewett first appears in his diary on December 13, 1920. She had been working as a stenographer with another company when, in late autumn, her older sister Olive, one of the senior secretaries at Gutta Percha, found her a job as switchboard operator. Olive was slender and dark-haired. Gladys had a striking, even sumptuous, figure and hair so light in colour that it seemed almost white. At sight, Sinclair admired her. "Hey, who's the new talent?" he asked Olive.

According to family folklore, much recalled in later years, Olive snapped, "She's my sister, and you stay away from her."

Sinclair at the time was known for his brash manner. Mae Hodgson, another worker at Gutta Percha, now lives in British Columbia. She told a newspaper columnist years later that in the office Sinclair "was a cheerful, laughing young man, and a great tease." Once he had told her, "Your teeth look beautiful today, Miss Hodgson. I see you use Sani-Flush." He'd have the office in stitches with such vaudeville-type barbs, to the extent that he'd been rebuked by management for talking too much. In contrast, he seemed intimidated by Gladys, although they saw one another at work every day.

The first mention of Gladys in Sinclair's diary doesn't describe her at all. But she is seen as fair-haired and shapely in photos of the time. Obviously he noticed. Only his shyness was uncharacteristic.

What she saw, in return, was a short and wiry young man whose reputation as a bizarre dresser was still in the future. He always reported to Gutta Percha in a three-piece suit with a handkerchief in the breast pocket, tie neatly knotted, and shirt clean (Bessie saw to that). The close haircuts of the time did nothing to disguise the way his ears stuck out. The buck-teeth of his school days had been brought under nominal control by the use of braces (the treatment cost $100, but Bessie insisted). Add to all that his cocky bantam strut and you get the picture. Still, his outward cockiness masked uncertainty.

Diary, Dec. 13: "Felt like asking Gladys Prewett to go out with me sometime but lost courage."

Dec. 17: "I summoned up my courage and asked Gladys Prewett to come out with me, which she did (to a movie). Gladys is a very nice girl. I would like to become good friends with her so we are going out again next Wed."

That is how their long life together began. Gladys had beauty and her own strength of character, but in comparison with Gordon must have come across as placid and easygoing. Her precise opinion of him then is unknown (but with her looks she must have had a lot of other options), and Gordon's approach was as respectful as she could wish. He bought her candy that Christmas. They chatted at the office over sandwich lunches. She was boarding with friends named Powell in the west part of the city. He told her about Bessie and Sandy and his two brothers. In addition to Olive, Gladys had two brothers, one a brilliant student headed for Oxford. Gordon found that her parents lived in Islington, where her father, Arthur Prewett, owned a market garden. Just before New Year's he picked her up one evening for a movie, and in his diary for that day noted: "Don't know what to think of Gladys except she is straight and on the level."

Soon they were seeing one another at night several times a week and things were developing on what seemed like a serious course. January 11: "Glad and I dropped in to see Ma, then I went up and met her mother at Mrs. Powell's on Grenadier." On Sunday, January 16, after teaching his Sunday-school class and dropping in on Bessie for a while, he took the Dundas streetcar west to Keele Street, "where Glad came down to meet me, then out to Islington. It was an awful night but worth it. Her mother is very nice and their place must be great in the summertime." He also met the formidable Arthur Prewett, who, like most Englishmen of his class and generation, insisted that his offspring have good manners, read the classics, and generally show the effects of careful upbringing. Sinclair, becoming a voracious reader, had common ground there.

For a time he seemed to join her circle of family and friends, rather than the reverse. Olive gave a party and there he met her sweetheart, Jim Pinchin, a Canadian National Railways telegrapher then working at Union station. Olive and Jim were soon engaged. There was no doubt about the romance between Sinclair and Gladys, either. Later in life Sinclair rarely, if ever, danced, but with Gladys he did; not only at parties but at dance halls. They were young, having fun, and developing a closer relationship. A typical diary entry states that Glad was at the Sinclairs' but some company stayed until 9:30, "so our fun didn't start until after." On Good Friday he went to her home and they came back in for the show at Shea's. Afterward, "I felt so full of pep, I think I showed my affection for her too much."

But with the coming of summer the focus shifted; he played tennis, pitched softball in the company league, paddled, swam, and sometimes turned to other women.

That summer Sinclair and four friends rented a boat-house at Toronto Island. The upstairs was rented to several young women, and in general there was a crowd around most of the time, with a wide variety of outdoor interests and pursuits. On foul days there was always a quorum for parties, dancing, poker, and crap games. Although Gladys was a frequent visitor, she seemed to distance herself sometimes from the free-and-easy ways of the others. Once in a while she'd consent to stay overnight with the girls upstairs, but she usually went back to where she boarded in the city. On a nice night, or when she missed the last boat, Sinclair might paddle her to the mainland to catch a street-car. She and Sinclair argued, usually over whether she should stay overnight. Sinclair obviously was completely recovered from his bashfulness with her. He apparently had to dominate, call the shots, and she, a well-brought-up young woman with a mind of her own, often wouldn't go along. When she rented a room of her own on the island in a family home, it lessened some of the pressures, but the first glow was over.

At the office, Gladys found herself the target of his wisecracks. Fellow-worker Mae Hodgson recently recalled a time when Gladys, who had ambitions to be a milliner, came in wearing a new hat that she might have made herself. It was as red as a mailbox. Sinclair said, "That's a terrific hat, Glad. But when you're standing on a corner don't leave your mouth open or somebody might post a letter in it." He confessed to his diary, " . . . afraid I'm getting tired of Glad, too familiar with her anyway." And: "Think my little romance with the blonde girl is about over, she didn't speak to me and I did likewise to her on the ferry, which may seem childish but Ann and Mae are both coming over next week so I better not run after Glad too hard."

These entries indicate not only Gordon's lack of real commitment, but his apparent indifference to whether he hurt her or not. Could she have loved enough for both? That seems doubtful. Whatever the case, that first summer of their long relationship—when he sometimes loved and admired her, but as often picked fights, chased other women, and didn't consider her side of a question unless it suited him—pretty well defined their life to come, the fateful positions hardening with each passing year.

By this point, for two years he had been writing about games in which he participated or watched from the sidelines, taking the reports to the papers and seeing them in print. Judging by the few samples available, they weren't much, at least as published. He was feeling his way along, using the accepted, plodding style he saw in the papers every day. But he was being published, he liked the feeling, and when he read books he liked or flashy front-page local stories, he daydreamed a bit. He also was bored with his career as a bookkeeper. It offered regular raises and good security, but no excitement unless he made it himself.

There is no record that anybody said to him, "Gordon, you're wasted in what you're doing . . . why don't you try newspapering?" But on New Year's Day, 1922, one of his resolutions was that he had to find a more interesting way to spend his life. He applied at all four newspapers, asking for a reporting job.

The *Star* gave him the only encouragement, calling him in for an interview with H. C. Hindmarsh. On February 22, 1922, at the raw, dark hour of 7 a.m., he walked through the front door of the old *Star* building at 18-20 King Street West and reported to the city editor, who waved him over to share a desk with another cub reporter who had been engaged the same day, Foster Hewitt.

CHAPTER THREE

STAR DAYS

For seven years, he never had a byline.

From Sinclair's first day he showed at least faint signs of what he was to become—but that didn't mean anybody noticed. By his own account, confirmed by the *Star* reference library, it was seven years (sometimes he said six) before his byline appeared on a story. This will seem incredible to students who work a few summer months for a newspaper today, get bylines immediately, and may never work as journalists again. Later in life he told different versions of almost every major event in his career, but it is quite easy to believe that in those days he put in six or seven years with no byline. A reporter might have years of routine assignments until a chance to show talent—or more often a lucky break—caused editors to remember the writer's name the next time a good assignment came along.

The upright telephone at the city desk would ring and the assistant on duty would grab the receiver off the hook and bark, "City desk!" A rag factory was on fire, or a monkey had died, or two cars had crashed at the prime downtown Toronto corner of King and Yonge, which had neither traffic lights nor stop signs then. The city editor would lift his eyes from the note he'd made and let his gaze roam over the scarred desks between aisles crowded with reporters moving or talking or phoning or even typing. The stars were safe. No rag-factory fire or monkey's demise would go to the likes of Gregory Clark, Ernest Hemingway, Morley Callaghan, Fred Griffin, Claude Pascoe, or C. E. Knowles. But who are those two new guys sitting at the same desk?

"Hey, you!" The assistant city editor, Harry Johnson, could have chosen Foster Hewitt, but he was pointing at Gordon Sinclair. This was about 9 a.m. on Sinclair's first morning at the *Star*. He'd reported as ordered at 7, and had been ignored until now.

"Me?" He hustled up there, all five and a half feet of him, sandy hair, long upper lip, with a somehow cocky look in his eyes. Harry Johnson was scribbling an address on a slip of paper and handing it over.

"This guy had two monkeys and one just died. Get out there and, you know, see if the other monkey is in mourning or if the guy is going to try to find another mate for the other monkey, or whatever."

The monkey story actually provides an excellent context in which to understand the journalistic era that Gordon Sinclair entered in 1922. Most newspapers in town at the time (no doubt some even now) would have perceived this item as the *Star* did: a potential human-interest story along the time-honoured line of "Bereaved Monkey Mourns Dead Mate". Such a story might even have a future. A combination of skilful handling and a slow news week could keep such a story going for days. The *Star* had performed such feats of news-making in the past, and would again before Sinclair was much older. A perfect example was the *Star*'s donation of a baby elephant named Stella to the Toronto Zoo. When Stella turned out to be bowlegged, was found to have rickets, and died, even that made news—the name Stella was on a lot of lips. But was the story over? Not on your life. The *Star* asked Toronto kids to send in their votes on what creature should replace Stella. Then, since it had a line on a white peacock, it "conned" (Sinclair's description) the kids into voting for a white peacock as a replacement. However, Sinclair wasn't senior enough to handle that job; Ernest Hemingway was assigned to welcome the peacock to Toronto and to orchestrate a contest to find a name for it.

The point being made is that nothing to do with the monkey story was impossible. If Sinclair did a good job on the opening story, he might be told to get on the phone and try to find another monkey to help the sorrowing survivor carry on the family name. Then he might be assigned to run a contest asking readers to name the new monkey. The possibilities, although not infinite, were many, tried, and true—they had worked before with everything from lost budgies ("Pensioner Pines for Feathered Friend") to lady cats suckling orphan pups.

Back to Sinclair's first assignment: he grabbed a pad of copy paper and headed out along with Fred Foster, a photographer (Foster Hewitt's Uncle Fred). Soon they were standing on the snowy veranda of the surviving monkey's owner, apparently a Tory. He admitted the death had upset the whole household, then suddenly grasped who his visitors were. "Get out of here!" he growled. "That Liberal rag you work for isn't going to print any picture of *my* monkey!"

Sinclair and Foster argued, but eventually retreated. Whereupon Sinclair, on his very first assignment, showed at least a glimpse of what he was made of. As he told Fred Foster, monkeys looked pretty much alike, and he knew exactly where the monkey-house was situated at the Riverdale Zoo. They went there, found a suitable monkey, and hurried back to the office. Sinclair's story, written in longhand, didn't mention the difficulty with the monkey's owner. His story made the paper, along with Fred Foster's picture of the zoo monkey, identified as the bereaved monkey. Within hours after the paper hit the streets, the owner of the real monkey was raising hell with the *Star*'s managing editor, Harry C. Hindmarsh, about this impostor. But very little of the criticism filtered down to Sinclair. Indeed, it might have marked him down as a man of enterprise.

Once, he was given a different sort of assignment: to help Foster Hewitt. The *Star* had its own radio station, CFCA, established a few months after Sinclair and Hewitt arrived. Reporters covered regular newspaper assignments mixed in with radio jobs. Foster Hewitt at that time had not called his first hockey game. For the paper he covered courts and speeches, anything that was going, as well as filling in on radio news broadcasts and, since he had some experience as a radio engineer, supervising broadcasts from outside the studio.

One Saturday morning Sinclair read in the assignment book that he was to help Hewitt set up equipment in Walmer Road Baptist Church for the *Star*'s weekly church broadcast the next day. His job included checking the batteries, which he either did not do, or did not know how to do, or did not do well. When the service began, the batteries were stone dead. It was the only time ever that the *Star*'s church broadcast didn't get any farther than the roof of the church. Hewitt always claimed that Sinclair did it on purpose, hoping the precedent would get him blackballed from the church broadcasts. If so, it worked.

He didn't have any such luck two or three years later when he was assigned to be women's editor, but coped in true Sinclair style with such things as a story attempting to explain the difference between a frock, a dress, and a gown, and survived to go on to better things.

That and other wildly varied early assignments at the *Star* were standard not only for cub reporters like Sinclair and Hewitt, but for older men who were experienced and capable. When someone made headlines and no photo of the principal (anyone from a murderer to a crime victim) was readily available, reporters were dispatched to the person's home or to the homes of relatives. Family photos might be borrowed, bought, or in extreme cases (such as if the *Telegram* had been there first) stolen.

In such situations it helped to travel in twos; one could engage the unsuspecting family while the other scanned the walls, the mantel, and family albums for anything portable. Sinclair did it, Gregory Clark did it; it was a particularly aggressive part of news-gathering. Some victims of this larceny sued and some laid theft charges. But when trouble came over photos or anything else, the early Sinclair learned to recognize another master at work, a hefty and haughty English ex-major named Claude Pascoe, who sat out in the newsroom and spent a lot of time on the phone, always opening with a lofty "Major Claude Pascoe here." Pascoe, among other chores, was a *fixer*. Sinclair wrote, "When people got angry at the paper and threatened to sue, it was Pascoe who combined the mannerisms of an archbishop, a chief justice and a hangman who calmed them down. He had a way of knowing which disguise to adopt and he had a batting average of at least 99%."

Much that engaged Sinclair in his earliest *Star* days was exciting and fun, partly because it was all new to him. However, the other side of the coin was obits. Everybody had to do them, but cubs like Sinclair and people who were in the doghouse got the most. Forms were filled out by people wishing to insert notices in the *Star*'s daily Deaths columns, and each included a spare copy, called a flimsy, for the newsroom. An assistant city editor would distribute these, a handful here and a handful there.

Reporters were expected to fill spare time by telephoning relatives or friends of the deceased and finding out more about them: any medals, awards, interesting achievements, or crimes; why the dear departed lived such a long time or such a short time; whether he or she had any famous relatives or was a member of any clubs or lodges. Two or three paragraphs might be printed under headings such as "Fought at Vimy" or "Father of 17". Sinclair did his share.

It was boring work, but to ditch a handful of obit flimsies meant taking a chance that the *Telegram* would turn up a good story that the *Star* had missed.

As time went on, Sinclair sometimes had a chance at an interesting story, but then, as forever after, human interest was his specialty. He wasn't interested in the abstract, in anything that required examination in depth, or in arcane items that only a limited number of people were interested in anyway. Something that he could be flip or funny about (and therefore have a chance for a good play) was his meat. Even without his name on a story he could always point it out to friends, or tell Bessie, "Hey, Ma! That's mine! I wrote that!"

In those days, when a person was hanged, the hanging was always attended by reporters—and it was a newsroom gag to send a cub who might faint, throw up, or otherwise distinctively mark forever in memory this milestone in his progress to becoming a "real" newspaperman. When Sinclair's time came, he found that his opposition from the *Telegram* was none other than the Sinclair family's neighbour, Harry Passmore,

> a wordy workhorse among the scribblers of his day,
> [who] could cover any story from wedding to hanging
> and indeed, did both on the same day. He used to
> keep a fragment of rope from every hanging he
> attended and once, when he was elder statesman of
> the craft and when I was a green beginner, we were
> assigned as rivals to a gibbet. . . . The execution was
> slated for early morning. . . .

The execution was in a small Ontario city, to which they travelled by train the night before the hanging. Because of the long friendship between the Passmores and the Sinclairs, Gordon apparently dropped his know-it-all stance to watch the master at work.

He was an observant bystander as Passmore did what Sinclair would not have had the nerve to do: ordered breakfast for a time hours before the dining-room would normally open. The innkeeper argued, but, after Passmore quoted him obscure portions of the Innkeepers' Act, gave in. When they rose well before dawn, breakfast was ready.

> As he was about to tuck in, Passmore let go with the
> hint that he was a hangman and I was his assistant and
> this would be a good day. The waitress, already in a
> state of emotional opposition [because of the early
> call], ran screaming from the room, and the cook
> served us.

A hanging, the only occasion on which a reporter could justifiably charge a bottle of whisky on the expense sheet, was a happy event to Harry, and his collection of rope strands grew steadily.

This and other reactions to his early work indicate that the excitement of it all often got Sinclair even when the stories turned out to be routine. It was fun to be going out of the office on the run and speeding in a photographer's car to where, with the magic words "The *Star*," he could get through the crowds that were being held back.

Not that he was always as keen as his employers would have liked him to be. In print years later he confessed, "I was a duty reporter, unshaven, sometimes drunk, now and again spending mornings, when I should have been on the prowl, in a card joint or bootlegger's, and sometimes in both."

Rookie reporters often learn their trade by filling in for the top men. Sinclair was sometimes teamed with ace police reporter Athol Gow. He also was sometimes assigned for a day or two to help out at the legislature. Augustus Bridle was the *Star*'s towering critic for music and plays. If Bridle was ill, or on holiday, Sinclair sometimes took his place.

Once he not only was the lone customer at a play with a cast of nine, but was also on a pass. He sat through the whole work. "To my feeble applause at the end, the nine players took bows. Gutsy actors!" Later in life he could have had some fun with that situation, but at the time he didn't.

Some days he would be assigned to cover a luncheon where some local or visiting bigwig was speaking. He would amble down to the King Edward or the Royal York, have a good free meal with the usual hungry kids and thirsty veterans at the press table, and then perform what to some young reporters could be a nightmare. Texts were rarely available, but the speeches had to be covered in time to make the *Star*'s late editions—the *Evening Telegram* would be doing the same. This meant that as soon as the speaker got through his opening platitudes, the *Star* and *Tely* men not only had to listen and take notes, as others at the press table did, but write their stories simultaneously in longhand.

Running copy, this was called, and Sinclair soon could do it with the best of them. His confidence, or cocksureness, whatever it was, made him quick to spot what was new or arresting and to get it on paper. The paragraphs, scrawled in pencil, were picked up page by page by office boys who ran them back to the office a couple of blocks away (the *Star* was on King Street between Bay and Yonge, the *Telegram* at Bay and Melinda). Within a couple of dozen minutes the words of the speech went to clattering linotypes, and in another half-hour they were on the street.

Like both his colleagues and his competitors, Sinclair used running copy to cover many events—trials, inquests, weddings, city-council sessions, the sittings of the legislature. Newspapers, the only source of news (radio was an infant, television unknown), fought like tigers to be first.

From city hall, running copy and complete stories were sent to the newspapers in leather cylinders placed in pneumatic tubes that worked by suction. From the legislature, the racetracks, and hockey and football games, the stories were sent by telegraph. The Morse operator with his eyeshade, arm garters, and clattering telegraph key was as much a part of Sinclair's life as a typewriter. Sometimes Sinclair and Jim Pinchin yarned over stories that both had worked on, Sinclair as reporter and Pinchin as telegrapher.

Early in Sinclair's *Star* days Olive and Jim Pinchin had married, and for a year or two Gladys boarded with them. Details of the relationship between Gladys and Sinclair for four or five years after that first summer when both had spent a lot of time at the Island range from sparse to non-existent. His diaries of those years are not to be found, either lost or destroyed. But some details are remembered by others.

Two or three years after he started at the *Star*, still living at home, he bought his first automobile. It was a Grey Dort, for which he paid $100. He sometimes would take Gladys for a Sunday drive, once or twice all the way to the town of Mount Forest in western Ontario, near where Gladys was born. It was quite a drive for those days of narrow mud roads, but probably coincided with the period when they were getting serious about marriage. Most of the Prewett relatives lived in the Mount Forest or Arthur area.

Gordon was still virtually unknown outside of the Toronto newspaper world when he and Gladys were married on May 8, 1926. The *Star* described it as a "very quiet ceremony", with only family present. Announcements were sent to friends when the newlyweds returned from a honeymoon in Quebec City. As a wedding present, Gladys's father, Arthur Prewett, gave them a building lot at the edge of his market garden in Islington. There they built their first house, about which Gordon once wrote:

> We planned a small bungalow which two brothers, Ed and George Watson, with help from ourselves, would put together on a plateau over a creek. . . . In its first two winters the house was bitterly cold, as the wind got a sweep at it, and we spent every spare copper plugging it against drafts. We had no floor coverings or paper on the walls, only the barest of furniture. . . .

Sinclair's own role in the do-it-yourself line of house-building is unclear. By common consent, he could not be trusted to drive a nail. There, in 1928, their first son, Gordon, was born, and the following year their second son, Donald. Before marriage he had bought a new Ford for $850, one day when the old Grey Dort gave up the ghost and had to be towed away. At the beginning of their marriage they owed a little on the Ford and a few thousand for their mortgage. His years of living at home, and the gift of the building lot, made their financial circumstances better than those of many young couples. By 1928 or 1929 Sinclair's pay had reached $50 a week, keeping them comfortably. Also, he didn't know it then, but he was about to become a favoured son around the *Star*.

Sinclair's first seven years there included remarkable contrasts in situations and people. The tall and stately figure of managing editor H. C. Hindmarsh marched the halls, exuding a dry and not always kindly power in person or through notes signed HCH. At the *Star*, only one man's word outranked his, that of Joseph (Holy Joe) Atkinson, the paper's publisher and Hindmarsh's father-in-law. Both were heard from frequently in the chain of command, two men who believed in themselves and their right to judge others when the good of the *Star* was at stake. A note or a few words passed by phone from Atkinson to Hindmarsh to news editor to city editor to reporter made or ruined careers.

That's how it was when Sinclair got his first big break. There is no telling exactly when someone Up There (which at the *Star* meant Atkinson or Hindmarsh) first noticed Sinclair seriously. Ruth Atkinson Hindmarsh said in a 1986 interview that her husband, HCH, "always liked and trusted" Sinclair, which was at variance with many stories that came to make up the Hindmarsh-Sinclair legend. But the fact remained that in seven years he never once had written a story that caused an editor to suggest to HCH, "This is worth a byline." Favourable decisions in that line were said to have come hard to HCH, who believed that the road to hell for a managing editor was paved with prima donnas, who had gotten that way by being given bylines. He wasn't going to make life any harder for himself than he had to.

Aside from well-known critics and featured department heads such as sports editor Lou Marsh, news and feature bylines and big play through much of Sinclair's early years went mainly to the *Star* "stars": Hemingway, whose fiction Sinclair liked but whose journalism he found no more than adequate and whose personality he disliked; Gregory Clark, a friend for life; Morley Callaghan the same; and Fred Griffin, whom Sinclair respected tremendously as having all the dedication and good sense that he felt he himself lacked, although he felt that Griffin "usually wrote too long."

These were household names. Few outside of relatives, fellow-workers, and friends had ever heard of Gordon Sinclair. He just plugged along—fairly happy, it seemed, he and Gladys with their car, their house, and the two young sons. Downtown, Sinclair might be a swinger, hanging around city hall and police headquarters, indulging in booze, women, and poker, but at home he had become an ardent photographer and was thinking of getting into home movies. Olive and Jim Pinchin, with their son Robert, born in 1924, lived only a few blocks away. The Pinchins and Sinclairs were often in and out of each other's homes for meals or cards.

Home was a warm place and there was no other job Sinclair wanted, no other city he wanted to live in. He could have used more money and a little fame, but if he felt any thwarted ambition it wasn't obvious. These might have been the happiest years of Gladys's married life. Years later, when faced with Sinclair's celebrity and asked to be part of it, to go where he would be lionized, she just shook her head. The celebrity life was not for her, she'd explain. "When I married him he was just an ordinary reporter."

But the ordinariness was to change very rapidly. Sinclair saw the change as beginning here:

> I was covering the police beat one routine day when I heard of a downtown house that had not been opened for many years, disgorging a treasure in art and foreign money together with a will leaving all of this plus hundreds of cases of liquor to a bachelor bank manager who barely knew the eccentric lady who'd left him this largesse. . . . I decided to take a look and found whole rooms filled with packing cases [containing] tapestries, sculpture and paintings. The wine cellar had at least a thousand bottles that had gone bad . . . beer so old that it was in bottles with permanent porcelain tops. . . . I went back to the desk with what I thought was a good human interest story about this banker's lucky strike and arranged for a

photographer to go up and take pictures of all this loot.

Alas, on a plea from the banker and maybe a nudge from those near the top of the bank's hierarchy, this story was played down and someone else . . . wrote it . . . in such dull style and hidden so deep in the sheets as to be ignored. No other paper picked it up.

It was the kind of encounter between newspaper politics and a reporter's good nose and hard work that makes cynics out of journalists. The contents of the house did eventually go on sale and brought a modest $100,000, most of the foreign money having been worthless because of changed boundaries and governments. The bachelor banker, whose wish for privacy had been part of what had scuppered Sinclair's lively story, sent him a dozen heavy crystal tumblers as a consolation prize.

This didn't do much to lessen Sinclair's annoyance, even despondency, at the fact that something he'd thought really good hadn't made the paper. He wondered if it was a sign to which he should pay attention. The *Star*, which not long before had built a new building at 80 King Street West and had done some retrenching financially, was famous for firing people during its economy waves. If he could be that out of tune with the paper's management, Sinclair thought, couldn't he be fired in the next economy wave?

But apparently someone of consequence at the *Star* had read and remembered the killed story, finding genuine human-interest appeal in Sinclair's approach. About the same time a shipment from Britain arrived in Toronto, bound for a much-ballyhooed three-day auction of suits of armour, silver, crystal, paintings, and other sale items, all supposed to be from stately homes—or at the very least, from sturdy manor-houses. Promoters dropped around to newspaper offices hoping for free publicity by playing on Canada's known reverence for all things British.

The *Star* didn't bite on the advance publicity, but did assign Sinclair to cover the first night of the auction. His approach was not unlike the one that became part of his celebrity persona years later; he strutted in with a "you gotta show me" attitude.

> The hall was a-swarm with shills making fake bids and since I was making no progress on the paper, and liable to be thrown out in the next economy wave, I slammed into this sale with all the sarcasm and cynicism I could muster.
>
> This struck a responsive chord and the story got page one treatment.
>
> To my astonishment there were turnaway crowds the next two nights and everybody seemed delighted. The promoters sold out (and gave me two water colors), the paper liked the stories, and apparently the buyers appreciated their purchases.

Sinclair hadn't intended to do the promoters a favour and hadn't been trying to draw big buying crowds, but he did feel good about the paper's liking the stories. "I hadn't scored any triumph with these yarns, but I had been noticed. . . ."

Being noticed meant that when a story came up that might be first-rate if given the right treatment, some people were beginning to think, Clark? Griffin? *Sinclair*?

Within a few days that first-rate story presented itself—although it had one of the longest and slowest fuses that ever was linked to a potential celebrity's booster rocket. He told the story many times, including twice in books. The most complete account is in *Will the Real Gordon Sinclair Please Stand Up*.

The background was that in June of 1929, a few days after Sinclair's twenty-ninth birthday, Toronto police raided an area near the railway tracks and charged more than one hundred men as vagrants. They were the sort of drifters called in those days "hoboes". So-called hobo jungles were common in almost every big city, usually handy to the railway tracks, since freights were their normal form of transportation. There was little or no public sympathy for

48

the hoboes. Jobs were plentiful. If men chose to be hoboes, the general attitude was to move them on. H. C. Hindmarsh figured correctly that when this hobo throng came to court, the order would be, "Get out of town," and he thought there might be a story in sending a reporter along with them. He first considered Leonard Knott, later to become prominent in public relations and advertising, because Knott was big and strong, and had a heavy beard. The trouble was, he couldn't be found.

HCH's second choice was Sinclair, who, by Sinclair's own account, qualified on the grounds of slovenly dress and Grade 8 English, even if he was rather small for tough company. The assignment was for Sinclair to pick up the regiment of bums outside the courthouse and go where they went.

Sinclair instantly felt that this might be a bad idea.

> I was married and father of two boys at this time, and I carried the assignment to Bessie for advice. Boxcars were risky, hoboes were often nutty. "Don't go," she cried. "I didn't raise you to be any bum. Who does this Hindmarsh think he is?"
>
> "If I don't go, I'll be fired sure."
>
> "So you'll be fired. . . . But don't go. No hoboes, no boxcars, no bums."
>
> I took her advice, went to a Ronald Colman movie, stayed home the next morning, and when Gladys asked how come I wasn't at work, I told her the facts. No comment. Hours later, fidgety, I said to my blonde wife, "Don't like it, eh?"
>
> "Your mother says don't go; you don't want to go. You're Bessie's boy, so who am I?"
>
> I went.

He joined up with the hoboes on University Avenue, lounging on the grassy boulevard and mingling eventually with four men who said they were going to New York. He went along, later remarking how strange he found it that in all that trip, four days and nights, there was no talk about sex. But there was a lot of other talk. One night when he and the others had joined a throng of other hoboes lounging under a bridge in upstate New York, he mentioned that he was a newspaperman and was going to leave and go back. They said they had known that all the time. Then Sinclair made his first gaffe.

A large hobo in the group got talking about "his happy days lying in the sun in Australia, gazing up at the Himalayas", with sheep and kangaroos all over the place. Sinclair pooh-poohed that. The Himalayas were in India, he pointed out, not Australia. The world traveller responded to this geography lesson by clubbing Sinclair over the head with a stick, giving him a very bad bruise and a black eye.

When he got back to the *Star*, he said there was no story, to forget it, wash it out. He was sent to cover a court case, and when he came back, he encountered D. B. (Dave) Rogers, that day's duty editor, later to become a news executive on papers in Regina and Winnipeg. Rogers, spotting Sinclair's bruises, "pointed with a pair of shears he was carrying and said, 'Walked into a strange door, no doubt.'"

"No, I got bashed," Sinclair replied and told Rogers about it, happening to mention that the bum who'd hit him had been lounging around on a bed made out of black stockings, boys' woollen stockings. The kind of touch Sinclair always had.

Rogers asked if he'd written about it. Sinclair said no, what the hell, there was really no story.

"Write it!"

"Write what?"

"About the bum and the trip and the black woollen stockings. Where did they get the stockings?"

"They didn't get them, they were just there from some other bums. All sorts of bums gather at that place. I don't even know where it was."

"Write it, especially about the crack on the head."

Sinclair wrote a few hundred words, not even enough to fill a single column, dropped it into Rogers' mail pigeonhole, and went back to his court case. For several days he heard nothing and spent his off-time in brokers' offices watching stock prices go up out of sight. This was months before the 1929 stock-market crash. He had bought stock and was making money.

Then one day around the courthouse he was approached by *Star* photographer Fred Davis (much older than, and not related to, the Fred Davis who nearly thirty years later was to be Sinclair's colleague on *Front Page Challenge*). Davis said he had a memo telling him to photograph Sinclair and asked what it was for. Sinclair said he didn't know, but he leaned on an automobile while Davis told him a dirty joke to get a smile and took the picture.

Sinclair then went upstairs to the newsroom to find a note from Rogers saying that the hobo story he'd written was a natural. Could he extend it to six pieces, one a day for a week?

CHAPTER FOUR

FOOTLOOSE REPORTER

A funny thing happened—he met Hitler.

It was in these circumstances that Sinclair first became a name to be reckoned with on the Toronto newspaper scene. Complete with his first byline and his photo, his hobo series started on the front page of the July 6, 1929, editions of the *Star* under the heading "Star Reporter Sees Life as Member of Hobo Club". The subhead read: "Star reporter relates gypsy-like experience with human rolling stones—travelling deluxe on a freighter with plenty of air on the roof."

Then, along with a photo of Sinclair, there was an editor's note:

> A roundup of hoboes by Toronto police on the waterfront about a week ago disclosed the fact that the Knights of the Road is by no means an extinct species. Following their arrest a reporter of the *Star*, unshaven and attired as a tramp, joined the hobo family to obtain first-hand information as to the way they lived and to learn something of the motives which impel men to follow such a gypsy-like existence. He travelled with the crowd from Toronto almost to Albany, N.Y., hoofing it part of the way, riding the bumpers of trains and freight-cars for the rest of the distance. The following is the first of a

series of articles in which he relates his experience
for readers of the *Star*.

His byline then and for a year or two later was Gordon A.
Sinclair (until Gregory Clark told him to drop the initial; "it
makes you sound like a banker"). In the lead, after repeating much of the *Star*'s intro, he lays out what he was trying
to learn: "Who are they? Where do they come from? Where
do they sleep at night? How do they get the money to live
on? Where will they go in winter? Are they vicious characters? Are they morons?"

His anecdotal answers to those questions and graphic
descriptions of how he and the hoboes covered the miles
was very good Sinclair—slangy, sharp, with flair and colour.

He fell one short of the six stories that Dave Rogers had
requested, but for five days the stories with his byline and
his photo ran on the *Star*'s front page. The final story ended
with the hoboes going on and Sinclair taking a train home.

Immediately letters poured in. What the hell, Sinclair?
Why did you stop? Why quit, leaving the readers in thin
air? The *Star* printed many of the letters, and Sinclair was
told that those that were printed were only a fraction of the
number received.

But more powerful than any bag of letters was a note from
publisher Joe Atkinson asking his son-in-law, managing
editor Harry Hindmarsh, why Sinclair didn't go on.

Hindmarsh immediately sent out runners to hunt down
the unimpeachable source. "Why *did* you turn back?" he
asked.

"You've got to be kidding! I had no money, no passport,
no health certificate . . . nothing except a family at home."

The appeal of the family at home didn't grab Hindmarsh
at all. Joe Atkinson's dictum was that Sinclair never should
have left the hoboes—family at home or no family. "Get
what you need and catch up," Hindmarsh ordered.

That was easier said than done. Several weeks had gone
by, and the joint resources of all the police forces in hobo-
flooded north-eastern North America could not have

located the exact band of hoboes that *Star* readers had come to know and love. So the immediate follow-up was abandoned. Still, the idea was remembered, and soon was to start Sinclair on his real journalistic career. After seven years and four months of relative obscurity, he was about to be launched.

He was to spend the next ten years travelling around the world. As an inevitable side-effect, that profound change in his life also started him on years spent as an absentee husband and father, away from his home more often than he was in it.

Two months after the hobo series he was sent to England, his mandate being to find out what hoboes were like there. That series was rather tentative Sinclair. England did not seem to be the place for his brand of common-man exotica. He couldn't have known it then, but his real forte was to lie in painting vivid pictures of man-eating tigers, cannibals, bare-breasted native maidens, bodies being gathered every morning in the streets of Bombay or Shanghai, the fury of Hindus when he, an infidel, dared to cool off in their sacred Ganges. Sinclair in England was like Babe Ruth looking for vicious curves and getting balloon-balls. His first story from Liverpool was about the custom of leaving one's shoes outside the door at night to be shined—his, of course, were stolen. Toronto was so British then that anything about the Old Country would sell papers. Certainly the very tame headlines wouldn't have done it on their own:

STAR REPORTER RELATES FURTHER EXPERIENCES AFTER REACH-ING ENGLAND

YOUNG RECIPIENTS OF DOLE UNGRATEFUL, PROFANE

BOXCAR IN ENGLAND GIVES HOBO NO CHANCE

Even the story promised in "The Diary of a Canadian in the Badlands of London" was disappointing:

SECRET PASSAGES, MURDEROUS ATTACKS AND CONSPIRACIES, STAR MAN FINDS, ARE MYTHS

His own critique of that trip was that he had written "the usual tourist stuff but dressed it up in slang." Still, when he got home he was immediately asked if he would like to keep on with foreign travel. He would.

Features about the home front written in his lively style took up the winter, but early in 1930 he was off again, this time starting in Germany, writing about the Kiel canal, Hamburg, and Berlin. Then in Munich a funny thing happened, as it sometimes does to a journalist blessed with luck.

In what he described as a crowded second- or third-class restaurant where he'd been taking his meals, he was ushered by a waiter to a large table that had a small swastika flag on it. The Nazis then had been gaining in public support, but seemed far from power. They ranked an unimposing ninth in Reichstag seats, and therefore they were not big on the average journalistic agenda.

However, they were pretty big on their own agendas. Sinclair was well into beer, food, and a newspaper when four large Germans turned up, wearing brown tunics with swastika armbands. They pounded his table and pointed at the swastika flag on it. Couldn't he see that the table had been reserved for them? He was about to leave when the waiter intervened in German to identify Sinclair as a journalist from Canada. Suddenly "everybody became polite. I was to stay. The little swastika was slapped on another table, whereupon everyone at that table moved out and the four in uniform moved in." Soon a young woman joined the four men. Sinclair knew he was being discussed. Then the woman came over and asked if he would care to interview Herr Hitler. They established that his German was not equal to the task and that she would be his interpreter.

He met Hitler the next day at noon "in a large carpeted room on the second floor of what had been a bank building." Hitler did not shake hands and offered "no small talk about Canada, no questions about how long I'd been or would likely be in Germany," but began to speak immediately.

"He said that anybody who thought a large, strong nation like Germany could be sentenced forever to no army, no navy, no air force, kept in a kind of quarantine, was crazy. When he began to talk about what had to be done to force the rest of the world to allow Germany to get on its feet again, he got more and more excited and repetitive. I think he forgot that I was there. The interpreter was having trouble keeping up. . . ."

Sinclair had not been asked if he wished to sit, but after a while he sat anyway. He took a few notes, then stopped. The interpreter also stopped.

"After more than an hour I looked with an appeal towards the girl, who nodded silently in the direction of a large double door." Sinclair edged out, the girl with him. Hitler was still talking.

Sinclair wrote the story, but the *Star* apparently found it lacking his usual zing; it was cut drastically and very little reached print. A few months later the *Star* would have reacted differently. In elections that September of 1930, the Nazis amazed Germany and the world by jumping to second place among German parties, the springboard from which, less than three years later, Hilter began to rule Germany.

Sinclair was back home that August for a few weeks, was sent to the United States in September, and in November sailed from New York for Cuba. A footnote to that trip is that he travelled on the same ship as Aimee Semple McPherson. She was on vacation and using an alias, but Sinclair recognized her—besides being a famous evangelist, and Ontario-born, she was exciting and attractive as a woman, and her photo was often in the newspapers. In a note asking to see her he mentioned that he had interviewed her several years earlier. That meant, before he had a byline.

Tracking down that unsigned story in the *Star*'s voluminous files on Aimee was no great problem; the style leaped out, pure Sinclair. His lead stated that in the previous year Aimee had "won the open American Headline Sweepstakes for yardage gained" because of a five-week disappearance that ended when she reappeared in Douglas, Arizona, claiming that she had been kidnapped; a court case later all but proved that she had been away with a lover.

Another clue identifying the story as authentic early Sinclair was that in stories years later, when he did have a byline, he would quote an imaginary someone called the Demon Statistician. In this first interview with Aimee, published in February 1927, he used the same technique. Taking off from the fact that during Aimee's first four years at her Angelus Temple in Los Angeles her conversions totalled 12,000, or about 3,000 a year, the Demon Statistician's figuring was that "if the reputed wealth of Aimee and her mother is correct at $750,000, it would make the unit value of one conversion $65 net. On a turnover of 3,000 a year this seems a sound business proposition." In that interview Sinclair described her as "youthful-looking, curvilinear . . . . When she speaks an attractive mouth opens widely and shows white teeth. Her eyes are clear and alight."

A few years later he was to know her, by his own account, intimately. But in Cuba she was "neither gracious nor accommodating" and would not be interviewed or photographed.

As "consolation prize", he treated himself to some dabbling in voodoo (which became one of his specialties) and, returning to the real world, wrote about thirty girls from a Havana brothel going on strike and picketing nude. In appearance they ranged from "white to tawny to black". They were striking "because the price of a lay was too low." The picket line he described as a motley display of bare skin "from demure little kids to brawny women who would have been just right for the wrestling ring." However, "the people passing by, except for me, didn't pay much attention."

There were riots in Cuba when he was there, with bullets zinging around. He did manage to get home from that assignment in time for Christmas. A few months earlier, he and Gladys had decided that they needed someone in the house with her and the children when he was away. On a friend's recommendation, they had asked a slim, blonde, and pleasant fifteen-year-old high-school girl, Doris Loach, to stay there that winter.

Doris was glad to accept, because it shortened her daily

walks to and from school. After she finished school and took a full-time job, she did occasional baby-sitting and for many years was a family friend, later Sinclair's special friend. Meanwhile he was on the road: Europe again, the United States, Cuba, Mexico, Africa, Spain, and Italy—the trips growing longer and longer and solidifying his reputation as a roving reporter. One indication of his high estate was an order from on high that his copy was not to be changed except for spelling.

Yet an incident early in 1931 must have caused some raised eyebrows at the *Star*. He wrote about it but said in his 1966 memoirs, "The article was never used. In fact, it's never been in print until now." The *Star* could have had at least two good reasons for not printing the story. One was that in the strait-laced social attitudes of the time, the paper was not quite ready to let Sinclair fans in on his attitude toward casual sex outside of marriage. The second reason was probably to protect him—and indeed it is thought-provoking to estimate the fury with which Gladys and Bessie would have reacted had the story been printed (although later in life Gladys might have been merely resigned).

When he left home on that 1931 trip, Gladys was expecting their third child. Although his schedule on leaving was to visit some German cities, then Prague and Venice, once in Europe he decided to visit Vienna for a few days paying for the trip himself. Yet when he was leaving addresses for Gladys, for one time period he had told her that he would be picking up mail at Cooks in Vienna. As he hadn't consciously intended, at the time of leaving, to go to Vienna, there was no reason for him to mention that city. "It was a slip, perhaps a Freudian slip, and I should have said, 'Cooks, Venice.' "

He arrived in Vienna by train late one cold and rainy night to find no taxis at the station, but a few "oldish, dispirited men" slumped sleepily in horse-drawn carriages for hire. As he was using his own bankroll, he asked one of the drivers to take him to a hostel for medical students that he'd heard was cheap and good. He figured he could pass for a medical student.

The driver said that that place would be closed because it was 1 a.m. Sinclair insisted, but the driver was right. When they reached the hostel, they found that no amount of hammering on the door brought a response. By then he had told the driver his real reason for insisting on the hostel: he was short of money. The driver replied that he knew just the place, and trotted the horse back into the centre of the city. Sinclair had no idea where he was being taken. Suddenly the carriage turned a corner and the driver urged the horse into a gallop for a grand arrival while simultaneously ringing a bell by pumping a foot-pedal in his carriage, as drivers did to summon hotel doormen to greet arriving guests. They pulled up in front of a substantial-looking four-storey building.

When help poured out to unload bags and carry them inside, the driver identified Sinclair as a young doctor who needed a room. The "young doctor" was surprised that the driver would accept no payment. Inside, "a picturesque man in a green apron" told him the carriage charge would be put on his bill. He was conducted to a warm and comfortable room which contained a lot of mirrors. Soon a man in a white uniform came to run a bath for him, and to take a food and drink order. A waiter arrived with a table, another with a tablecloth, a third with the food and drink, and then:

> The original waiter was back to see if all was well and my thoughts were on nothing but the cost. This would surely set me far back.
>
> "Is there anything further the Herr Doctor would require?" No.
>
> "Some company perhaps?"
>
> Herr Doctor looked interested.
>
> "Ah, yes, company. Would Herr Doctor find a blonde

desirable, or perhaps a Titian, or would it be inopportune to fancy a brunette?"

This was indeed a pimp in the grand manner. . . . The company problem was arranged: blonde, and she arrived discreetly, whereupon there was a complete rearrangement of the housekeeping scene. Everything left of what I'd ordered was taken away, a new collection of viands provided.

It was now somewhere around three in the morning, but the original waiter was not quite finished with his chore. "Would the young doctor admire to enjoy her company for the evening" pause "or for the night?"

The cost was in no sense high, and it turned out I'd been taken not to a hotel but a lively house of assignation. . . . I was never asked to sign a register, never asked when I'd be leaving, never pressed to use the services or the personnel of the establishment. . . .

When it came time to leave, I was *told* a price. It seemed very low and many of the staff lined up to say farewell. I thought this was the usual tip parade, but of six who stood there to say *Auf Wiedersehen* three refused tips. . . .

Sinclair had an instinct, as well, not to push an idea beyond its limit, although obviously his idea of a limit was based on his own mores. Still, once he had mentioned ordering up a blonde in the Vienna brothel, and that she duly arrived, he said nothing more about her. No doubt he knew that the story was borderline for the *Star* anyway, and that further details would doom it for sure.

But another Vienna story was told in full detail. He had written before about the high suicide rate in Vienna—there had been twenty-seven in four days while he was there— and about how, beneath its façade of gaiety, Vienna was full of hopeless people, some starving.

He wrote (subhead: Starving Woman Dies in Arms of Star

Reporter) that he'd gone into an automat to get a sandwich one midnight and

> I had just bitten into the sandwich when there was a commotion outside. I went out and a grey-faced hollow woman of about sixty was quivering on the ground. Another woman stood over her crying, "Verhungern," and repeating it. That means starvation.
> A man picked the woman up and carried her into the automat. A girl dropped three coins in the slot and a little wine trickled into a glass.
> I held the head while someone pushed the wine down the woman's throat. She did revive a little. I was thinking of that poem, *Somebody's Mother*, and gave her all the coins I had and she took hold of my wrist with a bony hand and tried to whisper something. I felt the bony hand grip my wrist tighter and tighter then it relaxed slowly and the woman toppled over dead.
> I took her shoulders in my arms but she never opened her eyes, never said any so-called last words. She was dead with the other one still muttering "starvation, starvation."

After Vienna he did go on to Venice, tried one hotel on the Grand Canal, objected to the canal's smell, and after a day or two moved to a place on the sea front, where he was given a cramped little room, said to be all that the place had available.

For days he called Cooks-Venice for mail before he remembered he'd given Gladys the Cooks-Vienna address, so he arranged to have his mail forwarded from Vienna to Venice. A few days later, when he came in from a swim, he found he'd been moved to a spacious suite.

There he found a pile of letters and telegrams. These, it turned out, had been the reason for his move to the larger room, since the management had decided that anybody with that much mail must be important. He opened the telegrams first, finding one from Gladys to let him know that while he'd been in Vienna he'd become the father of a baby girl to be named Jean. If he felt any remorse at living it up in a brothel while Gladys was giving birth, he didn't mention it in his memoirs.

With his career then approaching high gear, a whispering campaign began that followed him almost for life: that none of these things really happened, that he made them up as he went along. The truth is that some journalists could have travelled—some *have* travelled—the same route as Sinclair without possessing the instinct, the sheer curiosity about the human condition, to find what he found. He wasn't exactly the good Samaritan type, but when something interesting presented itself, he never crossed to the other side of the road and hurried on. Some of it was fun and he wrote that as fun; when it was tragedy or something close to it, he had a very clearly sensed, open-eyed, often dispassionate way of relating precisely what happened, and what happened next, until his readers had the picture as he saw it and felt it. He often lucked in to his kind of story, large or small, wherever he went.

Once in Montreal, en route to do a piece about hunting porpoises from aircraft, he happened to encounter Greta Garbo and interviewed her at lunch. When they were parting, she gave him a package of her very long and distinctive cigarettes.

A day later in a café he was smoking one of them when a passerby stopped and asked where such cigarettes came from.

Sinclair said, "Well, Greta Garbo gave them to me."

The man looked at him a little strangely. When Sinclair didn't elaborate, he asked, "What are you doing here in Montreal?"

"I'm going porpoise-hunting."

A searching look, then, "Well, when?"

Sinclair: "Not sure exactly. I'm waiting for my airplane."

The man left, looking back two or three times.

In New York he interviewed Earl Carroll, who at that time had the most famous girlie show of its time, *Earl Carroll's Vanities*. Carroll therefore was looked upon as one of the world's leading experts on beautiful women. Sinclair drew from him, among other things, this:

> I think the average age of our girls is 18 or 19. Of course, their mental age runs lower than that, about five years lower. Beautiful girls can only stay beautiful as long as they never think. Therefore the showgirls and the ladies of my ensemble ought to be beautiful for many years to come. Blondes are just a little goofier than brunettes, but I may have that all wrong—see, I have more blondes than brunettes.

Even when he was home, Gordon was on call by the *Star* for personal appearances. The paper naturally wanted to take advantage of the virtual hero-worship that by now surrounded their roving reporter. Canada was in one of the lowest points of the economic depression of the time. Sinclair's stories (the Vienna one apparently the only piece considered not fit for publication, although it was exactly in the Sinclair tone of self-revelation that sold papers) seemed to help people forget their troubles. Whenever he did get home to great fanfare, Bessie was bursting with pride and Sinclair enjoyed every minute of it.

He apparently ignored, or was unaware of, the profound effect that his travels were having on his family life. This was enunciated in a 1986 interview with his oldest son, Gord, who left home immediately after high school to become, in time, as famous a radio figure in Montreal as his father was in Toronto: "He'd be gone for seven months. There'd be the great homecoming and then the *Star* would send him on the banquet circuit. Next thing we knew we'd be down at Sunnyside station waving him goodbye again. It was Mother who held things together."

Gord's first memory of those departures dates from when he was three—and he'd seen a lot of them even by then. He was to grow up with memories that stamp his father as uncaring or even cruel in some family situations. This might have been caused partly by something Sinclair recognized as well: his inability to declare his feelings to those he loved. He once told Betty Kennedy that he didn't think he had kissed his wife more than twenty times since they were married, and that using endearments was simply unknown in his own family childhood. Gord's recollection is that Gladys and Gordon never hugged or kissed in front of their children.

However, in such recollections there are bound to be anomalies. If Gord's first memory of the hoopla of one of his father's departures dated from the time he was almost four, it would have been in January 1932, when Sinclair was setting out for the Orient by way of Europe. Gladys had done all his packing, and whatever he would need in 30,000 miles was stowed away somewhere. He would be gone until late August, seven and a half months, but the first leg of his trip was to New York to board ship. From New York, a day after leaving home, he sent a story to the *Star* about his departure.

> This business of coming away at the last possible second on the first 500-mile leg of the world jaunt is lots of fun, too—but hard on the self-control.
>
> There comes that moment when you put the boys to bed and all but blubber.
>
> It's an effort to say, "Now, Gordon, you sit in the big chair, you see that none of the big boys hit Donny. You take care of Momma and Jean," and Gordon swears with his big brown eyes that he will. Gordon is three and he tells me that he will look after the Sinclair women and keep the home from invasion. Don says that he wants to come with me on choo-choo. The baby cries. I try to act like a gay and gallant adventurer.
>
> There is the silent ride to Sunnyside station. A last look at familiar objects. The gang to see me off. I try to be flippant and friendly and the bird you think I

am. They make a newsreel and I feel important. My mother and dad get lost in the shuffle and I only spot them as the train moves off.

CHAPTER FIVE

"THE BIRD YOU THINK I AM"

*"I had seen many Hollywood newspaper pictures
and to me Sinclair looked like the star of them all."*
—Jocko Thomas, police reporter.

Sinclair's phrase "the bird you think I am" was deeply
symbolic of his life. He and the *Star* between them created
the image that the true Sinclair lay somewhere between
one of his own self-descriptions ("I'm just a hobo who
writes") and the public's hero-worship. The readers voiced
their gratitude by buying the *Star*. Sinclair met them halfway by never missing a chance to say somehow or another,
"Look at me, folks, I'm just an ordinary stiff like the rest of
you." By then several Ontario schools from London to
Oshawa, mainly in communities where the *Star* was sold or
Sinclair's stuff was printed in local dailies, were using his
stories in class. "I must be getting efficient," Sinclair said.
"Gosh, I hope efficiency never grows on me. What a terrible end for a guy."

One with a ringside seat to watch Sinclair's progress from
anonymity to stardom was still, in 1987, working the police
beat for the *Star*. Gwyn (Jocko) Thomas was hired as a
copy-boy in 1929, one of twenty-eight under head boy Red
Burnett. His earliest memory of Sinclair was "of a thin-
faced, good-looking guy who wore his fedora at all times
inside the office. Most reporters did. Even some deskmen,

like Alf Rubbra, wore hats while they sat on the rim writing heads and editing stories." (Rubbra had been a famous reporter once himself, which is probably why Jocko Thomas singled him out; Rubbra had covered for the *Star* the arrival of the *Titanic* survivors in New York in 1912.)

The first time Jocko Thomas worked with Sinclair, he recalled, was just before the hobo series. Sinclair had been assigned to cover a Presbytery meeting of Toronto-area churchmen. Hugh Garner, later one of Canada's better-known short-story writers and novelists, was the copy-boy assigned to go along and phone in Sinclair's running copy, but he begged off and Jocko Thomas was sent instead.

Their fifty-five-year friendship dated from then. As Sinclair's star rose, Jocko Thomas was an admiring onlooker. "Sinclair was one of the fastest typists I ever saw. Once he got going he could rattle off take after take, a bit wordy, the desk claimed, but in his heyday desk men had orders not to touch his stuff other than to make sure of spelling." In those days copy-boys, after a couple of years' service, were given a choice: they could become reporters or printers. Printers were better-paid. "It was watching guys like Sinclair at work that stopped me from becoming a printer when my time came. I had seen many Hollywood newspaper pictures and to me Sinclair looked like the star of them all. I thought what a great thing it would be if I could be a reporter."

That is only part of the evidence to show that, very quickly, Sinclair's image had taken on a life of its own. Better still, it was appreciated by management. Joe Atkinson had a talk with him one day, found out about his mortgage and the interest he was paying, and arranged to pay off the mortgage and get it back through weekly pay deductions; then promptly raised Sinclair's pay by enough to cover those deductions! Some idea of the public interest was indicated when the *Star* asked its readers where he should go next. Promotion material, possibly written by Sinclair, kidded that this survey was some kind of a contest: "Get your letter in fast. It might even win the gooseberry-flavored toothpaste." Within a few days 516 readers cast their votes: Italy and Spain were at the top of the list, India third, Russia fourth. That is what had led to his European trip.

Later that year, standard pre-trip promotion for Sinclair had developed to the point where not only would he write about the trip, talk it up on radio, and give interviews to newspapers in other cities that carried his work, but *other* stars of the *Star* would be assigned to interview him on his departure, on his return, and occasionally by cable in between.

For Sinclair's take-off for the Orient early in 1932 his own "so-long-folks" piece was told with typical Sinclairian breeziness (for these purposes he had a style derived from equal parts of the *Boy's Own Annual* and the 1928 Hecht-MacArthur play *Front Page*). His faithful sea-going type-writer, he wrote, had been in the shop getting all tuned up for

> the biggest, farthest and best news chase that it ever
> faced or ever expects to face any place, any time. . . .
> This footloose reporter with the inseparable pal in
> the much-labelled box will head around the world to
> all those glamorous spots you have dreamed about,
> read about, or seen in the movies. Will take the road
> to Mandalay and roll eastward from Suez. Will show
> you Rangoon and Singapore and Benares; that weird
> and spooky city on the Ganges where magicians make
> you see things that never existed. We'll float down the
> Nile together. . . .

He was not alone in warming up the crowd. Gregory Clark was assigned to the going-away interview (Sinclair the man, Sinclair the good friend, Sinclair the great adventurer). The story ran under Clark's own famous byline. And, as it turned out, everything that Sinclair had done before his January to August odyssey of 1932 was covered in a vaudeville saying of the time, "You ain't seen nothin' yet." Europe, the United States, Cuba, Mexico—even Vienna—

had not afforded him the kind of raw material that he turned out to be best at. Exotic adventure was to be his gold mine, his promised land, and the 1932 trip showed the way.

Newspapers in the United States, especially the huge weekend jobs that specialized in diverting alternatives to the joblessness, the bread lines, and the grindingly grim prospects that faced so many readers during the Great Depression, ate up all the Sinclair adventures that the *Star*'s own syndicate, the Star News Service, could provide.

Mad panthers, scared elephants. A scorpion in his shoe when he already had a broken and splint-bound hand. Preparing to face Chinese pirates on a diet of boiled beetles. Fragrant bowls of soup, featuring what he thought to be particularly tasty sausages until he noticed the horns on one and found it was a huge slug. A Canton admiral. A bobbed-haired pirate queen. A dying Chinese boy asking, "Is Daddy hurt?" while Sinclair gave him a blood transfusion, in vain.

Which brings one to Mohandas Karamchand (Mahatma) Gandhi, the man most responsible for India's independence and the most famous Indian in history. It's remarkable that inside of two years in the early 1930s, Sinclair met both Hitler and Gandhi, one to become the symbol of inhuman horror, an ultimate failure, the other devoted to attaining India's independence by non-violent means, an ultimate success. However, Sinclair's own published recollections of Gandhi are not quite in accord with the facts. In that part of his 1966 memoir which deals with his first visit to India in 1932, he says, "The first assignment outside of Bombay was Mahatma Gandhi's salt march to the sea, a walk of peaceful protest whereby he'd draw attention to Indian grievances for three weeks, then . . . make salt from sea water and get arrested."

This sounds like an unusual crime, but it was real. The British had declared that they had a monopoly on salt production. Gandhi announced well in advance that he was going to defy that monopoly. Then he took three leisurely weeks to walk to the scene of the crime, by which time

69

India was in a turmoil of suspense to see what the British would do. Also, more importantly to Gandhi's courtship of world opinion, the long march gave the world's press time to get there and cover the event.

But the fact is, Gordon Sinclair was *not* there. The famous salt march took place in April 1930, when Sinclair was in Germany. He was nowhere near India until two years later.

So Sinclair obviously erred when he wrote of talking to Gandhi during the salt march. Perhaps he confused it with another Gandhi march, or he was victim of a simple lapse of memory over the thirty-four years between meeting Gandhi and writing his memoirs. Whatever the reason, he had blended what he had heard or read with what he really knew firsthand. One is reminded of an introduction by British historian A. J. P. Taylor to John Reed's famous book about the Bolshevik revolution, *Ten Days That Shook the World*. Taylor points out that Reed could not possibly have been an eyewitness to everything he wrote about as being firsthand observation, yet his account captured the *sense* of the revolution better than any other. Sinclair's Gandhi recollections can't quite be classed with Reed's *Ten Days*, but telescoping events, or delivering different versions at different times, was part of Sinclair's method.

Ironically—considering Sinclair's own reputation—when he finally did meet Gandhi in the Poona prison in 1932, he accused Gandhi of being a fake! Sinclair had with him newspaper clippings of Gandhi in top hat and cutaway coat, attending a conference on India's future in London a few months earlier. Now here he sat in a cotton loincloth, much publicized as something he had made himself. Wasn't this phony?

As Sinclair reported: "He looked at the clippings, chuckled a bit and said one word . . . 'Yes.'"

Sinclair also chided him about having a car, while he urged others to ride bullock carts or walk; about going to Switzerland for an appendectomy instead of having it done in his beloved India. "He took it all without comment and over a series of more meetings over the years, I came to realize that this was a man of greatness."

In time, Gandhi came to recognize Sinclair each time they met. Although he'd never been in Canada, he had seen Canadian newspapers and was amused by real-estate ads, which often included a line about the availability of plumbing, usually expressed as "two baths", "three baths", even "five baths". In these subsequent Gandhi-Sinclair meetings, "Gandhi always greeted me with, 'Ah, the man from the country of many bathtubs.'"

Apart from Gandhi, what ensued as Sinclair met India and the Orient head on may be communicated most simply by *Star* headlines. A selection:

VULTURES, GRAVE-DIGGERS IN HINDU BURIAL CEREMONY

WITH BARE HANDS, PARSEES SQUEEZE OUT SNAKE'S VENOM

SMOKE OF FUNERAL PYRES HOVERS OVER BOMBAY

HINDU ROADSIDE SURGEON SAWS OFF LEGS FOR QUARTERS

AGA KHAN'S BATHWATER SELLS FOR $3.30 PER GLASS

DEAD MARTYR, TIED ON CHAIR, BORNE BY MOB TO HOLY SANDS

HID IN DEATH HOUSE TO ESCAPE HOT FURY OF GANDHI DISCIPLES (In that one he suffered a head wound during a riot and "vainly" sought relief from rioting Indians.)

TOM-TOMS, NAUTCH GIRLS VIE IN BENGAL WEDDING

CRAWLS FROM BOAT TO BOAT TO SEE DOPEY SNAKE IN TREE

STUNG BY BLACK SCORPION, SINCLAIR RACES WITH DEATH

OPIUM FED TO CHILDREN IN INDIAN SWEAT SHOP

KHYBER PASS, ADVENTURE, WILDMEN, BECKONS SCRIBE

Of course, the stories that went with the headlines all were told from Sinclair's point of view as the ordinary guy from Riverdale, 117 pounds of blood and guts, that his readers had come to know and love—or hate.

Once, in central India, he heard a noise outside his lodgings and went to the nearest window, which was high on the bathroom wall. With nothing else handy, he moved a tin bathtub over to the window to stand on.

As I moved it the head of a brown viper came around the edge with a menacing sweep and I jumped straight in the air as he pounced. He hit the side of the tub and it sounded like a drum. I was over the top of it marking myself down as a fool and an idiot. Here with a drain into the bungalow fairly coaxing snakes to come in, I was snooping around with loose slippers and bare legs.

He ran to his bedroom for high boots and leather breeches, grabbed a cane, rummaged in a bag for his pistol. Thus armed, he apparently had a sudden rush of what-the-hell-am-I-doing? As journalists tend to see almost everything in terms of story, no doubt Sinclair was thinking right then not so much about the snake as a snake, as about the snake as a supporting character in a *Star* front-page story. Of course, he *could* go back in and brave that big snake, perhaps kill it. Good story. Or, he could leave it as a going-away present for the room's next incumbent. Different kind of story, but still okay, especially if he could find a next incumbent who had done him dirt somewhere, like those Brits who had called him an asshole colonial in that bar somewhere.

He did leave the snake alone for the time being. The next morning, cane in one hand, pistol in the other, he went back to the bathroom, to find that the snake was not in evidence.

I knew he was either under the tub or had gone out through the hole again. I went back and got the top of my typewriter. Just the case part. I threw this in and it crashed on top of the tub. The tub rocked and the snake came out, partly coiled and partly reared up. He was about five feet long and didn't seem to know where to look first.

I let go three shots and he went sliding back into the corner like a long rope of sausages. I'd got him in the coiled part and he was bleeding and twisting up and down. He still seemed blind because he never faced me but kept pouncing downward at unseen things and once he bit himself. He was right in the V of the concrete wall. It was easy shooting in there so I let him have three more and that was the end of the viper. I went up beside him and he got the seventh bullet straight through the head. Lots of fun if you have the proper equipment. But when they come on you unexpectedly. Well, you think it out.

These stories were usually printed in the *Star* about six weeks after they were written. There was no international airmail in those days. Cabling was expensive, so he mailed his stuff back by sea. But as he really had no competition in the field (the *Telegram* had no footloose reporter), the delay never dimmed the impact of his sometimes wildly improbable exploits.

Then there was a stiflingly hot day when he was drifting on the Ganges in "shocked fascination, past demented, diseased, deluded and devout pilgrims" who were bathing in the river's healing waters. It would make a story, all right, but how could he make it better? He found the way. The heat was unbearable. What would the old Don River swimmer do in such a case? He jumped in to cool off, causing hundreds of the faithful who saw this infidel befouling their holy river to chase him and threaten his life.

His final story of this trip was datelined Tokyo, June 25, published in the *Star* on August 15, 1932. The next day he announced himself to be home and wrote about walking in to find that his youngest children, Don and Jean, didn't know who he was. But Gord "still knows his Dad when he sees him." He was happy to be home and, apart from the reunion with his family, claimed, "I've got the right to be excited."

This was not only because of the hero's welcome he got at the *Star*, plus an offer from a book publisher to work his trip into book form for quick release in both Canada and the United States, but also because of a column written a few days earlier by J. V. McAree of the *Mail and Empire*. McAree was a jewel of Canadian journalism. He had been writing a column since 1903. His graceful and well-informed "Fourth Column" on the editorial page, often reprinted in anthologies or collected in book form, was respected throughout the country. Sinclair, returning home, had found waiting for him a McAree column which began,

This morning or some morning soon, Gordon Sinclair will walk into the *Star* offices and sprinkle his cigarette ashes on the floor or on somebody's desk in the serene confidence that, having completed a remarkably workmanlike job, he is entitled to some privileges. Which nobody can deny.

In fact, he has done one of the best jobs of reporting that we have noted, and we have been noting things like this for a good many years. For Gordon Sinclair is the kind of reporter we should like to be if we were a reporter. Shame compels the admission that when we were a reporter we were nothing like Mr. Sinclair. It is most unusual for a comparatively young man to be the kind of reporter he is, to have confidence in his own judgment, the instinct that the things which interest him are the things which will interest his readers; and, after all, not to care so much and find the chief satisfaction in painting the thing as he sees it for the God of things as they are. It is a rare thing but it is the right thing, and he is blessed in not knowing any other.

In that column, McAree sets up what Gordon Sinclair is ("quite young . . . quite a rebel . . . if there is a pose about him it is that he is hardboiled") and what he is not:

The old method for the travelling correspondent was for him to go to the local library for his local color, and then drop into the newspaper offices and either look at the files or chat to the editors. The visit would be completed by a call on the mayor or lieutenant governor or whoever might be accepted as the official spokesman for the community. Thus would be produced another of the ten thousand similar space fillers which have bored their millions of newspaper readers in all parts of the world for a hundred years. . . .

   Mr. Sinclair is an exemplar of the revolt against the old-fashioned travel diaries, amateur and professional. . . . Instead of bowing his head and regarding reverently what is supposed to be reverent, Mr. Sinclair has cocked his hat as if to say, "What the hell!" and has looked at things which, to him, seemed worth regarding. . . . To interpret Mr. Sinclair to readers would be like explaining a hoe to a market gardener. What he does is so obvious that elucidation would be childish. Yet since we are all children in a way, it may not be useless to comment upon it.

   The clue was given in one of his articles from somewhere in India when he said that he followed somebody down a street expecting that something would happen, or that he might see something that readers of his articles would like to hear about. So he tailed this bird and sure enough found that he led him into mysteries if not Eleusinian at least sufficiently startling to Canadians. . . . He has brought the world of Asia and India to his readers in a way that it has not been brought before. The most important thing about him is that he is always himself. He is not imitating any other writer. The world is divided between people who are themselves, and people who are modelling themselves upon others. A further division might be made, the first being people who are worth being themselves. To this, Mr. Gordon Sinclair undoubtedly belongs.

Sinclair bubbled over McAree's column in his hey-folks-I'm-home piece, telling of experiencing his family again and his cronies again and Toronto again and all the joys thereof, and "besides, look what McAree says about me in his famed *Mail and Empire* Fourth Column. He says I'm a mighty doggone good newspaper reporter and if McAree says I'm a good reporter then I must be a good reporter.

Some day I hope to be a doggone good editorial writer and I think perhaps I will be. If I ever get to be as consistently interesting as McAree I'll be happier than a finance minister with a big surplus."

However, acclaim from other newspapers was not quite unanimous. A few days after the J. V. McAree column, the Fergus *News-Record* confessed that on reading the McAree column,

> We wondered at first if the *Mail and Empire* was going to offer Mr. Sinclair a job . . . but concluded that his style of writing would hardly find room in the morning papers, which try to give the news, and don't bother much about supplying entertainment, except in the comic strips and political editorials. . . .
>
> Every night the *Star* contains a column or more from [Sinclair's] typewriter and always, it appears, [he] has been in some amazing adventure or some place where his life is in momentary danger. Undoubtedly, he exaggerates. We won't say he lies, but you get the idea. . . .

The book that he'd been asked to write was called *Footloose in India*, and he wrote it in nineteen days. The first printing of about 3,000 copies hit the stands less than two months after he'd arrived home (it was reviewed in the *Mail and Empire* on October 15), and sold out the first day. Other printings were ordered. Sinclair was mobbed at autographings; mobbed isn't too strong a word—photos show the slim, smiling Sinclair in the middle of jam-packed throngs in department-store book sections in Toronto and Ottawa. Meanwhile Sinclair's name was in the *Star* assignment book every day. Just as the *Footloose* book publicity reached its height, a riot erupted at Kingston Penitentiary.

About a year earlier, a crackdown on Canadian communists had led to the jailing of Canadian Communist Party leader Tim Buck and some of his associates. In prison he'd found many willing to listen to his ideas about what was wrong with Canada, and attracted some new adherents to the party. When the riot broke out one night in October, ten months into Tim Buck's five-year sentence, many police and prison officials believed that Buck was the man behind the violence.

That charge was not proved at subsequent trials, and parliamentary inquiries were to last several years, but one ugly fact was accepted: At the height of the riot, five shots from a pistol and a shotgun were fired by two prison guards into Buck's cell, the only cell fired upon in the whole prison. None hit Buck. But the shots were not even a rumor when Sinclair and another rising *Star* man, Matthew Halton, were called out late on the night the riot began and drove to Kingston, arriving about 7 the next morning. Reporters had been there all night, none able to get an interview with anyone in authority. What happened next was a triumph of Sinclairism.

Two lines of soldiers were patrolling back and forth in front of the prison gate. Some reporters from time to time had tried to dash through, but had been caught and turned back. Sinclair watched from a distance. In an outer ring, the soldiers paced in such a way that every minute or so they met face to face, did an about-turn, then marched away from one another, leaving a gap of nearly two hundred feet.

In all the earlier attempts to reach the jail, reporters had tried to run the gap. Sinclair did it his way. He waited until the soldiers reached the outer point of their walk and turned to march back toward one another, then

> I sauntered up to arrive just as the soldiers were coming together. I plucked an ordinary police identity card from my wallet and tried to sound the proper bureaucratic tones when I said to the soldiers, "Sinclair to see the governor." Nothing to it. They let me through. Seeing me passed by the first row of soldiers, the second row went on about their patrol, ignoring me.
>
> I have a peculiar toes-out walk which makes me

seem far more self-assured and confident than I am, and with such an arrogant walk I made a bold move toward the front door of the prison. A man with a face as red as a baboon's behind opened the door and when I said I was there to see the governor, he let me in.

I knew where the governor's office was, so deliberately went the other way to see as much as I could before they chucked me out. What I saw was a lot of broken plumbing, wet floors and nervous men. When guards came to hustle me in the opposite direction (and into the prison office) I told the exhausted warden that I'd already seen enough to make a pretty good yarn and it was to his advantage to tell me his side of what had happened.

He wearily said he couldn't do that without permission from Ottawa, but while we were talking an inspector of the penitentiaries branch arrived and we got along just dandy because he thought I was inside with permission. When I got out with a detailed yarn about two hours later [and reached telegraphers who had set up their Morse keys near by], I worked a bit of psychology, flashing off a wire to the city desk,

"THINK SINCLAIR GOT INSIDE. WILL ADVISE. HALTON."
Then I started to write my story. After about forty minutes I shot off another wire—"SINCLAIR DEFINITELY ON INSIDE. HALTON."

In another twenty minutes, with my story almost finished, I sent a third message. "HAVE COMPLETE STORY; INTERVIEW WITH WARDEN. MUCH DAMAGE. SAW BUCK IN CELL. SINCLAIR."

By the time the story did arrive, only five or six hours after Sinclair's 7 a.m. landing in Kingston, the *Star*'s editors were ready with their biggest type: EXCLUSIVE! EYEWITNESS!

His reward was a telegraphed message of congratulations, which also instructed him to return right away to Toronto. He was just in time to catch a fast westbound train from Kingston. Also on the train was a photographer friend who had a bottle of gin. They began to celebrate Sinclair's scoop, which in those days, when radio news was in its infancy and television unknown, was total. Well into the gin, "only then did I remember I hadn't eaten all day." The two headed for the dining car, had to wait in line, and drank more gin from the bottle. "When the food came . . . I couldn't eat, and when I tried to get up and leave, I couldn't make it. For the first, last and only time of my life, I had to be helped out of the dining car . . . ."

When he staggered off the train in Toronto, it was back to having to dance not only to what the editors wanted, but to what book publishers and the book-buying public wanted. He was in demand for speaking engagements, all of which were covered euphorically by the *Star*. A rare firsthand description of such an event comes from a man with whom he would share hundreds of evenings in the future on *Front Page Challenge*.

"The first recollection I have of Sinclair is long before I met him," Fred Davis said.

> I was in high school and he was just back from his trip to India. In those days high school assemblies sometimes featured illustrated lectures with slides— except he didn't bring slides, *he* was the slide.
>
> He was in costume—pith helmet, safari jacket long before they were in style, shorts and puttees, and a lot of memorabilia, spears, swords and that sort of thing, and did a very engaging morning assembly. Here was this colorful little bantam rooster strutting across the stage brandishing these exotic instruments of war. . . .

When the book came out in the United States, columnist Lewis Gannett's review in the *New York Herald Tribune* described Sinclair as "a brash young Canadian who writes like a merger of [American traveller and adventurer] Richard Halliburton, Floyd Gibbons [American journalist and

war correspondent] and [famous New York gossip colum-
nist] Walter Winchell, with occasional touches of Katherine
Mayo [whose bestseller of the time was a study of child
marriage in India] and the [movie gossip-mongers] Gra-
hams of Hollywood."

The book eventually made, by Sinclair's estimate, about
$50,000, some of which went to a new house, but which
also made possible Sinclair's first substantial stock-market
investments. He had dabbled a little in stock before the
1929 crash, writing late in life that he'd held at least two
stocks through the crash and didn't lose a penny on them.
But when his first royalties for *Footloose* arrived, he took
the cheque for several thousand dollars around the corner
from the *Star* to the office of Dominion Securities on Bay
Street, plunked it down in front of the first man he met, and
asked for investment advice.

The young stockbroker he chose, then in his early twenties, knew how to make money. He was John Angus (Bud)
McDougald, who became one of Canada's most influential
financiers. Later in life he headed great corporations, one
being the Argus Corporation, and in one sixteen-year
period paid more than a million dollars in personal income
tax every year. The Sinclair luck obviously seemed to
extend well beyond journalism. Bud McDougald handled
the Sinclair portfolio through its formative years. Later
Sinclair could and did call him, on occasion, when he
wanted an insider's private opinion on flaps or trends or
news in the financial world.

But that was later. When Sinclair was back home, it was a
certainty that Sinclair was soon going to be on the road
again. The flurry of excitement over *Footloose* came in the
midst of a series of long pieces in the *Star Weekly*. Then on
December 29 he announced that his next trip would be "on
the trail of romance through the South Seas". An accompanying picture layout, complete with map, showed scantily
dressed South Sea maidens and a preview of how he'd look
in his South Seas wardrobe, running heavily to breeches
and pith helmets.

For this take-off, *Star* promotion went into an even higher gear. Gregory Clark had written the send-off story for India and Asia a year before. This time an equally senior *Star* reporter, Fred Griffin, was assigned to organize a public farewell. He booked Massey Hall in downtown Toronto—and it wasn't big enough.

Headline:

TORONTO WRITES HISTORY IN FAREWELL TO SINCLAIR

Under the subhead "Ten Thousand Clamoured for Entry to Massey Hall Party", Griffin reported that three thousand jammed into Massey Hall while other thousands milled around outside hoping to catch a glimpse of the guest of honour. Sinclair was cheered as he reached the stage, pith helmet and all. Sinclair's parents and his own family were seated with the mayor, city councillors, and other notables on the stage behind him. With the aid of a map and pointer he traced his proposed route and speculated on what he would see and write about.

Griffin's story was backed up by a six-column photo layout. One huge photo showed the jammed interior of the hall. Another showed Gladys accepting a bouquet while chatting with the mayor's wife. Still another had Sinclair kissing his mother goodbye, Bessie beaming; and one showed the crowd at Union Station as he boarded his train to head west.

Of course, being Sinclair, he didn't go straight anywhere. He wrote several stories from Hollywood on his way through, and one datelined Tijuana, Mexico: "A mud-splashed news hawk tramped toward the United States in a driving rain tonight and on arrival got tossed in the guardhouse as an alien under surveillance. I ought to know because I am the mud-stained prowler and if I don't get this story dashed off in a big league rush I'll miss my ship for the South Seas."

The South Seas stories were in the now-familiar Sinclair pattern: blood, death, sex, danger, keep 'em guessing what comes next. Before leaving Toronto a priest had given him $25 with the injunction that he use it, and any more he could raise, to buy freedom for girls held in "paganistic slavery in the jungle badlands of Bathurst Island". *Star* readers had added another $35. Sinclair converted this into eighteen pounds, five shillings, of Australian money, enabling him to buy "18 brown-bodied brides" and to turn them over to a Catholic mission on the island, swelling the congregation to 128, "every member bought and paid for in the market."

Headline:

LANDS ON CANNIBAL ISLE AS DEATH DRUMS MUTTER

In a story from New Guinea, one of the last fading strongholds of cannibalism, he mentioned a man from Lucknow, Ontario, who had gone into the jungle and disappeared, only his gnawed bones being found. He ended that story, it seemed puckishly, "so do any of our readers know of any other Canadians who have been eaten by cannibals anywhere in the world, or who have had experiences with cannibals? If so, will they please write to the City Editor, Toronto Star, 80 King Street West, Toronto."

In those few lines is the faint echo of a man Sinclair knew and liked, James Curran of Sault Ste. Marie, Ontario, who owned and operated the *Sault Ste. Marie Star*. Curran steadfastly contended that wolves would not eat humans, and backed this opinion with a standing reward of $1,000 "for any man who can prove that he was et by a wolf."

Headline:

GHOULISH, UNPRINTABLE PRACTICES WITNESSED BY WANDERING REPORTER

The unprintable practices turned out to be printed anyway:

Cannibals say, only eat a strong man's arms because to eat them is to gain the man's strength. Even though man-eating has pretty well died out, the things you do see are pretty doggone blood-curdling. We climbed a tall hill here, for instance, to see dead men perched in trees. The bodies were wrapped in woven bark. Beneath the perched dead sat the wives, usually about three, and some of the sorrowing relatives.

The idea of this shocking [custom] it seems is for the descendants to acquire the dead person's strength by having his decomposing body drip greasily all over them. This, they say, is the very man himself. They will smear himself (sic) in his very body. And do you know it? Oi yoi! They do. I'm telling you.

One story was of a boy who had been eaten by a crocodile, whereupon the crocodile was killed, wrapped in white, and buried with the boy inside. All in one especially unlucky day, a cobra startled Sinclair so that he dropped his camera, which was swallowed by quicksand; he damaged his typewriter; then he suffered sunstroke. It made a good story.

But he did get home, as alive as ever, by June. His South Seas series ran until September, while the *Star*, as usual, was bedevilled by correspondents who claimed that Sinclair never saw or experienced or even was told authentically the fantastic stories that were his stock in trade. This time Sinclair, for once, was supported by a substantial local citizen. H. W. Phelan, of the family that had founded the Canadian Railway News Company (now called Cara Operations Limited), had travelled with Sinclair in the South Seas for a few weeks.

"Gord certainly earns his dough," Mr. Phelan told the *Star* in a lengthy interview.

He must have the constitution of an ox to live in those tropical lands and exist on the food he gets. He goes into regions no other white man would think of touching and you can take my word for it, all his thrills are genuine. Lots of places he finds no hotel at all and about all the decent food he gets comes from cans and you can figure out yourself what canned meat is like that's been lying in the sun at 115 degrees for a year or more. When I left him at Singapore he was doping up with quinine to ward off fever. All the time he was with us he carried a little medical valise on his wrist. . . . You know, he has to tone down his stories quite a bit to have them believed. He has a real big adventure every day because he goes right after it and doesn't give a hang about the risk. . . .

Immediately on his return home, Sinclair wrote his second book, *Cannibal Quest*. It was destined for the fall lists to catch those readers left panting for more after the previous year's *Footloose in India*. The *Star* reported that their wandering reporter now had four more books under contract. Soon after publication, *Cannibal Quest*, selling well in Canada, was doing even better in the United States. It was chosen "book of the week" by Macy's department store in New York, was ninth on the overall U.S. best-seller list, and was topping that in several places: first in Cleveland, Boston, Philadelphia, Scranton, Cincinnati, and Albany; second in Chicago; in a tie for third in New York City. One day Walter Winchell's column in the *New York Mirror* was headed, "THINGS I NEVER KNEW 'TIL NOW . . . (Thanks to Gordon Sinclair, author of *Cannibal Quest*)." On a couple of later occasions, Sinclair wrote guest columns for Winchell.

Meanwhile, Sinclair was missing the publication excitement because he was gone again, heading for Devil's Island for a series that ended early in February 1934. These he was to bring together in his 1935 book *Loose Among Devils*, which he started in the few weeks between his return from Devil's Island and his departure in mid-March for a 4½-month trip to Africa, and completed after his return from Africa in late summer. The speed with which his books were written may be slightly misleading. Microfilm of his stories in the *Toronto Star* files now shows that many of the clippings were edited in what appears to be his handwriting, and in a manner consistent with a man whipping a pile of his own articles into book form.

But also in the autumn of 1934 Aimee Semple McPherson came back to Canada, her birthplace, for a series of revival meetings. At the time, hundreds of churches in the United

States and Canada had been organized under her Four-square Gospel banner, in addition to the mother church at her Angelus Temple in Los Angeles, usually filled to its 5,000 capacity for her services. In Canada her first revival meeting was in Montreal, followed by one in Kingston and another in Belleville. Sinclair picked up the tour in Kingston and travelled with her to Toronto and elsewhere.

CHAPTER SIX

AIMEE

*"... . for twenty years Maitland kidded me for having
an inflammable love affair in the arms of the
evangelist."*
—Sinclair, writing about Aimee Semple McPherson.

In Sinclair's 1966 memoir the opening chapter is entitled,
"Aimee Loved a Party", and describes a couple of days
Sinclair and Aimee Semple McPherson spent together in
Toronto and in Ingersoll, Ontario. It seemed an odd choice
to lead off a book that was mainly about the Toronto in
which Sinclair grew up, his family, his early jobs, and his
days as a footloose reporter. Although that halcyon period
of his life when he was becoming famous did include Sister
Aimee, as her faithful called her, she had been dead for
twenty-three years by the time his memoir came out and
she was no longer topical. Only those who had been adults
in the 1920s had a chance to experience the full flower of
the Sister Aimee legend. Obviously she was something
special to Sinclair, and much of it was physical. In his 1966
opening chapter she is "shapely, curvy, seductive of voice,
persuasive", and apparently he took it from there, although
if it were a conquest there'd be some question as to who
conquered whom.

There is no attempt in his book to depict this as a major
milestone kind of affair for either of them. Indeed, it is
more meaningful simply as a glimpse of the kind of man
Sinclair was. His earlier diaries indicate that he was rarely
without a female favourite, whom he pursued assiduously,

and though he always stopped short of saying that they'd had sex together, his accounts were heavy with innuendo. He never mentioned the possibility of marriage to any of them. In other writings, some may point to his allusions to the availability of sex and his self-proclaimed disinterest in his late boyhood as indicating a languid libido , but it couldn't all have been that. When he did have his first sexual experience with the girl in the park, nobody was holding a gun to his head. His early relationship with Gladys, though restrained in the beginning, and respectful, soon resumed the tone with which he'd dealt with earlier girlfriends. The courtship lasted six years, before they married. Soon after, he was having sex elsewhere, and was to do so until the end of his life.

After marriage, Sinclair described himself in his travel writing as being shy in matters of sex. That might well have been a cover for the folks at home. Usually he made the claim of sexual shyness after describing encounters with women on some distant ship or strand which in many circumstances would have led to bed (slim Siamese girls ready to obey his every whim, a fräulein in night-dress slipping into his bedroom after midnight in Berlin, Sinclair always standing them off). So what to make of Sinclair and Aimee? Probably only that it was a casual affair, but, as it is his only casual affair open for conjectural examination, let's go.

Much of the evidence available about what happened between them in those ten or twelve days of September 1934 is circumstantial—but Sinclair did tell some confidants, usually with jubilance, that he and Sister had been up to (what is sometimes known as) no good. Certainly their meetings that September, drinking together, travelling together, provided propinquity well beyond his duty as a journalist and hers as an evangelist. Also, he had indicated in Vienna, and elsewhere, that he was open to sexual adventure as a form of random experience, almost as an offshoot of his news-gathering *modus operandi*.

As for Sister Aimee, since the age of seventeen, when she

first married, she had rarely been without a man in her life. But she was unattached when she re-encountered Sinclair, having been divorced a few months earlier by her third husband, David Hutton. She had married first in 1907 in Ingersoll, Ontario, her birthplace, leaving for China with her first husband, a missionary named Robert Semple. When he died in Hong Kong a little more than a year later, she and their baby daughter, Roberta Star Semple, returned to North America. Soon Aimee, working in various city missions in the United States, married Harold McPherson, a steady-living wholesale-grocery clerk in Rhode Island. They had a son, Rolf, but trouble began to develop because McPherson wanted a home with a wife in it, and Aimee wanted to be a travelling evangelist.

McPherson went along with her for a while, but finally he couldn't stand the barnstorming life, so he left her and went home. Years later, in the early 1920s, he filed for divorce, citing desertion and her "wildcat" habits. That marriage was long past at the time of her widely publicized "kidnapping" in 1926, which many were convinced had been a cover-up for a secret fling with a radio technician from her Angelus Temple; a friendship earlier so warm that it had worried staff members and some of her temple congregations.

This incident had been followed a few years later by marriage to David Hutton, a hefty actor and singer in an opera she had written. Hutton also in a short time filed for divorce. An acrimonious and much-publicized year of charges and counter-charges ended in March 1934 when she instructed her lawyers to allow Hutton's divorce action by default. She was in South Carolina that month when she was told that the provisional decree had been granted, and would become final a year later. In her 1977 biography, *Storming Heaven*, by Lately Thomas (William Morrow, New York), her biographer reported that she reacted to the end of her third marriage by "shaking her curls vivaciously" and saying, "I don't believe in marriage after divorce, but even if I did, I'd say *jamais* to the idea of another husband.

Love is a wonderful thing, but marriage . . . *jamais encore!*" (She had recently spent some months in Paris.)

Six months later when she landed in Montreal, Sinclair was thirty-four. Aimee was a few weeks short of forty-four, and by common consent everything Sinclair said about her physical attractiveness was true. This trip was an attempt to get back on a winning streak. The huge, unquestioning crowds that used to pack her meetings on the road and those in her home temple had been eroded by the years in which her "kidnapping", her muddled family life, and her other public sensations had made her seem less of a wonder-woman than an evangelistic question-mark.

The Canadian part of the trip wasn't helping, since crowds were poor in Montreal and Kingston. After Kingston, where Sinclair met her, and another meeting in Belleville, she was driven—one account says by Sinclair in his Ford coupe—to Toronto for two bookings at Maple Leaf Gardens.

Besides the local Ontario-girl-makes-good interest, her past was tailor-made for a feature writer of Sinclair's hard-boiled character, his technique of leaving out nothing and trying for more. When he asked for a private interview, she invited him to her Royal York hotel room. Sinclair arrived carrying the *Star*'s thick clippings-file from which to rehash old sensations.

The headline on his interview read:

SISTER AIMEE STILL INSISTS KIDNAPPING NO IDLE DREAM

He let the reader in on his system of sorting through the clippings as he led Aimee through many of the controversial parts of her life, obviously more interested in prurient sensations than in how many souls she'd saved. Regarding the kidnapping, he asked bluntly, "Was that a phony?" She contended, at length, that she had told nothing but the truth. The interview over, they breakfasted together in her room and seemed on friendly terms. When she mentioned that she'd like to visit her father's grave at Ingersoll, Sinclair offered to drive her there and she accepted.

Before that trip was due to take place, however, his

interview was published. It was milder than it might have been, but it still touched all the bases, including well-known, sworn-to, and previously published evidence casting doubt on her version of the kidnapping story. On the day it was printed, Sinclair went first to see Aimee and then to see his mother; it was her birthday. Bessie read the story and angrily denounced it to him. "You've deliberately set out to make this lady hated and cheap!" she raged.

He admitted that, in a way, Bessie was right, and confessed, "An hour before, Aimee had been crying on my shoulder about that same interview." He had taken the first edition to Aimee with the words, "Read it and weep." She had done both, and when he left she was still so upset that he thought their previous date to visit her father's grave together was definitely off. But Aimee had her secretary phone in a few hours to say that, as he had said some good things about her as well, the trip was on.

Sinclair has written two full-scale accounts of that trip to Ingersoll, the first in the *Star* the following day, and the other in his 1966 memoir. In the *Star* story Aimee, her blonde secretary, a *Star* photographer, and Sinclair started away in a car that broke down not far from the Sinclair home, where they proceeded on foot to pick up another car.

He had two cars then, a Cadillac sedan and a Ford coupe. Gladys was out with their three children in the Cadillac. The coupe had room for two in the front and could squeeze two more into what was called a rumble seat, an open-out, open-air seat for two at the back of the car with no shelter from the weather, which was threatening rain. Not enough room, Sinclair said. Nonsense, Aimee said, she'd ride in the rumble seat herself if she had to. In the *Star* story, Sinclair reported that he loaned Aimee a raincoat and, with her beside him in the front, his photographer and her secretary in the rumble seat, they set out—only to meet Gladys coming home in the Cadillac. Both stopped, Gladys looking Sinclair over "with vocal disapproval as she wondered who this smartly groomed woman was, coming from their house, in their car, wearing his coat."

In the *Star* story, the exchange went this way:

> "Gladys," I said, "this is Aimee Semple McPherson...
> you've heard of her?"
>
> "Yes, and I've heard of Rudy Vallee and Shirley
> Temple and the Prince of Wales."
>
> "Well, we can't argue now but this is Mrs.
> McPherson all right and I'd like that car because we
> have a long way to go."
>
> Gladys didn't look very happy about this but we got
> the car and away we went.

But the *Star* in those days was death on liquor. Even Sinclair couldn't have gotten away with—probably couldn't even have got published—the story as he told it in his 1966 memoir, and this is the version also remembered by other family members. In the unexpurgated (or less expurgated) 1966 version, Sinclair set out from downtown in the Ford coupe with Aimee alongside him and photographer Tom Wilson in the rumble seat with Aimee's secretary. Rain began when they were near Sinclair's home in Islington. He told Aimee they'd change cars, that his Cadillac would be a lot more comfortable.

> Sister Aimee looked with amused disbelief when I
> mentioned the Cadillac. She seemed to expect it
> when, on reaching the house, there was no such car.
> No person either. Gladys was out with our three kids,
> but the rain was now pelting at a windblown angle.
> There was no hope of continuing, so we went
> indoors.
>
> A fireplace was set so I put a match to it and asked if
> the ladies would like a short, sharp one.
>
> "A what?"
>
> "A drink. I have gin. Only gin."
>
> "No mix?"

"Lots of mix."

"Then gin and ginger for me," said Aimee.

We were away again. [The "again" is not explained.] The wind rose, the fires crackled, the bottle of gin vanished, and we opened another.

When Gladys came home, she looked in on this modest little orgy of the redhead [he described Aimee on various occasions as being redhead, blonde, or strawberry blonde] and the blonde, not to mention Wilson [the photographer] who was suffering no discomfort, and she carried a sack of groceries to the kitchen in silence. Aimee and I got up and followed her.

"This is Aimee McPherson," I said to Gladys. "You know, the evangelist. We got caught in the rain."

Gladys waited an awkward 40 seconds, then said, "I'm Cleopatra," and turned to unpack the groceries.

"Well, it is so Aimee McPherson and we're going to Ingersoll. How's the gas?"

There was no answer, so I picked up two raincoats, the preaching lady prudently carried the remains of the second bottle to the car, and we were westbound on Highway 5, stopping just once for a hot dog. Aimee left a startled cook at the stand after showing him clippings of herself and taking his chef's hat as a souvenir.

Legends among newspapermen at the time, and among Sinclair's friends later, had the foursome spending the next many hours in a Woodstock hotel. There is no way of checking. Sinclair's account in his memoirs was that after a few wrong turns in the wet and gloomy day, they found the right cemetery and eventually the right grave "with the square of granite saying, 'Semple'."

That must have been excellent gin, as Aimee's father's name was Kennedy, and her husband, Robert Semple, had been buried in Hong Kong. But enough of dreary technicalities. . . .

Aimee put on my white raincoat and Tom got ready for pictures in the gloom when Aimee exclaimed, "Christ! I forgot the flowers."

Happily there had been a funeral that day and that mound of earth was littered with an abundance of floral tributes, so we used those. . . . Tom got his tender pictures. . . . Driving back to town that night we were sleepy and quiet and Aimee . . . was girl-like and pensive when she asked, "Why did you do it?"

"Do what?"

"Write that terrible article. It was slimy with scandal and slander. Why don't people just ignore me? So okay, I made a mistake; I'm a phony, let's say. My career is wrecked. This pilgrimage has been a nothing . . . a costly nothing. Why can't people just leave me alone?"

I said it was personality. Some people had it just like she had red hair. Personality, I told her, was something you can't buy, beg, rent, steal, cultivate or inherit. "You've got it and you know it and you're going to be in the papers as long as you live."

The next day a headlined story from Ingersoll reported that vandals in the cemetery had stolen Aimee's flowers from her father's grave. In his memoir, Sinclair admitted who had done this dastardly deed: he and Aimee had carefully put the flowers back on the other grave, where they'd found them.

There was no hint of Aimee's late-night confession in Gordon's warm and supportive *Star* story the next day. He said he'd gone along on the pilgrimage to her father's grave "first as critic and cynic; later as an admirer". He wrote about driving her to the farm where she'd spent her girl-hood, and how they had sat by the farm pump in the rain while she told about "odd platform happenings in far countries".

They had visited Aimee's old school, heard how she had conducted her first revival meeting in Guelph when the

93

regular revivalist's voice "went dead", and talked about how she'd had three husbands but a total married life of just about the same number of years.

It was altogether a rather jolly story, ending with,

"It's been fun," she exclaimed. "All sorts of fun. Lots of troubles, of course; everybody has troubles. But mine get into the headlines."

When I got home it was still raining and Gladys was still sitting up wondering.

Aimee's first meeting in Toronto had drawn only 2,400, lost in the vastness of the Gardens. The second crowd was a good deal bigger. Sinclair attributed the better attendance to the impact of the way he'd reported the trip to her old home turf. He wrote nothing more about her for a few days. The Toronto visit ended, and Aimee went on to London. Their next meeting could have been a coincidence, or could have been planned; only the principals would know for sure.

Sinclair wrote about it. Again there were two versions, many years apart. The *Star*'s was somewhat the more squeaky-clean, the headlines reading

ON HIS WAY TO VISIT HUEY GORDON RUNS INTO AIMEE

His *Star* story, in which he borrowed a style then made famous by Damon Runyon, said that he'd been assigned to interview Huey Long, partly because Aimee had told him Huey Long would beat Franklin Roosevelt in the next U.S. elections. So he was en route to Louisiana, he wrote, the train on a siding at Hammond, Indiana, "when who walks out but a beautiful blonde [Aimee] who speaks as follows, 'Why, look who's here and where do you think you're going?'" According to his *Star* story she sat down, they talked awhile, and that was that.

The account in his 1966 book still had them meeting on the train, but Hammond, Indiana, had disappeared into limbo. The overnight train from Toronto to Chicago in those days always included several sleeping-cars. As all berths were curtained, the people in them out of sight, and the aisles dark and quiet, chance meetings were considerably odds-against, unless pre-planned.

However, Gordon was just riding along on the night train out of Toronto, he said, heading for Chicago and then Louisiana, passing the time before he went to his berth, when

> At London, Ontario, alone and woebegone, Aimee Semple McPherson, a picture of care and frustration, came into the nearly dark railway car and I didn't recognize her until she spoke to the porter. There was no sign of her blonde travelling companion, and she said she wanted to turn in at once. Obviously the London meeting had gone badly. If there was anyone to see her off, I didn't notice. In the morning she rang for coffee and when partly dressed, rolled out from the green curtains to recognize me and grunt a tired good morning.
>
> She brightened when I said I was on my way to see Huey [and they sat together while, Sinclair reported, Aimee talked enthusiastically about Huey Long's accomplishments]. Towards the end of this buildup Aimee was aglow again, starry-eyed. . . .
>
> No trains by-passed or even went through Chicago those days so, for me, it meant hanging around until evening. Aimee invited me to have breakfast in her room [in another reference to this trip he said the hotel was the Blackstone] and I spent much of the day there listening to that magic voice in snatches of her life story. Somehow George Maitland, editor-in-chief of the *Star*, got wind of this. Thereafter for twenty years Maitland kidded me for having an inflammable love affair in the arms of the evangelist, quite the way it was written in [Sinclair Lewis's novel] *Elmer Gantry*.

How George Maitland got that idea, no one can tell. Maybe Sinclair told him, or hinted, or mentioning it again was a way of keeping the memory green. A few years later

Aimee again visited Canada (writer and broadcaster Clyde Gilmour met her and danced with her in Lethbridge, describing her as a lively, witty, and "rather earthy" person), and Sinclair occasionally was in Los Angeles, where Aimee had rekindled her popularity. But there is no record that they met again after he left her room at the Blackstone.

In the early 1940s Aimee was found one morning, sprawled across her bed in a litter of powerful pills. A coroner's jury called it an "accidental overdose".

From then on, Sinclair wrote several times about Aimee Semple McPherson. There were lots of opportunities—a play about her life, the 1977 biography by Lately Thomas (in which neither Sinclair nor that 1934 trip was mentioned), and other less specific reasons.

The last was in September 1981, in a script for his *Let's Be Personal* program on CFRB. Some friends thought Sinclair was alluding, not so subtly, to his bygone days with Sister Aimee when, near the end of that item, he made a quite gratuitous reference to her sexuality: "*Variety*, the so-called Bible of Show Biz, gave Aimee a full-page obituary as 'The Redhead Who Couldn't Keep Her Legs Crossed'".

In the circumstances it seemed a little sad that, in 1966, writing about a woman who had been important in his life, even for a short time, he was shaky on the facts, saying their travels took place in 1935 when the year was 1934. And in his 1981 *Let's Be Personal* item he identified her as "the Ontario-born girl christened Aimee Semple". Of course, her family name was Kennedy, but he apparently had forgotten.

CHAPTER SEVEN

THE TIME HE WAS REALLY FIRED

His stuff from the Quetta earthquake was great (66,000 dead) but then he blew Ethiopia and got the axe.

It would be impossible to chart the number of times Sinclair was fired from the *Star*. Even before his reputation was made, he could be a difficult man to manage (self-confessedly "unshaven, sometimes drunk, now and again spending mornings in a card joint or bootlegger's"), and once he had become famous, he loudly questioned whatever he didn't agree with. Sometimes at the *Star*, someone who nominally had firing authority would say, "Sinclair, you're fired!" but in time they all found out that no firing of Sinclair would stick unless managing editor Harry C. Hindmarsh did it in person. Hindmarsh only did so once—and even that lasted only a few months. When Sinclair finally left the *Star* staff forever, the move was as much his decision as it was the *Star*'s.

Nevertheless, Sinclair, as part of his bag of tricks, often used to say that he had been fired from every job he ever had. True as that might have been, he didn't really take it very seriously—he seemed more amused at the pervasiveness of his own propaganda. A few months before he died, on the last occasion he was interviewed at length in a newspaper, a Regina *Leader-Post* reporter, Peter Edwards,

97

said he understood that Sinclair had been fired seven times from the *Star*. Sinclair laughed and said, "Yeah, I guess that's the going figure, isn't it?" *Maclean's* once said eleven times, the *Star* once put the figure at ten.

However, all of his firings by the *Star*, except one, were on a contingency basis—the contingency being that both sides would likely cool off. The only time the *Star* seriously fired him was for defying Hindmarsh's direct orders in 1935, causing the *Star* to be well beaten by the *Telegram* on Italy's invasion of, and war with, Ethiopia.

Perhaps some who had tried to fire him earlier wouldn't have been so bold if they had known something police reporter Jocko Thomas learned years later. After Hindmarsh died in 1956, his widow, Ruth Atkinson Hindmarsh, continued to hold, at her home in Oakville, her annual Garden Tea for *Star* people. One feature was an anteroom in which she displayed various archival objects, including the *Star*'s old paybook from Sinclair's time. Jocko read it carefully one day to find that in 1936 Sinclair was the second-highest-paid man on the *Star* editorial staff. Hindmarsh himself got $225 a week, Sinclair $125. Next was Augustus Bridle, the long-time critic, at $100 a week, while other senior writers such as Fred Griffin, Gregory Clark, Roy Greenaway, Bill Shields, and Athol Gow were listed between $65 and $80 a week. Earlier paybooks also showed that in one stretch publisher Joseph E. Atkinson gave Sinclair small raises week after week "because he was doing so much to sell the *Star*." This might have dated from the time when Atkinson was helping with the mortgage payments.

Once in 1933 Sinclair, feeling that Hindmarsh and Atkinson had not properly defended his honour in a lawsuit (indeed, had done much to dishonour him), seriously considered quitting the *Star*. This bind began as an indirect result of Sinclair's meeting George Vanderbilt, a young heir to that family's fortune, on a ship bound for Australia. Vanderbilt had with him an underwater film he'd made about sharks, manta rays, whales, and other exotic marine life. When this was shown aboard ship, Sinclair wrote about it so enthusiastically that it later played a four-week run in a

Toronto theatre, cementing the shipboard friendship—and causing Vanderbilt to say once that Sinclair was the "cat's pajamas" when it came to giving a poor little rich boy useful publicity.

A few months later in Paris, Sinclair was trying to cross the Place Vendôme when a red MG zoomed up to him and stopped. Someone called his name. One of three young men crowded into the MG was Vanderbilt, who (according to Sinclair's second book of memoirs, *Will the Real Gordon Sinclair Please Sit Down*, McClelland and Stewart, 1975, and Goodread Biographies, paperback, 1986) called, "Boy, have I got a story for you! Come on, we'll have lunch . . . tell you all about it."

They went to Vanderbilt's room at the Ritz and ordered up champagne, and Vanderbilt told Sinclair he had shot a new and exciting film in Kenya. He had *fished* for lions, he said. Sinclair, taking the bait as willingly as any mere lion, asked what the hell he meant. Vanderbilt explained: he'd dragged aromatic zebra meat behind a vehicle through lion country, attracting lions which would grab at the meat within close camera range.

A matter of debate between lawyers months later was whether Vanderbilt had or had not said that the zebra carcasses were on big meat-hooks which sometimes snagged a lion; hence the phrase, fishing for lions. But one element of that day in Paris was not in debate: that at first Sinclair had not taken notes, doing so only when Vanderbilt kept urging him. Sinclair frankly suspected the story. He knew that Kenya had licensed guides and particularly strict rules in game parks.

"Did the park wardens know what you were doing?" he asked, and reported Vanderbilt's reply in this passage:

> "We had the best of guides; permits, good
> equipment. The picture hasn't been fitted together
> but it's going to be a smash. Take notes."
> Vanderbilt handed me some Ritz stationery and I
> took notes.
> About a week later I sailed for home from

Cherbourg in the *Bremen*, having no intention of writing the story.

When he got home he was assigned to write an article a day of his own choosing. It was not a column as such. The *Star* felt at the time, and for decades thereafter, that columns, with only one or two exceptions, were a drug on the market; let the *Telegram* have columns. Sinclair's daily story would be used prominently, but wherever in the paper the editors thought best, each time under a news headline. One day, having trouble finding a subject, he came across his Vanderbilt notes and used them, making no judgments himself, but quoting Vanderbilt throughout.

The *Star* put his piece on the front page, entitled, "The Man Who Fished for Lions". Next morning the Toronto Humane Society was on the line. Was this shockingly inhumane story true? Sinclair replied that he didn't know for sure, which was why he had put almost everything in quotation marks. The matter was raised in Britain's House of Lords. Quickly thereafter some guides in the game preserve where Vanderbilt said he had made the pictures were suspended. They sued Sinclair and the *Star* for libel. So did Vanderbilt's mother, on behalf of her son. The total at stake was $100,000.

At this point, publisher Atkinson, seemingly amused, called Sinclair in and told him not to worry.

> "We'll take care of this. To do anything these people must all come to Toronto, a long, expensive journey. There will be delays. I can't imagine any Toronto jury awarding money to one of the most privileged of young Americans to be paid by a local boy who was born in our own Cabbagetown. There would be so many interested people they'd have to stage the trial in Maple Leaf Gardens."

But for once Joe Atkinson was wrong.

Five weeks later the guides reached Toronto from Africa and marched straight to the *Star* newsroom to deny everything, a story published prominently by opposition papers. At the same time, the libel suit's statement of claim was amended to say that Sinclair had been drinking when he'd been gathering the material for his story. A Toronto tabloid published the headline "Was Sinclair Drunk?"

With the *Star*'s attitude to booze, this suspicion changed everything. Atkinson asked Sinclair if he had been drunk. Sinclair said that, if anybody had been drunk, it was the others; they were mere kids, while he could hold his champagne. Atkinson asked if he had witnesses to back up his account. Sinclair said the two young men with Vanderbilt had seemed decent enough and that he had their names and addresses in his notes. He was sent the same night to track them down. He found that one, named Hard, was visiting the Vanderbilts in Florida, so did not seem a likely prospect to support Sinclair in court. The other, named Borden, a scion of the milk family, Sinclair found in Worcester, Massachusetts, working in one of the family's plants. Borden said sure, someone had sent him Sinclair's story and it was true. He signed a statement to that effect, adding that he, Borden, had heard Vanderbilt urging Sinclair to take notes and write the story.

Sinclair took that back to Toronto. Nothing further had been heard from the Vanderbilts. The guides were a different matter—they were in Toronto for the duration of a case that might take months even to come to court. Amazingly, Sinclair was then told to go on a writing trip back to Africa and while there to nose around Nairobi and see if he could get anything on the guides that would discredit them in a court case. Judging by what soon happened, Sinclair later felt that the *Star* was just getting him out of the way for a planned cop-out. As his ship neared Gibraltar, a wireless message told him to turn around and come home, everything had been solved.

At first he was relieved: no more worries, and a few days of paid vacation in Europe to boot. But he'd been given no details. What he found on returning home infuriated him. The *Star* had capitulated, settling out of court for $37,000 and a lengthy front-page apology (Sinclair called it "crawl-ing, grovelling"), which said that when their wandering reporter had met Vanderbilt in Paris he had been exhausted from his travels, was weak with various ailments, was not himself, had got the facts on the safari wrong, had been drinking, and the *Star* regretted, etc. . . .

For a day or so, Sinclair wrote in 1975, "I was in a funk; a drained feeling of having been betrayed. I talked vaguely of suing the paper and might, today, have done just that. . . . I felt depressed, but this experience was seldom mentioned again [at the *Star*]. At the house Gladys shrugged, 'So you weren't spiffed, but you did cost the paper money. Who's to worry?' "

Surprisingly, Sinclair finished his long-after-the-fact account of these events with kind words about Hindmarsh, who had been chief executive officer in the settlement that caused Sinclair to feel betrayed. Perhaps Sinclair was sim-ply being revisionist, or perhaps, because Sinclair never could stand to be a part of a mob decision, and mobs of old *Star* reporters, including Ernest Hemingway, insisted that Hindmarsh was a monster, Sinclair had to find good in him. Anyway, after relating the depressing outcome of the fish-ing-for-lions story Sinclair called Hindmarsh "a more com-passionate and sentimental man than many of his staff thought," and cited some of his kindnesses to *Star* people in difficulty.

But, at the time, Sinclair continued to brood. The *Star*, in effect, had labelled him an untrustworthy journalist just so they could weasel out of the libel case. He went in and told Hindmarsh how he felt.

Hindmarsh didn't soft-soap or rationalize or hold Sin-clair's hand. He just said, "Where would you like to go? Pick a place."

It was then that Sinclair headed for Devil's Island, France's infamous penal colony off the coast of French Guiana in South America. Apparently Hindmarsh was well aware that adventure, headlines, being on the move once again, in character "as the bird you think I am", worked as a wonder drug for Sinclair.

Such setbacks as the lawsuit didn't seem to bother Sinclair much in the long run, but there is evidence that his non-stop travelling did. This probably didn't show a great deal around the *Star*, for he always had the faculty of being "on" when he was there, answering summonses from on high, coming back to walk cockily through the newsroom in the colourful clothes he had just then assumed as his lifetime style, calling out to his older buddies, hammering out a story at breakneck speed, showing the kids what a star reporter looked like. He was unsurpassed at handling even minor stories that depended on touch as much as on facts; in clumsy hands they'd never have made the paper. There is something of a sense that the *Star* had type-cast Sinclair in a way that accentuated the jungle drums side of his journalism, but even when not engaged in that pursuit of the exotic, he was bright, inquisitive, a fearless thrower of fast-balls and curves alike in interviews, and had an almost incredible facility for making stories out of unlikely encounters.

Once, in London, he noticed on the street a man whose face he was sure he knew, and, hoping to strike up a conversation and find out who the man was, he asked him for a match. However, he didn't know until he saw a newspaper photo the following day that his cigar had been lighted by Toscanini. Beefed up, Sinclair style, it made a story.

In Toronto he was lounging in the empty seats during a rehearsal in Massey Hall when the internationally famous soprano Amelita Galli-Curci hit a wrong note—an event almost unprecedented for her—became extremely upset, and confessed she'd been having trouble with her throat. Did anyone know a good specialist? Sinclair did, at St. Michael's Hospital about a two-minute walk away, and escorted her there. Sinclair wrote it up, for all it was worth.

At one stage his local stories seemed to concentrate on

unlucky experiences. He was good at realizing that one person's bad luck might be another person's belly-laugh. That made him the one who wrote about a man with a new derby hat, whose friends pulled it down hard over his ears as a joke—and severed one ear. Also, there was a schoolteacher, late for class, who grabbed a cab, jumped out in front of the school, tossed the money to the driver, and slammed the door on her skirt. The cab drove off, dragging her skirt, leaving her on a crowded street trying to take shelter behind a telephone pole. Sinclair was the one who could make you see it; and also see driver after driver going by goggle-eyed but not stopping, until a truck pulled up and the driver threw the door open and called, "In here, lady, quick," and gave her a burlap bag to cover herself while he drove her home for another skirt.

When a reporter gets on a streak like that, people call in with additional stories. One was from a woman who thought her experience was even unluckier than the derby hat man, or the skirtless schoolteacher. Her husband had died. He'd been an extremely difficult man, but still she wanted to get him a good gravestone. She saved for some months before she could pay for it and have it installed. On the day when she went to the cemetery to have a look at the tall stone marker and tidy around the grave, the stone toppled over on her and broke her leg.

In all this, the record doesn't indicate that he had much time for loafing, gardening, fishing—or getting to know and enjoy his family better. Away, he was lonely for his family and could be gravely affected by bad news from home. When a message reached him in the African interior in 1934 (naturally by jungle drums, making another story) that a truck had hit his children while they and June Bailey, one of two live-in housekeepers at the time, took an evening walk on his home street, he sped for the coast to phone home.

Before he could contact Gladys, a mix-up led him to believe that his little daughter had lost an arm. Waiting for him at the coast he'd found a letter from Gladys saying, "It is really too bad about Jean's arm." But he hadn't received an earlier letter saying it was a fracture and she would be okay. Without notifying the *Star*, he hurried home by boat and rail and got off the train in Hamilton (that way the news of his arrival was less likely to get back to the paper) to find that all was well.

But he didn't handle the yearning for home and family well when he actually *was* home. Sometimes the streak of self-pity in him, the other side of his public cocksureness, made him feel that he was regarded as an interruption in his family's normal life. They had a routine when he was away; it was all shot when he was with them. His battles with Gladys apparently by then had settled into a rigid pattern. It didn't help that, having met him as a three-piece-suit man, she was now embarrassed by his outlandish clothes and public demeanour and so tried to avoid accompanying him to public receptions or other events unless absolutely necessary. She once said that, without his career, their lives would have been much different, leaning to quiet evenings with friends, and a lot of bridge. So they fought about that, and about bringing up children, going out in public, his frequent absences, and almost everything else that came along. He was tough on her and their sons, making an exception only for Jean.

As Jean recovered late in 1934, he made a couple of long trips to the United States, and then in February 1935 headed again for India. A feature of that trip was a Chevrolet that General Motors had provided in a private deal with Sinclair, hoping to get a few mentions of the car as he carved his way through the usual life-threatening obstacles.

There was no shortage of material. The Chevrolet was there in the background when an elephant grabbed a loaded gun with its trunk and swung it around until it went off and killed the elephant; verdict, suicide. And when a leaping tiger missed him and the Chevrolet by inches. And when he was snow-blind for a day on a Kashmir ski trip. He and the car narrowly escaped death in a Kashmir rock-slide. He could never have made his perilous trip to the Khyber Pass without his trusty Chev. It was only much later that he found the *Star* had been cutting every mention of the Chevrolet, forcing General Motors to write its own handouts.

Random headline:

LEECHES "LIKE HOTDOGS" FEED ON SINCLAIR'S BLOOD

For a while he travelled on the Kashmir-Tibet frontier with the Yale-Cambridge Upper India Geographical and Anthropological Expedition. The leader of that expedition was so impressed with Sinclair that he nominated him to be a fellow of the Royal Geographical Society. The decision came through in time for him to put F.R.G.S. after his byline on his next book. The honour was a matter of pride for Sinclair all his life.

After leaving that expedition, according to his 1975 account (which is given here briefly only as a curiosity, because it did not jibe with the truth, let alone with the vivid account he wrote at the time), he drove southwest until he bedded down "in the suburbs"—they actually were very distant suburbs, something like 1,000 miles away—of Quetta, a city which is now in West Pakistan. According to this 1975 account, early the following morning he was sleeping soundly when a disastrous earthquake hit Quetta.

He wrote that he had been feeling ill for some days and might have taken a sleeping-pill. Anyway, "hard to believe, neither the noise nor the shake of the 'quake wakened me. I was awakened by clouds of dust and was coughing and choking when people came running around to say Quetta had been demolished."

If it was hard to believe, that could have been simply because it was untrue. The truth is a good deal more interesting, but takes longer to tell. The real story was printed at the time in the *Star* and more completely in Sinclair's book *Khyber Caravan*. He had been a day's drive from Quetta a few days before the earthquake, but was in Bombay when it struck late in May. The first Bombay headlines estimated the dead at 1,000; the final figure was set months later at 66,000, about three-quarters of the population. A few minutes after he'd seen the first Bombay news-

106

paper headlines, a Cook's runner delivered an urgent message from the *Star*: Go to Quetta. Banks were closed. He borrowed money from friends and boarded a train that would get him to Ahmedabad. From Bombay by phone he had arranged for an aircraft to take him from Ahmedabad to Quetta. At Ahmedabad he found the plane had left without him. He took another train to Karachi, twenty-four hours away, but before reaching Karachi found a three-seater plane at Hyderabad. Then he had to fight the authorities, threatening to fly the plane himself if they wouldn't clear the flight, and got to Quetta early in June for the finest reportage of his life.

Telescoping the event for consumption forty years later in his 1975 memoir would have been forgivable. But why he drastically changed his real connection with the event, as if to give it some spurious punch of immediacy, and why he carelessly said that it happened in August rather than in late May—perhaps because when he reached Quetta in June the temperature was around 120°F—is beyond comprehension.

When he did get there, he worked in his own best traditions, walking into the shattered city to see and smell for himself. Climbing over the rubble, he helped dig for the dead and injured, noting among other things a distraught man doggedly going from body to body and turning it over to see the face, and the fact that among search parties when a body was suspected to be female, it was examined behind a makeshift curtain by another female.

When he'd seen enough, his next task was to get the story out. This was front-page news that should be cabled, especially as he was the only western journalist with an eyewitness account. Telephones and cable facilities, scarce at the best of times, were out. He drove south nearly five hundred miles to Hyderabad, where he managed to get off a short cable. He cabled again from nearby Karachi but, unsure that his cables were getting through, at last arranged a phone link through Turkey to the *Star*, which after receiving his cables was staffing the phones on a twenty-four-hour basis.

Then, ill, tired, and shaken, he drove on to Bombay, more

than 1,000 miles from Quetta, to find a *Star* message. This instructed him to proceed immediately to Ethiopia. The 1936 war between Italy and Ethiopia was still months away, but it had seemed imminent after a shooting incident between Ethiopian border troops and a unit from Italian Somaliland.

The urgency of the *Star* message had a particularly Toronto angle; the *Telegram* had the burly, enterprising, and imaginative Robinson MacLean already in Ethiopia, and he was writing the pants off any Ethiopian correspondent the *Star* could pick up. The *Star* explicitly explained that, while Sinclair's stuff from India was great last week, sure, this other story quickly had become the only game in town: woefully weak Ethiopian forces against crack Italian army troops and air force. (Mussolini's son-in-law later described a bomb landing in the midst of a spear-waving black army below as looking like a rose opening.)

In the prelude to this David-versus-Goliath conflict, the tiny emperor Haile Selassie was embattled in his capital of Addis Ababa. The *Telegram* had a good man on the spot. Go, Sinclair, go! But they'd caught him at the wrong time.

> I cabled that Ethiopia was impossible. I was exhausted and in a state of nerves. There were further messages [that] appealed to my loyalty; said I had to pass the place on my way home. They understood my position but I should understand their position, too.
> Nuts!
> I sailed for home. At Aden; another wire. At Suez, two wires. Drop dead!
> I went home, took a week off without reporting [to the *Star*], felt better and went to work.

When Sinclair marched into the *Star* newsroom, he was expecting a storm. It didn't happen. Obviously, Hindmarsh knew that a blow-up and a disaffected Sinclair would solve nothing. He would bide his time. So when Sinclair reported, the fact that he'd disobeyed orders was never mentioned. The *Telegram* was still giving banner headlines to Robinson MacLean and the *Star* was still limping along with whatever it could find—but what it could find was not in MacLean's class. Or Sinclair's. Weeks went by—obviously a cooling-off period—during which Sinclair's battered Chevrolet was on show at the Canadian National Exhibition, and Sinclair wrote a few inconsequential local stories.

Then late in September a *Star* headline read,

SINCLAIR OFF TO ETHIOPIA TO SIZE UP WAR OUTLOOK

What had happened was that after Sinclair was judged to be back in fighting trim again, Hindmarsh, "who didn't often try to con his clowns, he gave orders, talked me into going back." The *Star* obviously was trying hard to get their star on track again. It was a form of bribery. They sent Gladys along on the first part of the trip, booking the Sinclairs first class on the *Normandie*, then the newest and fastest ship in the world. Then there was a week for the Sinclairs in Paris at the Grand Hotel at *Star* expense, with "lunch at Maxim's, dinner at the Tour d'Argent, boats on the Seine, Folies Bergère." At the end of a week Gladys (who was pregnant with their third son, Jack) left for England to visit her brother Frank at Oxford, where he was teaching. Sinclair saw her off and then hopped a train for Marseilles, where he would board ship for Djibouti in French Somaliland. That's where a pile-up of correspondents had gathered to await visas, all trying in vain to get to Ethiopia. Sinclair described them as "Bums posing as journalists or journalists posing as bums. I was soon as drunk as the rest. To hell with the war! . . . most newspaper people couldn't get close enough to really describe what was going on. So many invented stories."

Sinclair didn't invent any stories, but it was a hopeless situation. The only way to Addis Ababa in landlocked Ethiopia was over 487 miles of single-line, narrow-gauge railway, already clogged with war supplies. Battling officials for permission to ride the train was a daily frustration, and Sinclair's Hindmarsh-imposed ambition to play catch-up soon evaporated.

For once, he was becalmed. He was also despondent, not

the least of the reasons being the nagging knowledge that if he'd obeyed the *Star*'s summer instructions he could have been among the first on the spot in Addis Ababa. After several weeks he did manage to get into Ethiopia as far as Harar, but that was it. He wasn't surprised, he said, "to be angrily recalled" to Toronto.

For public consumption, the *Star* hid its anger well. On December 14, an introductory note to a new Sinclair series confessed that the journey that had started with such fanfare in September had not gone as planned. "The *Star* had instructed Mr. Sinclair to go to Addis Ababa, but [later] cabled directing him to land at Djibouti and not to run the risk to life or health which a visit to the Ethiopian capital involved. Mr. Sinclair has prepared a series of articles, of which this is the first."

He'd written the series in Rome on his way home, so once in Toronto he had no work to keep him from facing the music. He reported to Hindmarsh's office. The door from the anteroom to the inner sanctum usually was open for Sinclair. This day it was closed. Sinclair waited. Hindmarsh would not see him. A few hours later news executive Glen Ogilvie handed Sinclair a note saying he was fired.

But from the *Star*'s send-off, published December 19, no one could have guessed Sinclair had been fired if he hadn't spread the news himself. The *Star* couldn't face admitting in public that, after Sinclair's years as everybody's favourite wandering reporter, he'd been hung out to dry.

Instead, his departure from the paper was announced in a long celebratory piece about his career. If he'd been dead it could have been his obituary. In a superlative-larded review of "The Sinclair Years", the *Star* proclaimed that he'd travelled 160,000 miles for *Star* readers, visited 38 countries, and written three books.

Other warm passages depicted him in the bosom of his family as a man who raised collie dogs, enjoyed table-tennis, golf, riding, and romping with his young children. But he now had decided to pursue another career, the story said, as if it had been entirely his idea, and "had been

110

appointed a member of the staff of Maclaren Advertising, to assume his new duties January 1."

On March 27, 1936, just fourteen weeks later, the *Star* ran another front-page piece under this headline:

GORDON SINCLAIR RETURNS TO STAR AS COLUMNIST IN SPORTS DEPARTMENT

Amazingly enough, in Sinclair's brief absence his travels had been treated to a recount. "Gordon has travelled 340,000 miles and visited 73 countries for the *Star*," the welcome-home story stated—a marked improvement on the mere 160,000 miles and 38 countries mentioned at his farewell.

CHAPTER EIGHT

SINCLAIR . . . A SPORTS-WRITER?

Conn Smythe wanted to fight him, the Star *slashed his salary, but his new book was getting rave reviews.*

Why, with all his options, did Sinclair pick advertising as his landing-place after the *Star* fired him? He could probably have written his own ticket with one of the other Toronto newspapers, and by then, from his travels (and from being Sinclair), he knew what British and American writers at his level were being paid. If he'd wished to move to the United States or England he might have doubled, trebled, or quadrupled his income. No Canadian journalist before or since has reached Sinclair's fame internationally. His work was syndicated to a steady string of about twenty North American newspapers, plus some in Britain, Australia, and Africa. At its peak, his Devil's Island series reached "about 300 papers". His books, all being outcomes of his journalism, were reviewed in the United States and elsewhere in the English-speaking world, mostly with enthusiasm.

The most likely explanation for his temporary rejection of journalism at that time is that his defiance of Hindmarsh's original orders to go to Ethiopia was the result of what today would be called burn-out: too many earthquakes, man-eating tigers, funeral pyres for the dead, slugs in his soup, and snakes in his bathroom, and not enough tender loving care of a personal nature (as distinguished from the adulation of fans). His subsequent failure at Djibouti and Harar, especially Harar, only two hundred miles overland from Addis Ababa, was uncharacteristic; there'd been a time when he was the acknowledged master at beating such odds, by luck, enterprise, bribery, or whatever it took, but on that assignment he was fresh out of the old Sinclair magic.

Another possible answer really has several layers, all bearing on one heart's-core fact: Toronto was his city, Canada his country, and he wanted a job that paid well, had a future, and had him home every night for dinner just like a bank manager.

A clue is that, as early as 1930, on the last page of that year's diary he listed his trips during the year and totted up that he'd been 177 days away, 188 home. With two baby sons and his relationship with his wife not yet completely in ruins, that year he had sounded out Charles Vining, a senior executive at another advertising agency, Cockfield Brown Limited, for a job that would keep him at home.

Five years later, little had changed for the better except his income. He'd had little chance even to unpack in the new home that he and Gladys had built and moved into during October 1934. Between then and December 1935, he had been home sixteen weeks out of sixty. When the *Star* fired him he wanted to stay home without the constant threat of a train whistle calling him back to his wanderings.

The new house was not far from their smaller original. Gladys had chosen the site, a large double lot fronting on Burnhamthorpe Park Boulevard and bounded at the rear by the fast-running Mimico Creek. Across the creek the well-treed rolling fairways of the Islington Golf Club virtually guaranteed that the view would be pleasant for life. Also, golfers being what they are, an almost inexhaustible supply of balls landed in the back yard. What Sinclair didn't use himself he sold (or so he said) to fellow members. Before environmental concerns, and before the area even had regular garbage pick-up, the creek bank was where Sinclair threw his empty wine bottles. He wanted to garden,

113

to pave the driveway, to play golf and poker and drink at the club, and then come back to the solid and comfortable house that would be *home* for the rest of their lives. So, in his emotional state at the time he was fired, it was quite in character that he would take the first job offered him.

In the background was the fact that he'd had extra expense in connection with the new family home. Proceeds from his books had paid for it ("the house that words built" was one of his lines), but because of his sense of having had a hand-to-mouth childhood, he was uneasy, sometimes nearly frantic, when his financial situation was uncertain. The offer from Maclaren was fast, and his acceptance was faster. A photo of Maclaren's Christmas party that year, taken only a day or two after Sinclair left the *Star*, shows him prominently among the tables of celebrating admen.

With travel behind him for the moment, he romped happily in the house, and in the snow by the creek, and with sleds on the golf course, with his children, Gord, seven, Don, six, and Jean, four, endlessly filming them with his 8-mm home movie camera as well as with the still camera he'd learned to use with skill and imagination at the *Star*. His fascination with their developing personalities at that time was that of a man who'd been away from his children a lot and was trying to catch up.

He did treat Jean differently than he did his sons. This was not in a way that the boys resented, but, his son Gord said many years later, was "just a little more softly". Sinclair's diary late in 1930 had revealed that when Gladys learned she was pregnant for the third time, she was upset at the thought of another child, and "I didn't think much of the idea either." But when that child, Jean, was born and grew into a bright and quick little girl, the first female Sinclair child in fifty-six years, he lavished love on her.

Some of this is recalled by Doris Loach, who, after first entering the Sinclair household in 1930 as a companion for the pregnant Gladys and as a helper with the two toddlers, was often around later as a baby-sitter, a guest at mealtimes, and a family friend trusted by Gladys.

114

Doris remembers that when Jean was young, Gordon would straddle the foot of her baby carriage ("he didn't weigh much, you know") and talk to her by the hour. But he was no hand with baby care. Once when he took Jean for a drive, she wet herself and began to cry. He removed the diaper but didn't know how to put on a dry one, so sped home for help. Although from the earliest memories of his sons, the loving-father role was rarely front and centre, it was certainly there for them as well as for Jean at this stage—just before he went back to the *Star*. Only when they grew up a little did he become the stern father they were to remember.

Why did the *Star* take him back so quickly? There are various accounts. One is that Joe Atkinson had been opposed to his firing. Although Atkinson hadn't exercised his veto, the story among *Star* men was that he had asked Hindmarsh flatly, "Who are you going to get to replace him?" The answer, after a few earnest tries, was that nobody available had Sinclair's touch—or anything near it.

While the search for a substitute Sinclair was going on, *Star* sports columnist Lou Marsh, as famous in his field as Sinclair had been in his, died suddenly. Now, with two major *Star* personalities to replace, the Hindmarsh door eased tentatively open for Sinclair again. Inquiries were made as to his state of mind regarding his new job. The answer was that he wasn't enjoying advertising at all, despite a good contract and a number of projects in which he was involved.

An invitation was extended by Hindmarsh for him to "come in for a little discussion". Sinclair had enough friends at the *Star* that he knew in advance the subject for the little discussion would be the possibility of his replacing Lou Marsh. Still, James Y. Nicol, by 1987 one of the few *Star* people surviving from that period, was told by Sinclair of how it went when he and Hindmarsh met that day: "Hindmarsh was humming and hawing until I said to him, 'Mr. Hindmarsh, what the hell am I doing sitting here? Did you ask me to come up so you could do a little window-shopping or what the hell are you doing?' And I pounded the desk."

The job was offered to him there and then, and he took it, a mistake on all sides. Sinclair's brand of fire-wagon journalism depended to a great extent on what he saw and what he thought about it. Rarely had anyone been able to argue authoritatively with him who had a first-hand experience of his subjects equal to his own. When it came to working with Foster Hewitt on hockey broadcasts, dealing with Toronto Maple Leaf boss Conn Smythe, writing about baseball, rowing, football, and other sports, he was out of his depth. Writing sports was the lowest point in his career, a flop emphasized when his pay was cut from $125 a week to $100 and then to $75.

During the year or so that Sinclair wrote his monumentally unsuccessful sports column, he was home most of the time, but unhappy with his work. When he was unhappy, as he confessed occasionally in his diary, he would be crabby and inclined to get into rows with Gladys and anyone else who got in his way. One was Conn Smythe, manager of the Toronto Maple Leafs, who recalled in his memoirs, *If You Can't Beat 'Em in the Alley* (McClelland and Stewart, 1981), Sinclair's sports-writing incarnation:

> In one column he said my Leafs were yellow. I met him in a hotel lobby that day and handed him the key to my room. "Yellow, eh?" I said. "Meet me up there and the one who comes out alive wins the argument."
> He didn't take me up on it. Said I outweighed him. . . . Anyway, it proved that he had a hell of a lot of nerve to call anybody yellow.

Whether it would ever have come to a fight is another matter. Both Smythe and Sinclair could be hotheads, but Sinclair's heart wasn't in it; he was trying in the only way he knew (outrageousness, which served him well all his life) to make an impact in a new field. In subsequent years as a Maple Leaf Gardens shareholder and hockey fan, he sometimes would twit Smythe but, for a personal reason, never did more than that.

The personal reason was that one Sunday in New York a few years after the hotel-room-fight incident, he had a call from a distraught friend, one of whose relatives had died in Florida. American money was required to bring the body back to Canada. Sinclair didn't have enough—at the time, under Canadian currency regulations, travellers were allowed a bare minimum for their own needs. Sinclair's New York connections were all in business and publishing. He had no home phone numbers. Then he remembered that the Leafs were in town for a game with the Rangers in Madison Square Garden. He telephoned Smythe, who simply growled, "How much do you need?" That kind of favour, from a man who was by no stretch of imagination his friend, Sinclair would translate into an indelible mental memo which read: Don't shaft this guy.

While he was flopping in sports he was being reminded almost daily of the kind of journalism in which he'd never been a flop. His 1935 book about Devil's Island, *Loose Among Devils*, had been published in England by Hurst and Blackett. Late reviews were still arriving from such papers as South Australia's *Adelaide Mail* and Bombay's *Times of India*.

More importantly, by early June, only two months into his sports job, his fourth book, *Khyber Caravan* (New York, Farrar and Rinehart), was published to excellent reviews in the United States. A syndicated book columnist, Bruce Catton, called it a "thoroughly entertaining" book by "a species of Richard Halliburton minus the smart-alecky-ness" told with "all the pleased surprise of an irreverent freshman loose in the faculty club". The *Brooklyn Citizen* called it "a volume for your library, not just a snatch-read-and-forget item." The Savannah, Georgia, *News* said "what a tremendously interesting book this is." The New Orleans *Tribune* remarked that he "tickles his prose with a delicious sense of humor", some of it containing "the most humorous bits of writing in English literature". The *New York Herald-Tribune* claimed "his book's very unpretentiousness helps to make it one of the best of its kind."

In another few months, reviews began to show up from

Britain, where Hurst and Blackett again was his publisher. The reception was as dazzling as an author could hope for. J. S. Collis in the London *Sunday Times* of November 15, 1936, under the headline "A Brilliant Traveller", led off with

> It is a long time since I have come across anything written with such sustained brilliance as this new travel book by Mr. Gordon Sinclair. . . . remarkably few travellers can write with half his direct nail-hitting skill. This book is a finished example of the vitality colloquial English can gain by the bold introduction of American idiom.

The London *Daily Mirror*, the *London Evening News* ("Gordon Sinclair stalks adventure while adventure stalks him"), the *Evening Standard*, the *Reynolds Illustrated News*, the *Sphere*, *Everybody's Weekly*, and *Books of Today* gave warm reviews, as did the Glasgow *Daily Express*, the Nottingham *Evening Post*, the Liverpool *Post*, and the Birmingham *Gazette*.

Canadian publication seems to have followed the foreign success by at least a year. The *Star* library's list of his publications has *Khyber Caravan* (the original hard-cover edition is still found in public libraries) published in 1937. Unaccountably, the 1975 and 1986 publishers of *Will the Real Gordon Sinclair Please Sit Down* list *Khyber Caravan* as coming out in 1940. At any rate, when Sinclair was labouring fruitlessly to make his name as a sports columnist, he kept being reminded that his real calling, the one that was drawing the sort of acclaim that few writers ever experience, was as a footloose reporter.

This message, constantly hammered home by the contrast between his heralded past and his humdrum present, led him to decide early in 1937 that nearly a year in sports was more than enough. He asked to be returned to general reporting. It was a relief all around (including for the readers) when the *Star* agreed. Within weeks he was travelling with some hoboes in the Southern United States, edging back into the kind of adventure that had made his name in the first place.

After that, for a couple of years he managed to keep long trips to a minimum, except for an interesting series from Yellowknife about Canada's latest gold rush. Then, late in 1938, he took off on his last major journey as a *Star* staffer—to the Far East. This began as an attempt by Hindmarsh to have Sinclair and Gregory Clark meet in the middle of the Soviet Union, Sinclair travelling from the Pacific by way of Vladivostok and Clark from the west, through Poland. This project in its original form eventually was aborted because neither could get a Soviet visa, but the *Star* told Sinclair to head out anyway and try for the visa at consulates along the way.

At that time the Japanese had overrun much of northern China, including all of Manchuria. Sinclair started in Yokohama, then moved to Shanghai, displaying all the old Sinclair pizazz.

Headlines:

CHINESE GIRLS OF 14 SOLD INTO SLAVERY FOR $.50

SHANGHAI CHINESE PEACEFUL. BOW, RAISE HATS TO JAPS

THROW AWAY 59 CORPSES A DAY NEAR SHANGHAI

SAW JAPANESE ARMY BULLY SMASH OUT WOMAN'S TEETH

In Shanghai he was introduced to Chiang Kai-shek's personal pilot, who "let fly with a left jab and blacked my eye." He wrote a piece about Japanese reporters having a casualty rate higher than soldiers because they "try to get into the most dangerous bits of action every time the guns bark. These are brave men who die with their boots on for $16.50 a week and never once dream that they're suckers." In one stretch he wrote a story or two about the Japanese being fairly easy to get along with, and the very next time he tried out their patience he was gashed by a Japanese bayonet—a story picked up by international news services.

But this wasn't getting to Russia, and Sinclair cabled the *Star*.

SLIGHTLY INJURED JAPANESE BAYONET RIGHT
SHOULDER CANTON STOP BROUGHT HERE AMERICAN
GUNBOAT MINDANAO CAMERA SEIZED STOP CAN NOW
PROCEED CHUNGKING NEW CHINESE CAPITAL OR LIKE
NORTH MANCHURIA MONGOLIA THINK BEST PLAN WAIT
ORDERS STOP WOUNDS UNSERIOUS

While awaiting the *Star*'s reply—which was basically, "Go, Sinclair, go"—he was reached by telephone for a long *Star* interview by Gregory Clark, during which Sinclair said the incident was not serious enough to qualify as an international incident. This didn't fool *Star* readers; they knew their boy was on the fly again.

While he was looking for a ship heading north, some of the most interesting pieces he wrote from Shanghai were about Jews; in them he exercised both his eye for bizarre situations, and his hard-headed understanding that many of his Toronto readers were Jewish.

The world was in the earlier stages of realizing the horrors that were befalling Jews at the hands of Hitler's Nazis. Many Canadian Jews were frantic with concern for relatives. Jewish refugees from Germany were trying to get out through many border stations in Europe, but Sinclair had found something else: they were arriving in Shanghai at the rate of 110 a day, some with money, many without, to sleep on narrow bunks stacked four or five deep, floor to ceiling. However, everybody was happy to be there, because

> This is the biggest city on earth where they can land without a passport. And as you mingle with them and hear their talks you realize that these people are not down and out! These people are not whipped! These people are almost happy! Shanghai's famed Bund now looks more Jewish at noonday than it does Russian or Chinese.

Refugee-aid money flowing in from Jews around the world was badly needed, he wrote. The Shanghai government's food allowance for these refugees "is $2.50 per month per man. This is Shanghai money which is our money divided by six. They try to keep a white man alive on 40 cents a month—less than you would pay for a single meal."

He had almost always been a loner on his trips, mainly in the sense that he didn't hang out with other reporters and especially shunned press clubs, mindful of the eternal verity that everybody at the bar of a press club winds up with the same story. On Christmas morning he joined the regular crew detailed to pick up the dead in the streets, and accompanied 157 bodies to where they were burned. It was a story.

Eventually he boarded a British ship in Shanghai and headed north, hoping to get to Manchuria and then Siberia. Right on cue (Sinclair needed each story more than he needed sea air) the ship was intercepted by the Japanese Navy. Cue Charles Laughton: The good guys' haughty captain, Charles Cater, was charged by the Japanese with running some kind of covert operation and in turn charged the Japanese with a long list of offences against international law. Cut to Sinclair, not risking further bayonet wounds from the touchy Japanese but keeping his eyes and ears open, grist for the mill, as passengers were held under armed guard for thirty hours. Sinclair's readers got it all, short on technicalities and long on adventure, danger, suspense.

Sinclair was eventually released to a British warship, HMS *Sandwich*. He made it to the Siberian border and crossed a bridge into that country, where he stayed a few hours before the Russians sent him back over the bridge. Then he made his way back to Japan, writing that the strain of years of war showed in the "grim, determined nature of silent midnights in Tokyo", a startling contrast to "the uproarious nighttime revels in Shanghai".

"You look around you here and wonder how long they can stand this. I watched light standards being taken down to be melted down for guns. Concrete poles go up in their place. Manhole covers are all of wood. The steel ones went into shells." If he'd ever lost his touch, he had it back.

When he returned to Canada early that summer to help cover the royal tour of King George VI and Queen Elizabeth (now the Queen Mother), nobody knew that it would be his last major job for the *Star*.

At that time, too, there was a change that would be with him for life. Doris Loach by then was twenty-four, small and pretty. Not many of his friends found much warmth in Sinclair, but Doris was a lifetime exception. As she grew into womanhood, with her own job, they met often and had been within a breath of being lovers several times. When it finally happened in 1939, neither could have guessed the relationship would last until his death.

He was a *Star* employee for another four years, but when the Second World War began that autumn of 1939, the *Star* decided not to accredit him as a war correspondent. Gregory Clark, a few years older, had served in the First World War. He got the nod to sail with the first Canadian division for Europe that December of 1939. In time many other *Star* reporters were accredited, but not Sinclair. If there was a plot outside of the *Star* to keep him a civilian, it has never surfaced, but Sinclair thought someone in the armed forces had given him a thumbs-down. If so, he didn't exactly put himself out to get back in the brass's good books. Sent to Halifax to interview a senior naval officer, he asked what the officer's initials, S. S., stood for. The officer declined to give that information, on the grounds that his initials were all that Sinclair needed, his names were his own business. "Okay," Sinclair said. "Now I know what they stand for. Stuffed Shirt."

The officer's complaint was duly lodged with H. C. Hindmarsh—with no recorded result. But his work during that part of the war was mainly on the fringes, writing about the home front, about army training, about women war-workers, occasionally getting off a nostalgic piece when a ship was sunk that he had sailed on or someone he knew became a war casualty. His style, many thought in retrospect, would have given Canada some memorable war coverage. He never quite got over being passed by when the biggest story—the only story—was the war.

But, given a chance, he could show his mettle in a spectacular way, whether he won or lost. One of his losing tries is remembered by both photographer Norm James and reporter James Y. Nicol. Their recollections differ slightly in detail, but agree on the denouement.

A hush-hush area of Ontario then was a Canadian Industries Limited explosives plant at Nobel, near Parry Sound, about two hours' drive northwest of Toronto. One morning there was a huge explosion at the plant. Rumours were that eighteen workers had been killed.

Norm James, a hawk-nosed and unexcitable operative with just about the same inventiveness in getting good pictures as Sinclair had in getting good stories, was in the first wave of news people to arrive. Sinclair came later. James's *modus operandi* was to be pleasant, Mr. Good Guy, when he encountered opposition; at least until he figured some way, perhaps even legal, to get around it. When he and others went to the plant, they were told by a shaken security man that they couldn't get in until the place had been cleaned up a bit.

"Don't clean it up so much that you eliminate all signs of an explosion," James said.

"There's no possibility of that," the spokesman said. "But to put it crudely, we want to clean up blood and guts and all that stuff."

"How long?" James asked.

"Give us an hour or two."

So the first wave retired to lounge around in the sun outside. In a short time Sinclair came along with Nicol, and demanded, "What are you doing out here?"

James told him.

"Well, I'm not taking any of that crap," Sinclair said, and barged in, everyone following. Nicol knew one of the security men, a former policeman, who gave him the same story: not yet. But Sinclair by then was nose to nose with the security chief.

James told the story later: "Sinclair says, 'You say we can't get a story and pictures?' and the other guy says, 'That's it.' 'Well,' Sinclair says, 'do you realize we're fighting your kind overseas now?' You'd think Gord just came back from the trenches or something, this was striking at the very roots of democracy, and the upshot of it was that we all got tossed right off the premises. We didn't get a story, pictures, or anything, nobody did. He'd picked on somebody he couldn't push around."

(James's own way would have been more subtle, and perhaps more effective. One night at a prison riot in Guelph, with prisoners in control inside and while guards outside played fire hoses on the scene, he'd arranged to have a stream of water directed by a friendly guard in such a way that he could climb through a broken window, unseen. James got his pictures, still undetected: he had a prisoner hold a blanket over a window to prevent the photo flashes from being seen outside. He was back outside in the complaining media throng, looking innocent, his photos long gone on the road back to Toronto, when the warden announced to the others that some photographer had sneaked in there, they'd found the flash bulbs, so in half an hour everybody could go in. James went back in. None of the others knew he was the bad guy until they saw his exclusive stuff in the *Star*'s first edition.)

Even when the *Star* seemed to be wasting Sinclair's talents by keeping him relatively idle, handing him only routine assignments, his brash initiative could come in useful.

In December 1939, the German pocket battleship *Graf Spee* had been chased by British and New Zealand naval units into the harbour at Montevideo. While news services around the world stood by for the outcome, the *Graf Spee* was told that if it didn't get out of Montevideo, the ship and men would be interned, the ship perhaps winding up in Allied hands. The captain's only options (aside from scuttling his ship) were to accept internment, or to sail out into the guns of the British warships. Either way he'd be risking possible capture of the ship and its equipment.

While the world waited for the denouement, Sinclair, on his own, thinking that someone at the British consulate could tell him what was happening, telephoned the consul and got an eyewitness account as the Germans scuttled their ship. He wrote it fast and gave it to the editors. The *Star* didn't believe it was real.

> When the story was turned in [to the *Star* desk] a subeditor was assigned to call Montevideo again to see if Sinclair in truth had been talking to the consul. . . . The surprised consul said, "Certainly he was talking to me! Why did you ask?"

This majestic shafting of nervous editors quickly became part of Sinclair's by-then-lengthy dossier of ways to deal with brass hats—in and out of the *Star* offices—and win. It was a triumph reminiscent of one of Gregory Clark's anecdotes, which was served up from time to time when newsmen gathered in fishing cabins and told truths, or lies, about their traditional oppressors, the editors. After Sinclair had returned from India in 1935 following his sensational stories of adventure and soldiers and bandits in the Khyber Pass and environs, Clark had an assignment in India. As he told it, Hindmarsh said to him on leaving that, while in the area, he might go up to the Khyber Pass and meet that army fellow Sinclair said he was so friendly with and just, ah, check out some of the letters the *Star* had been receiving claiming that Sinclair had never been seen at the Khyber Pass at the time he wrote about.

In Clark's story, the Khyber Pass was a thousand miles out of his way, and it took him a week to get there. However, he finally did arrive, and requested an interview with the commanding officer of the British force. After some delay he was ushered in to the presence of the seated, stiff, correct officer in question, who looked up and said, "Yes?"

Clark introduced himself: "I'm Gregory Clark of the *Toronto Star*, sir, and . . . "

The officer jumped to his feet, rushed around the desk, and grabbed Clark's hand. "The *Star*, hmmn? Then you must know a man who was here a while ago, wrote some fine stories, Gordon Sinclair!"

CHAPTER NINE

SO HOW WERE THINGS AT HOME?

*Remark to the Sinclairs' oldest son, Gord: "He told
Betty Kennedy once that he didn't think he had
kissed your mother more than twenty times in their
married life."*
*Gord: "If he kissed her twenty times, I never saw any
of them."*

As the war wound on into gasoline shortages and a mild
food rationing on the home front, the verdicts on Gordon
Sinclair as a husband and father by many of those who knew
him most intimately ranged from tyrannical to unfeeling to
hurtful, except specifically in the case of his daughter, Jean.
Robert Pinchin, Olive's son, was around the Sinclair home a
great deal. He was four years older than his cousin Gord,
and five years older than Don, but he and the Sinclair boys
were chums. Cousin Robert remembers times when he had
joined them at mealtime and "we'd hear the gravel crunch
when the car came in, and Aunt Gladys would grab the arms
of her chair, her hands white and tense, until he came in
and she found what kind of a mood he was in. It was a pity
to see."

None of this was known by the public, of course. Indeed, the Sinclair family was viewed as a fond and close-knit group when, as sometimes happened, a piece for the *Star Weekly* called for family photos and the three boys and Jean would pose with their father. Jack, born in 1936, was the youngest in any such groups. Also, he seems to have been the least scarred by the ongoing family battles as he moved through boyhood and into his eventual career in television production. "If someone were to ask now about *particular* instances of bad times with my dad, I could certainly remember them, but they don't ring often in my mind," he said during a 1986 interview.

The second son, Don, is reserved on the subject. Others say that well into his own adult life he so deeply disapproved of much that his father did (including his extramarital relations) that he rarely, if ever, listened to his father on radio or television. But at some point, perhaps when he learned that his father had chosen him to be executor of the estate when that time came, he more or less came to terms. By 1986 he preferred to temporize, while still suggesting between the lines that life with Father could be mighty tough. People should realize, he said, "that Dad was a temperamental individual and that his outbursts of temper were more prevalent at home than they were on the job or anything like that, among outsiders. Yet I think he did not want the family to be destroyed. So during those periods my mother developed a pretty good resistance or pretty good method of handling his more outrageous outbursts."

While Gladys held the line, Doris Loach had a different approach. By the late 1930s (leading up to the time she and Sinclair became lovers), Doris had her own room or rooms close to the city centre, but most Sundays both she and Sinclair's parents would come out by streetcar for Gladys's big Sunday dinner. Doris became known in the family for loyally taking Sinclair's side in time of battle when he was usually outnumbered. At any rate, she blamed much of the difficulty on the fact that Gladys frequently lined up with the children to thwart Sinclair. A son might want something and Sinclair would refuse, but Gladys would circumvent the ruling somehow.

Gord, the eldest son, denies that any such anti-Dad alliance existed—at least as long as he lived at home. "We were all in a kind of conspiracy against him in many ways, the three brothers and my sister, when she was alive, and people like cousin Robert, who was almost like a fourth son, but my mother was never a part of the conspiracy.

"She was a 1920s wife. What he did was right and he paid the bills and [when] he'd done something outrageous, *we* could talk about it but she wouldn't—she didn't criticize him. But he was a tough son of a bitch as a husband, no doubt about it. He was not easy to live with as a father. Also, especially at first we weren't used to having him around."

It's not known precisely how, or at what point, the relationship between Sinclair and Doris affected the family generally, but Gord seems to have been quite affable on the subject. He used to introduce her to friends with, "This is my big sister." If asked, Don was more direct: "She's the old man's girl-friend." Jack says he was too young to notice.

All agreed on the point that there were often quite hectic discussions at the table. In Don's words, "It didn't matter who was there, he would sometimes take exception to other people's statements and attack them." Gord saw such situations as being like some kind of pre-ordained storm, as if when his father was in the mood for a fight it couldn't be avoided. "I can't really explain except that maybe he'd look out and say, 'It's starting to clear up,' and you knew that was a provocative statement. It didn't sound like it, but you knew, here comes trouble. So you think to yourself, now what do I do? Do I say, horseshit, it's not going to ever clear up? Or do I say, yes, it's great. It didn't make any difference, you knew that this was what we were going to fight over, and it was inevitable, and it ended up in screaming matches really, so that it was most unpleasant. It was certainly most unpleasant for anybody who was there with us."

Gord's memory of a specific incident illustrates another facet of the Sinclair family life as the 1930s moved into the

1940s. "When we were kids we didn't dare admit to being sick, ever. The only time I recall admitting even to having a cold was a lie, I didn't have a cold. That was a day when some new houses were going up on our street, which had lots of open spaces then.

"My brother Don and I, I suppose we were thirteen to fourteen years old, were climbing around in a three-storey house after the workmen had gone for the day. We were both up on the roof, having gone out through one of the dormer windows, when Don started to slip. He grabbed me to save himself, which was natural. However, that saved him and started me going and I did fall off that three-storey roof. I recall to this second seeing my hat floating above me as I landed on a pile of rock, or gravel, or whatever, building materials.

"I literally could not walk, I was hurt so much, and my brother dragged me by one foot to the house. My mother decided right away, we're not to tell the old man. This decided, they put me to bed because I couldn't move. For three days I could not move—they had to bring me a pot to pee in—but no doctor was called. I was supposed to be sick with the flu and the old man didn't come to say hello because sick with the flu was disgusting and inexcusable.

"Years later I had some X-rays and the doctor said, 'When did you break your back?'

"I said, 'To my knowledge I never broke my back. What are you talking about?'

"He said, 'You've definitely had a broken back, there's no doubt about that.' Then I recalled it. But this was typical of the old man. You did not admit to illness. No way, ever. He wouldn't tolerate it."

It might be argued that, as Sinclair didn't know about his son's injury, he could scarcely be blamed for not reacting to it. But one fact remains: his family was so indoctrinated with his set of rules, including his attitude to illness, that almost anything was more endurable than chancing his wrath.

Gord recalls one other incident that emphasizes even

more poignantly the bitter nature of everyday events, which left such a mark on at least this one of his sons. Gladys had been ill and was considered to have a heart condition. "Among us kids the great terror was that Mother would die and leave us with the old man. One day in high school the principal came to the door and said I had to go home at once on a family matter. Naturally I thought of Mother first. I got on my bicycle and pedalled home as fast as I could, two or three miles, with tears running down my face, because I was afraid that my mother was dead.

"I got home and the old man was standing there. I had left the garage door open, when he had told me to close it. He said, 'When I tell you to close the fucking garage door, you close the fucking garage door. Now close it.'

"That's the sort of thing, for a kid, that sticks. . . . Pretty hard to explain when I got back to school that the urgent family matter had been that I hadn't closed the garage door.

"I left home as soon as I could after getting out of high school and getting a job, and I think that if it hadn't been that he was so hard to get along with, I wouldn't have. On the other hand, I think my brothers would agree that I handled it maybe better than anyone else. I could outshout him sometimes. He could be pretty hurtful when he was in one of his rages—there was no other way to describe them, they were rages—and I was pretty good at hurting back."

Jack was six years old, Jean eleven, Don thirteen, and Gord fourteen in 1942 when two events changed their parents' lives. One was the dawn of a new career for their father, the other a tragedy for the whole family.

At 4:50 a.m. on August 19, 1942, almost three years after the first shots were fired in the Second World War, Canadian troops made up most of an Allied force that sailed across the English Channel for a disastrous raid against the French coast. The target, beaches in and around Dieppe, turned out to be the stuff of nightmares. The alert and well-prepared defenders reacted so fast to the first Canadians splashing ashore that the element of surprise was virtually non-existent. Guns that had been positioned to fight off any invasion by sea did exactly that, pouring a withering fire on the beaches. The first wave of troops, and later many reinforcements, were pinned down a few yards from where they landed. Roads leading from the waterfront were so well covered that only a few troops ever reached their objectives short distances inland. Casualties were heavy. By afternoon all survivors, except for those who had managed to get back to the ships, were in German hands. When German guns fell silent about 2 p.m. after only nine hours of fighting, Canadian casualties included more than 900 killed or fatally wounded, many more wounded, and 1,944 taken prisoner.

Dieppe for years thereafter was defended as an essential rehearsal for invasion (and certainly was rich in bloody lessons that saved lives in later invasions of North Africa, Sicily, and Normandy). But at the time in Canada—when the eventual casualty toll was unknown—it was simply a profound shock, producing huge newspaper headlines and frantic activity among news broadcasters. At first only bare official communiqués were available on the story. By the following morning the first eyewitness accounts were beginning to fill in some of the brave and tragic human details—and Sinclair received a phone call at the *Star*.

On the line was Harry (Red) Foster, a broadcaster who had a daily news program just before noon at CFRB.

He also had his own advertising agency, which he'd started because he was hustling up his own sponsors anyway. His office was in the King Edward Hotel a couple of minutes away from the *Star*.

"I got a problem," he said. "I want you to listen to something. Can you come over?"

Foster had recorded two excellent broadcasts from England about how bravely the Canadians had fought at Dieppe. He wanted to use them on his noon news. The trouble was, they had been done by an American war correspondent, who had no problem with most Canadian regiments in the attack, but each time he mentioned the heroic deeds of the South Saskatchewan Regiment, it came out "Saska-*chew*-an".

In those days, recording was done on wax discs of various sizes. If anything went wrong, you just threw the record away and did the whole thing over again. There was no way a proper pronunciation could be spliced in, as would have been simple years later on tape. Records were played the same way—using a needle at the end of a control arm.

Foster's original idea was to time things so that whenever the offending "Saska-*chew*-an" was about to occur, the arm could be lifted and Sinclair could come in for a few words, including the correct pronunciation. However, when they tried this, it sounded almost as bizarre as the original, and the morning was wearing on.

Then Sinclair said, "Look, since that guy did his broadcasts there's a lot of new stuff. Why don't I write an entirely new piece, quoting him where it fits, but bringing the rest of it right up to date?"

Foster asked when Sinclair could do this.

"Now. In twenty minutes."

That twenty minutes changed his career. He sat down and reeled off the story at his usual record speed. It brought him $25, and when he read it on the air, it was so successful that he and Foster discussed what he could do for the next day.

Sinclair suggested two pieces, one on Lieutenant-Colonel Cecil I. Merritt, officer commanding the South Saskatchewans, and another on Honorary Captain John W. Foote, chaplain of the Royal Hamilton Light Infantry. Colonel Merritt's men had been unable to move through heavy fire that met them just after scaling the sea-wall. Finally he walked forward himself toward a bridge where they were held up, waving his helmet and calling, "See, there is no danger here!" He led his men across the bridge into a series of fierce attacks, and later in a bloody rearguard action in which he was among those taken prisoner. Foote had spent much of the morning among those who'd never made it past the beach, helping wounded men to shelter, giving first aid, bandaging, administering morphine injections, and staying with the wounded until he was also captured. Sinclair's instinct on picking subjects for his second and third broadcasts turned out to have been unerring. Both Merritt and Foote later were awarded the Victoria Cross, Britain's highest military honour.

It didn't do Sinclair any harm, either. The series he began with his Dieppe broadcast continued five times a week on CFRB for forty-two years thereafter, first under the name *Headliners* and then as *Let's Be Personal*. It is unclear how often he made the early broadcasts himself. He wrote them all, but in the first year or so many were read by others, so that, in effect, it was a simple matter of moonlighting. As the *Star* had a rule against reporters' doing outside work on a regular basis, he didn't mention his radio work around the paper. So no one in authority paid attention until early in 1943, six or seven months after Dieppe.

Then one morning his photo and name appeared in newspaper advertisements announcing a new series of programs sponsored by Shreddies. As he told the story in his 1966 memoirs,

> a note came through channels—publisher to
> managing editor to city editor: "We understand Mr.
> Sinclair is being heard on radio in violation of a
> standing order. Please ascertain from him when, and
> by whom, this contract was arranged, what he is being
> paid, how much of the payment comes to this paper,
> and how long this contract is to run."
> The managing editor to the city editor: "Do so."
> The city editor to me: "Please explain."
> I guess I'd been on the slosh—I don't remember.
> But I went along with the other notes and scribbled,
> "None of your damned business."
> Of course that did it. I was given two weeks' notice.

On the news that Sinclair not only had been fired, but was actually going to leave this time, other reporters decided to give him a going-away present. Dennis Braithwaite, later a popular columnist with other Toronto dailies—the *Telegram*, the *Globe and Mail*, and the *Toronto Sun*—was a young reporter at the *Star* when all hands assembled in the newsroom to present Sinclair with something to remember them by—a bicycle. The gathering included big names as well as desk men, editorial writers, office boys, and secretaries, and Gregory Clark stood on a desk to make the presentation. Braithwaite's chief memory is one of surprise that, although Clark was already known as a great off-the-cuff raconteur, he had the speech all written out and *read it*!

This could have been to guard against showing emotion about the departure of a long-time colleague—he and Sinclair were to remain friends for life—or it could have been written out so that the *Star* could print it, which was done in a long and warm going-away story published on February 18, 1943, and headed:

GLOBE-TROTTING SINCLAIR EMBARKS ON RADIO CAREER

"Yesterday," the story began, "Gordon Sinclair walked out of the city room of the *Star* for the last time. . . ." Again, as when he left for his brief period in advertising, and when he returned to write sports, there was no stinting. Sinclair was quoted at length about what he hoped to do in radio. Clark's text seems to have made the paper in its entirety, recounting how "all over the world he went, round and round in those troubled tragic years of depression and of meanness of spirit amongst all mankind. With nonchalance and impudence and a deep underlying sense of pathos and irony, he described all the other peoples of the world, in the far, unknown corners. He carried us out of our own little selves."

Then he gave chapter and verse, starting with the hobo series of 1929. It was the warmest send-off for a fired reporter in journalistic memory, and the manner of it still stands as a compliment to the *Star*. Firings there could be tough, too, but Sinclair was special.

A characteristic fact is that Sinclair, in his perversity, knowing how much rope the *Star* had always given him, staged a loud public showdown with Hindmarsh just before the official farewell. One account is that on one of Sinclair's final few days at the *Star* he got drunk and came in carrying his old, well-travelled typewriter, the one he had written about from a hundred exotic pit-stops as Tippy the Typewriter. His plan was to carry it to Hindmarsh's office, lean it against the door, and then knock, so that when the door was opened, the typewriter would fall in.

James Y. Nicol says that it didn't turn out that way. Sinclair might have had the typewriter, along with some such plan, but Nicol's recollection is that Sinclair waited around the hall near Hindmarsh's office until Hindmarsh appeared, then confronted him with, "Well, Mr. Hindmarsh, everything going well now that you've fired Sinclair? I guess you're pretty proud of yourself for getting me out of here, eh? Well, try to fire me now! Would you like to fire me now? Would it make you feel better?"

It was what Nicol called "a real razzing". Hindmarsh waited it out. When Sinclair ran out of breath, Hindmarsh said mildly, "Well, Gordon, if you go up to the fifth floor you'll find there's a cheque there waiting for you, in appreciation of past services."

The cheque was for $5,000. Severance pay was unknown in those days. Sinclair acknowledged this parting bonus in his memoirs, without giving the circumstances.

But part of his uncontrolled behaviour at the time of the firing, his "none of your damned business" note, his confrontation with Hindmarsh, even his reference to being sloshed, no doubt was influenced by another event that was to cast a long, sad shadow on him for life.

His daughter Jean, the apple of his eye, was eleven coming up to Christmas of 1942. She petitioned her parents with great persistence to agree that she was grown up enough to do her own Christmas shopping. That year, as usual, she had helped to decorate the family tree. She had wrapped a few gifts and placed them on it. Finally, on the Saturday before Christmas, December 19, a cold and raw day, she and her mother went out to shop, with the understanding that Jean would do her own picking and choosing.

When they came home after the strenuous hours of

136

battling crowds, she said she didn't feel like supper. Everybody agreed that probably the excitement of the day's shopping in heavy clothes, getting overheated, and then going outside to try other stores, had been too much for her. No one saw it as more than that. She went to bed earlier than usual. In the middle of the night Gladys woke to a strange sound.

When she got up to investigate, she found that Jean was having great trouble breathing and had a high temperature. Gladys and Gordon had separate rooms. Gordon had wakened, too, and after an hour or two, as Jean seemed to be getting worse, they bundled her up warmly and drove downtown in the pre-dawn dark of Sunday morning to the Hospital for Sick Children, which was then on College Street near Bay in an old and drafty building.

When Sinclair carried her in to the admitting area, certain events occurred that stayed with him for life, and he often mentioned them bitterly whenever anyone referred to that hospital's slogan, "Where No Child Is Ever Turned Away".

"I was turned away!" he wrote in his 1966 memoirs, referring back to the time his mother had taken him there as a child. "My daughter was almost turned away. . . ."

> . . . She was left on the floor of the lobby on a low stretcher until I paid cash in advance to have her admitted. I had no cash. It was Sunday and I had rushed from home without cash, but there was little at home anyway. I was by then a relatively well-fixed man, but they wouldn't take a cheque. I had to make several telephone calls to have the admission of my daughter guaranteed.
>
> When we got her in the hospital bed but before the doctors had arrived, Jean asked for a drink. She was a positive kind of a girl and she said, "I'd like orange juice, please."
>
> The nurse . . . said she would have to wait. Jean turned to me with dark-eyed dismay. "Daddy, I always

thought that if I went into a hospital I could have anything I wanted, whenever I wanted it."

That was the last sentence she ever spoke to me.

Leaving Jean in an oxygen tent later that day—the hospital by then was doing everything it could—Gordon was optimistic. Doris had joined him and Gladys at the hospital. Her memory is that he was convinced Jean would be all right. She'd seemed to be delirious earlier, but she had been started on oxygen soon after admission. The diagnosis was viral pneumonia. Sulpha drugs were being used at that time, but penicillin had not been discovered.

All three felt that the crisis was past, and when Sinclair left Doris late in the afternoon he told her, "I think she's a little better."

But medical help had come too late. The virus already had entered Jean's bloodstream and hampered or wholly shut down the functions of her vital organs. She died that evening, not much more than twenty-four hours after she'd first complained of feeling unwell.

When the news came to the Sinclair family, they were all together. Gladys and Gordon clung to each other in grief. One family member said years later, "It was the only time I ever saw my mother and father hug each other."

The next morning about eight, Gordon phoned Doris to say that Jean was dead. Doris wanted to know if there was anything she could do. Sinclair told her no, she should carry on, go to work.

The funeral was on Christmas Eve. There was no Christmas at the Sinclair home that year, and there were tears each time anyone passed the Christmas tree that Jean had helped decorate, and on which, with giggles, she had put the presents she had wrapped. A few days later, Gladys carried the tree, exactly as it was, to the attic. It was not an artificial tree but a real one, and for years thereafter, the needles all dried and fallen, the tree stood, a decorated skeleton, in the Sinclair attic.

Sinclair's grieving despondency without doubt affected

his behaviour, not only in his final break with the *Star* but elsewhere. Some months later, James V. Nicol was looking for a bicycle for his own daughter. Thoughtlessly, he realized later, he phoned Sinclair to ask advice, figuring he'd know, he'd had all those kids to buy bicycles for . . . "and he said, 'Yeah, I have a bicycle here that my daughter used and you can have that, it's a good bike . . . ' and all of a sudden he started to cry and said, 'Jim, I could never let that bike go.' "

After that, Sinclair often took time off work at Christmas. It became known as one of his depressed periods. He would start drinking a few days before Christmas and keep it up until early January, sloshed (to use his own term) most of that time.

Sinclair's eldest son, Gord, said in 1986 that opening gifts was a bad time. "He was sentimental, but he couldn't handle it, it didn't go with his own tough-guy image of himself, so he'd escape into the bottle. The death in the family had its effect forever, as long as he lived, and the same with my mother until she couldn't remember."

CHAPTER TEN

I TOLD THEM I COULDN'T DO NEWS

His first sponsor was kind enough to come and fire him in person.

Looking at Sinclair's life for the year or two after Jean's death and his departure from the *Star*, it helps to understand that at first he saw radio not as his glowing future but simply as a living and an escape hatch from his dead-end at the *Star*. He was uneasy about his voice, his delivery, his pronunciation, everything. His lack of confidence was quickly confirmed when his first sponsors said they liked the stuff he wrote for *Headliners* but not the way he gave it on air. As a result, an announcer named Mike Fitzgerald was assigned to read *Headliners* at $5 per program.

That was okay with Sinclair. With someone else to read his pieces, he could dash them off two or three at a time and get someone to drop them in. He even tried (in vain) to have CFRB mail his cheques out to him. He seemed to shrink from people he didn't know, even the ones at work—anyway, they were on staff and he was not. When Fitzgerald complained to a Foster executive, Wis McQuillan, about the agency's taking its customary fifteen-per-cent cut from his daily $5, he was replaced by a more amenable young announcer just in from the prairies, Jack Dennett. But

Sinclair hadn't left his old truculence behind at the *Star*. CFRB tried to cut his pay to $20 per item on the grounds that someone else had to be paid $5 to read it. Sinclair told them either to keep on paying him $25 "or get another hack".

The grieving loner in him, often at odds even with his own family, showed distinctly for many months. At home sometimes he would be sitting at his typewriter in the small study just off the front hall, lost in thought, and would start at some sound and for an instant think it was Jean. His emotional state, as exemplified by his reaction to James Y. Nicol over Jean's bicycle, was more than simply grief. Jean's death caused him to question many of his beliefs. His Methodist upbringing, church services twice every Sunday as a boy, midweek prayer meetings, and revival meetings, as well as his experience teaching Sunday school, then teaching a Bible class until he was at least twenty, had not prepared him for this, even though none of what he had been taught could have promised him immunity from personal suffering.

Sinclair often said in later years that his questioning of a powerful God's existence began in India when he saw how people suffered and died in the streets every day, but Jean's death brought this unbelief to another dimension. Bill Baker, who had started at CFRB in 1924 before the station went on the air and was Sinclair's first friend there, said that after Jean died, "Gord got so he just couldn't believe that there is a God. He talked about it a lot. He'd say, 'Here's a girl, she's eleven, she never did anything wrong, she never had a chance,' and he'd go away brooding."

Now that he no longer had to report anywhere daily, he went on long, melancholy walks on the golf course with the current dog, a predecessor to the often-mentioned four-legged buddies that he later made into such characters for his public. In winter sometimes he'd take a gun and hunt rabbits. In summer he'd play golf and then take a few drinks, often on a weekend staying for bridge in the locker-room or on the veranda. This would lead to fights with Gladys when he got home hours late for the big Sunday dinners she had spent hours preparing.

There was a reason that he gave no more time to broad-casting than he could help. More than ever he wanted to be known as a writer. The book reviews that he most cherished were the ones praising his writing. He would declaim late in life to his son Jack, whose field is television production, that television wasn't creative, that the only really creative pursuit open to man is writing: sitting down to a blank piece of paper and creating something from nothing, either as fiction or as what the writing and publishing world terms "non-fiction", thus delicately carving a fine line between that and "fact".

His ambitions went far beyond what he was ever able to accomplish. He wanted to write fiction and kept trying from time to time, but as early as 1935, he acknowledged that it seemed beyond him. He was in Kashmir at the time, "among personable young officers on leave from their stations and gay young wenches out from England, a gland-stimulating climate and all those lakes and streams full of flower-decked houseboats combined to create wholesale amour. . . .

"So I sat down and tried to write a love story—it was a colossal flop." The failure was

> not from the usual laziness or lack of time, but
> because I simply dried up when it came to a love
> scene. Perhaps dour Scots ancestry and upbringing in
> a home where outward signs of affection and amour
> were a scandalous indication of weakness had
> something to do with it. So far as I know, neither my
> parents, my brothers nor myself have ever used the
> words dear, darling, sweetheart or any of that other
> rot.

It wasn't that he was uninterested in sex. Quite the contrary. Many women he knew well or even intimately, from Doris Loach on through chance acquaintances, secre-taries, and friends, said he often tried out sex-related ideas or anecdotes on them, as if trying to find out how they would react—in effect conducting a research into female attitudes. In these sallies, there would be no room for the warmth that might have turned sex talk into intimacy. He just didn't know how to bridge the gap, except with Doris, always a close friend as well as his lover. His overt sexual attitudes were simply male-locker-room gothic. When he discussed women in the abstract, apart from those near and dear to him, his approach was described by one as "sort of sniggering".

At home, it was the same. One time when son Gord was going out with a girl and Gladys called, "Don't forget your rubbers," Sinclair added mockingly, "Yes, don't forget your *rubbers*!" making it plain that he was using the word, as was common then, to mean condoms. With that attitude to relationships with females, he might not have done badly at some forms of fiction where women are seen mainly as usable chattels, but he had so many hang-ups on the subject that the only writing he is known to have done and thrown away was his fiction.

Now that he could no longer undertake the kind of travel that had produced his earlier books, he turned seriously to writing for magazines. He did a great deal of this in the next few years, mainly for Canadian magazines, including *Maclean's*, *Liberty*, and *Saturday Night*. Sometimes, simply for the money or to remind himself and others of where he'd been and what he'd seen, he would find a new reason to justify a rerun of one of his old footloose experiences. But he knew he was only treading water; he was a lot better than that.

The best magazine market in Canada was *Maclean's*, which then was published on the first and fifteenth of each month, featuring fiction and articles, a Canadian equivalent to the vastly popular U.S. slick magazines of the time: *Saturday Evening Post*, *Collier's*, and others. *Maclean's* had a few staff writers but mainly bought free-lance. He'd written once for *Maclean's* as early as 1932. He approached the magazine again, through H. Napier Moore, editor, and W. Arthur Irwin, managing editor, and within weeks of leaving the *Star* he was working on the first of his *Maclean's* assignments.

This was the summer of 1943. Some of the many thousands of young Canadians who had flown in the air war over Europe now occasionally came home on leave or for medical reasons. *Maclean's* editors kept a hawklike eye on the newspapers for leads to stories that would have national appeal. Sometimes this took the form of thinking up a title and then finding the right fighting-man to work with a good writer to produce something that would match the title. Sinclair's well-honed skills at making adventure come alive made him a natural for such work.

His first piece appeared as the magazine's masthead (lead story) in the issue dated October 1, 1943, as:

I BOMBED BERLIN
By Flying Officer Walter Scott Sherk, DFC and Bar
As told to Gordon Sinclair

When the manuscript was turned in, Sinclair's staccato style, his sense of suspense, and his skill with dialogue in the exchanges between the pilot and the other crew members in scenes of hair-raising danger, must have made the editors think they had died and gone to heaven.

The story is told in the first person, Flying Officer Sherk through Sinclair. In the first paragraph, Sherk and his crew are flying through the night in their four-engined Halifax for a bombing raid on Stettin, the pilot extolling the virtues of his navigator, "Mouthpiece" Morrison. (Morrison was a Vancouver lawyer, hence "Mouthpiece", the nickname itself probably being enough to make a place in Sinclair's lead.)

The crew's laconic exchanges as the pilot reports they are being shot at, Mouthpiece observing, "So what?", a gunner wanting to alter course and shoot back at the bastards, the pilot replying calmly, "Some other time, we're getting near target area," use only a few words each to make the crewmen into recognizable characters. This gives extra meaning to the action to come. The next passages read even now like a movie script, leading up to the bomb-aimer's words to the pilot, "Steady as you go. Left a bit. Left. Right . . . right . . . Steady. Bombs gone. Turn off."

Then the pilot's account as Sinclair wrote it:

> I started to swing off the target area and set the course for home but at that second there was a crash and a burst of bluewhite flame which slowly turned to orange. We spun downward. The chance of an aircraft being struck by explosives from another aircraft in its own attack group are about a million to one. But we had suffered that millionth chance. A plane 2,000 feet above dropped its bombs without seeing us below.
>
> I assumed we'd suffered a direct anti-aircraft hit and so did the other boys. The roof had been blown off. One bomb had crashed through my compartment. The back of my flying suit was on fire and the cockpit was ablaze. I struggled with the jammed controls. The idea of a prison camp kept flashing through my mind. . . .

With the big Halifax out of control, in flames, and falling five thousand feet in a minute or so, the pilot gave the order to bail out. The custom was that he would fly the aircraft until everyone else had gone, then jump last. Two did bail out, each reporting to the captain as he jumped, but the wireless operator, up next, yelled that he had no parachute. He'd ruined it beating out flames, so *he* wasn't going anywhere, he said. The pilot ordered him to hook up with another, smallish man, hoping one parachute would hold both. They were about to do this when suddenly the engineer got the controls working again—at least a little. Then the reader gets a blow-by-blow account as Mouthpiece, navigating by the stars through the hole in the roof (his maps all burned in the fire), directs them on a circuitous course, and the pilot gradually gains confidence. They head first toward Sweden (and sure internment), then swing over Denmark and the North Sea, finally turning back to England and touching safely down. One hour late.

145

It was a classic magazine article of its kind. Sinclair even achieved the goal of working in the full names and home towns of all the principals without ever slowing the action. Taken altogether, that piece stands up even now as a textbook example of what can be good about magazine journalism.

Sinclair didn't always have such dramatic material to work with, but another measure of a good professional is to get the utmost out of what there is.

He did that ten weeks later for a sister team of figure-skaters; then, in January 1944, for another airman (first sentence: "It was moonlight as we crossed the North Sea to Juist in the Frisian Islands that lie north of Holland. Our task was to mine the sea lanes . . . "); and in March 1944 for a story on test pilots. Each was thoroughly researched, and well told. The only problem from the standpoint of a man trying to make a living is that *Maclean's* didn't pay much, $300 tops at that time. Perhaps Sinclair made $1,200 in total from those four articles. In the United States or England, with his skill, he never would have had to work again at anything other than magazines and books. But he never voiced any intention of moving away from home to greener pastures. In the next two years he wrote eleven more articles for *Maclean's*, more than any other free-lance writer, the topics covering a wide range. Some titles: Steam Baths; Snakes Alive; Bee Business; I'm Reducing. As many magazine writers do, operating as a hired gun, he was one of the best in the trade.

Often he took refuge with Doris, then in her late twenties and a slender and attractive blonde, for plays and movies and dinners out. Gladys seemingly was aware of this. Both before and after Doris and he had become lovers in 1939, Gladys would sometimes say, "Take Doris," if he asked her to go somewhere with him and she didn't want to go. One of his *Maclean's* articles was about a mayor of Ottawa, Stanley Lewis. For the research, he asked Gladys to go to Ottawa with him. Again she declined, saying, "Take Doris." The manner in which she spoke those words might have suggested that she suspected what the relationship had become, but no one will ever know. This was the first time they'd gone away overnight together and marked a new stage in their lives. From then on their trips together occurred with increasing frequency.

But by then his radio career was about to blossom financially and otherwise. Late in May 1944 he was asked by CFRB to take on a news program that Red Foster had been doing for years at 11:50 each morning, sponsored by Acme Farmers Dairy.

Sinclair didn't like the new assignment at all. He figured it would tie him down too much. It would take two or three hours for him to put the news package together from wire-service copy, local newspapers, and whatever else he could find, to write it, and to read it. And, as he wrote in his second book of memoirs, "The style of news broadcasting in those days was genteel; pearly-voiced rounded sentences, contrived depth to the delivery. I had none of that and it was too late to learn. Also, I didn't give a damn."

He turned it down.

The station management—Harry Sedgwick as president and Lloyd Moore as manager—said he either did it or his *Headliners* show would be taken away from him as well and it would be "Goodbye, Gordon."

He said he'd do it.

The pay would be $12 per broadcast, which, added to his $25 a day for the *Headliners* series, made $37 a day, $185 a week. It would be done on a free-lance basis. There was one early hitch: a major local promotion campaign had been planned, but it was dropped because the head of Acme Farmers Dairy, the sponsor, didn't like Sinclair's voice and wanted a trial period first.

Sinclair mentioned many times later that his news show was supposed to start on Monday, June 6, 1944. This was one of his numerous and no doubt unconscious errors (getting the month wrong or the year wrong) in writing or talking about major dates of his life. This time he was only one day out. He did start on a Monday, but it was June 5.

However, to have been completely accurate in this case would have spoiled the impact of the story as he always told it: "Hell broke loose on the day I was to start because it was D-Day. Troops were swarming ashore on the beaches of Normandy and bulletins were taking over the radio stations, cancelling even the soap operas, as well as my debut."

Still, the program did get on the air the day before D-Day and survived the wild news day of the invasion itself. With Sinclair being Sinclair, doing it his way, his new career was under way.

Simultaneously came the complaints. Those listeners accustomed to Red Foster's dulcet tones and gentlemanly delivery—and to whose back doors Acme drivers delivered milk every day—phoned the dairy "to demand, by shriek or reason, that Foster be brought back and I get the heave-ho. I used slang, I fluffed, had no class . . . cancel my milk!" When the crunch came, it was after an item he did about the new styles in women's hats, ending with, "Frankly, folks, to me they all look like spittoons."

Sinclair always remembered appreciatively that the president of the dairy took the time to come and fire him in person. A phone call or a letter would have been the easy way out. "But this man, who was ill at the time and died soon after, came in and told me he was sorry, his customers just didn't like me. I'd be replaced."

It was the first of many times when CFRB would stand fast in Sinclair's defence. CFRB's president, Harry Sedgwick, a former movie executive with Famous Players, who had grown up in the same district as the Sinclairs, ruled that the sponsor could quit if he wanted to, but Sinclair would not be fired. The sponsor quit, exactly three weeks into the show.

A prospective new sponsor, Alka Seltzer, which had a local office but was run mainly from headquarters in Elkhart, Indiana, offered a contract. Sinclair said okay, he'd sign—but for $20 per newscast instead of $12. This weighty matter had to be taken all the way to Elkhart. He got his $20, and the routine that CFRB was to follow for decades had been established: the time from 11:45 to 12 noon belonged to Gordon Sinclair's five-minute *Headliners*, renamed *Let's Be Personal*, and his ten-to-twelve news.

Bill Baker, his control-room operator much of the time, liked this development from the beginning. "His voice was craggy, 'readable' as I call it, meaning it was a personality, it was solid, and he was consistent."

Those qualities, together with Sinclair's often off-beat choice of news, and pungent opinions, took hold. The audience began to climb, while, as Sedgwick told a reporter a few years later, "Sinclair causes us more trouble than all the rest of the staff put together." His battles with Sedgwick became a legend. As Baker recalls it, "He and Sinc were so much alike. Sedgwick would come down the hall and yell, 'You shouldn't have done that,' and they'd scream and holler at each other and then it was all over."

The CFRB studios were then on the second floor of a building at 37 Bloor Street West in downtown Toronto. Sinclair, since he was in the studio every day, quickly made it his own neighbourhood, and used it that way on-air. On the street floor below CFRB was Creed's, whose labels were to be found wherever a fashionable woman threw a mink coat or a sable stole carelessly over a chair (with the label carefully showing). Jack Creed was the boss. His son Eddie—eventually to succeed his father as head of the business—was serving as a Royal Canadian Naval Volunteer Reserve officer on a minesweeper in the Atlantic. In Creed's basement, where the fur-cutters worked, they knew Sinclair and sometimes had coffee with him.

On the Bloor-Yonge southwest corner was Frank Stollery's men's store. Sinclair knew all the Stollerys—Frank, with his big cigar and bow tie (like Sinclair's), and his three sons. Sam Rouse sold papers on the corner in all weathers. A few doors south on Yonge Street was Curry's, a jeweller about to branch out into art supplies. Sinclair would make the rounds after his noon broadcast, stopping in almost daily at Clapp's shoe store (which also sold live fishing-bait) for a game of cribbage with Cecil Clapp.

Everything that went on around the Bloor and Yonge corner worked itself one way or another into Sinclair's broadcasts, including "a rowdy group of Scotsmen" who lived in one of the decaying boarding-houses alongside the parking-lot behind the studio. One of these Scots, sitting on the running-board of a car one day to yarn with Sinclair, said he'd been a piper with the Gordon Highlanders in the First World War. Sinclair called him a liar, said he was too young to have been in that war, and, after an argument that included the Scot's getting his bagpipes and playing a piece or two, the man admitted it. But when the Scots were down and out, Sinclair sometimes would help out with a few dollars.

One day, sober and cleanly dressed, the original piper stopped Sinclair in the parking-lot after his noon broadcast and asked for $100. His son was coming on a visit from Cape Breton and he wanted to make a decent impression. "A hundred was too much and I said so. The fur-cutters from Creed's were on their lunch break and heard part of this conversation, and with what I provided, and I think Manny Feldman, the furriers' union man, kicked in as well, they chipped in and we got almost a hundred." The son arrived and the piper "did not let us, or his son, down. They had a good visit."

Sinclair's work at the station soon grew to sharing with Alan Savage a weekly interview show called *Ontario Panorama*. Each one would be lined up by an advance man with newspaper experience who'd go into a small town or village, hire a hall, and pick out five or six residents with good stories to tell (one in Richmond Hill had helped build the Empire State Building). Then Bill Baker, Sinclair, and Savage would arrive, the crowd would gather, and, Sinclair said, "We'd talk with people most of whom had never seen a microphone let alone talked into one."

Sinclair and Savage were a good contrast. Savage was a stylishly dressed and thorough interviewer, while the mussed-up Sinclair shook things up with the penetrating interview techniques that he'd perfected at the *Star*, and which ten years later were to lead to his television career. Money collected from *Ontario Panorama* audiences went at first to war work and, later in the four years that the program lasted, to work with ex-servicemen. One night their driver and advance man committed suicide when he got home to find his house empty and his wife and children gone. His body was found under the snow in his back yard a few days later. "I think about that sometimes," Sinclair said forty years later in a *Let's Be Personal*.

Radio in Sinclair's first years underwent a remarkable transformation. At CFRB he was on the leading edge, but was by no means the top dog he would become. The main newscasts of the day were done by the *Telegram*'s Jim Hunter at 8 a.m. and 6 p.m. Rex Frost had a half-hour farm show that started at 12 and was considered unmovable. As Jack Dawson, who had worked at CFRB in 1939 and returned there after his war service recalls, "In those days there was no CFRB programming as such; it was all done by an ad agency. An agency man would come along and say, 'I've got a sponsor, I want a newscast here,' and name the time. We'd give it to him. It was money. Eaton's wanted one at 4 and another at 11? Sure!"

In the late 1940s all CFRB announcers—Sinclair, Dawson, John Collingwood Reade, Jack Dennett, and Wes McKnight—shared one office, even a desk. Dawson remembers,

> Each guy would be allotted one drawer in this desk, and the one with the most seniority would get the top drawer, that sort of thing. Sinc would come in a couple of hours before he was due on air. If it was a slow news day he'd be busting and scratching for something he could get his teeth into.
>
> He wanted every day to grab his audience, and he was such a good digger that he often could do it better than the newspapers did. One day the *Globe* had a little story that there'd been a baby left on the

steps of the Children's Aid Society. No more information than that. To many that would have been enough, but not to Sinclair. He got on the phone and called the C.A.S. Was the child male or female? They wouldn't tell him! He got kicked upstairs on the phone to the head of the C.A.S. and still couldn't get an answer. By then he was mad. He told the top guy, last one he talked to, "You better listen to the ten-to-twelve newscast! I'm going to have something to say about you!"

A short time after that, with Sinclair typing away at his newscast, Lloyd Moore, the station manager, got a call in his office from the C.A.S. head, complaining. So Lloyd came down the hall and in to where Sinclair was typing his story and said, "Gordon, I understand that you have a little problem with the C.A.S."

Sinclair didn't look up, just said, "I sure have."

Lloyd started to say, "I wish you would . . ." but Sinclair, still not looking up, cut him off and said, "Lloyd, I'm a bit busy now so I haven't much time to argue with you, but just lean over my shoulder and you can read what it is I'm going to say on your radio station about them."

As Lloyd read it, Sinc just kept on typing and Lloyd was furious, really spluttering, so Sinc said, "There's only one person that can change this as far as I'm concerned and that's the sponsor, Alka Seltzer, and they're in Elkhart, Indiana."

When he went on the air, all worked up, he went blow-by-blow through the matter of the original report in the *Globe* and his phone calls and then said, "All I wanted to know was whether the child was male or female! That's *all* I wanted to know and these blank-blank bureaucrats wouldn't tell me!"

That set his ground rules right there. Sinc was staking out new territory in the news business, and every time he'd go right to the breaking-point, like he did with Lloyd Moore. He was also a good judge of

Always small for his age, and his mother's boy, his clothes were usually hand-me-downs. The style is pure Bessie, his mother, an expert at making a man's suit fit a boy. (*Gordon Sinclair Estate*)

The *Star's* roving reporter, his beat the world's most exotic corners. Before one trip, ten thousand people jammed Massey Hall and the streets around to see him off.(*Gordon Sinclair Estate*)

On the beach at Toronto Island.(*Gordon Sinclair Estate*)

He was bold enough with most women, but when he met Gladys Prewett, at first he couldn't get up the nerve to ask her out. (*Gordon Sinclair Estate*)

Gladys and Gordon on a Lake Ontario excursion steamer. Probably late 1920's. (*Gordon Sinclair Estate*)

The children in summer: Gord, Jack, Jean and Don. A year or two before Jean's tragic death. (*Gordon Sinclair Estate*)

The hat, typewriter, radios barking police calls in the background...his style both at home and on the road was that of Hollywood newspaper movies. Only his family didn't buy the image. (*Teskey—Toronto Star Syndicate*)

Another kind of religion: Aimee Semple McPherson was the most famous evangelist of the time. She and Sinclair were believed to be lovers. (*Gordon Sinclair Estate*)

FRONT PAGE CHALLENGE

Above: In 1957 the producers of a new game show called *Front Page Challenge* knew they needed a curmudgeon and a pretty lady: Sinclair and Toby Robins. Pierre Berton came later. (*Ragsdale—CBC Information Service*). *Below:* Betty Kennedy, a regular with Sinclair on CFRB and at *Front Page*, often was the one who could get him out of his depressions and back to work. (*Ron Bull*)

Longtime secretary Pat Morse (*above*) was what Sinclair called "zoo-keeper to the resident celebrity." (*her own photo*)

When Pat Morse resigned in 1981, the job was given to newsroom assistant Millie Moriak. Her memo blasting Sinclair for sexual crudities was an unpublished classic. Then they became friends. (*Paul Till*)

It was a proud moment for a Cabbagetown kid to be named an officer of the Order of Canada. With Governor General Ed Schreyer. (*Toronto Star Syndicate*)

Same tam o'shanter, sporran, and kilt, three years older—with his granddaughter Connie, at her wedding in 1981. (*Toronto Star Syndicate*)

Gladys with grandchildren: Jim, Allan, Jennifer, Connie, Susie. (*Gordon Sinclair Estate*)

Sinclair in 1978 with his sons, from the left: Don, Gord and Jack. (*Gordon Sinclair Estate*)

(*Toronto Star Syndicate*)

where the hell the breaking-point was.

After that, Sinclair's relations with Lloyd Moore were strained, to say the least. No boss likes to be shot down by someone he expects at least to be able to reason with. One day soon after this incident, Moore found him in CFRB at 2 p.m. writing letters and, according to Sinclair's second memoirs, "told me to clear out, that my stint ended at noon and I was to be gone at 12:05." Another time Moore found Sinclair putting letters in CFRB's outgoing mail and chewed him out. He was not to use CFRB letterheads. He was to put his own stamps on everything. Then, as Sinclair wrote in *Will the Real Gordon Sinclair Please Sit Down*,

> One day I happened to be walking past Station Manager Moore's office when he was on the phone red-faced and explosive about me—but *in my defence*!
>
> I thought he hated me and would have chucked me out except for Harry Sedgwick.
>
> But there was some screaming woman on the telephone and he was telling her that he as a person, and CFRB as a station, believed in free speech, that they were providing free entertainment and information and if Sinclair was so offensive why didn't she turn us off?
>
> This was heresy of the worst kind. Telling a cherished listener to go to hell? Oh, no!
>
> I don't think Moore ever knew I'd overheard that conversation but it sure changed my attitude toward him.

Sometimes, later, he would reflect on "what ifs"—that he might have married another woman (one he had considered was killed in a car crash at twenty-seven, the other married, childless, and dead at fifty); that he might have done better to knuckle under to various bosses instead of making a career of riling them; that he might have bought a weekly newspaper, a project that Gladys had predicted, probably accurately, would have resulted in his being run out of some small town on a rail; even that he might have chosen another career, and stayed in school past Grade 8 to become a doctor(!).

But in one of these musings, a deceptively simple one, he wondered what would have happened "if Gladys had been as tired as I was on Thanksgiving Day 1946, after we had spent three fruitless weekends in Muskoka looking for a summer place to buy." That day he'd given up and gone into the Windsor Hotel at Bala for a beer while Gladys and Don went to look at one more cottage. They returned to say that it wasn't much of a cottage, pretty skimpy, but the site on Acton Island, which had a bridge to the mainland, was beautiful. On their say-so he'd bought it sight unseen. For the rest of his life Acton Island was his beloved refuge.

At the time, he and Gladys for years had had separate rooms and, outside of the home, separate lives. On Acton Island he soon had a separate cabin built for himself, so that there they didn't even live under the same roof. Today, given their situation, a divorce might have been in their near future, especially as even then or shortly thereafter his trips with Doris included (unknown to Gladys until later) an annual jaunt for a week in New York to see the new Broadway plays. Whatever Gladys knew or suspected, she wasn't ready—yet—to force the issue. And in the memory of their son Gord, Sinclair, no matter what he did outside of the bonds of marriage, "preached to us that the family unit was the most important thing in society."

A *Maclean's* article he wrote about the women of Quebec may be taken as an explanation of that view. He said he was quoting someone else but the tone was his own, his vehicle a Montreal woman named Suzanne who

> had no use for that ridiculous and unworkable philosophy called romantic love. She didn't believe the Hollywood hokum that once a man and a maid go to the altar their amorous problems are automatically solved and they'll live happily ever afterward. Sue and

her sort identify that lie for what it is. The delusion that marriage is, or will be, a perpetual extension of courtship with children as some future possibility is not part of the Gallic theory. [These] girls realistically approach marriage with the realization that the family is . . . the very purpose of the union. And they are the better for it, spiritually and physically. The home is the foundation of the nation and of civilization. . . .

That attitude might well have explained the rules that Sinclair lived by, and had done since soon after marriage—even Doris said, "I knew he had other women." Country singer Dolly Parton many years later, when asked if she ever was attracted to men other than her husband, laughed and said, "I'm married, but I'm not dead." Sinclair lived his two lives on that concept. His family was to endure, but not to the exclusion of other excitements or tendernesses that he found along the way.

CHAPTER ELEVEN

ON THE ROAD AGAIN

Around the world for the Star, *a fragrant bedroom in Berlin, a showdown over Doris.*

In 1949 Sinclair wrote in *Maclean's* that he could lay his hands on $100,000 "without borrowing a nickel", noting correctly that no other reporter could make that claim. Neither could many publishers. Those were the days when a good magazine editor such as Pierre Berton at *Maclean's* made $125 a week, and a fairly new three-bedroom bungalow on a good North Toronto street could be had for $11,500. For a man who owned his own fine home, a Muskoka cottage, and two cars including a new Studebaker Land Cruiser, as Sinclair did, his kind of cash liquidity demonstrated bona fide upper-middle-class affluence. He was making $375 a week from CFRB, more from freelance jobs here and there, and he lived on his pay. His investments were the gravy. If he'd been as flamboyant in the stock market as he was in his daily life, he'd have been either broke by then or many times a millionaire. From the beginning, his stocks had been chosen for solid, rather than spectacular, prospects. He'd built by invariably reinvesting his market earnings—but he also had a loan arrangement with a bank so he could move immediately if something hot beckoned.

As to his state of mind, footloose and fancy-free wasn't

exactly the description, but it was close. His home life seemed to have become what it was to be forevermore; that is, no change. Wally Crouter, then fairly new at CFRB, went home with Sinclair one day for the first time and nearly perpetrated a gaffe of some size. It is cruel to have to say, but it was true: Crouter thought Gladys was Sinclair's mother. At the time Gladys was fifty, Sinclair forty-eight. She had the love of her children and of many of their old pre-celebrity friends, but while he had bloomed, she had aged.

More disturbing to Crouter was the gap between Sinclair and his sons. "Whatever had happened before, by the time I met the family Gladys just didn't want to go anywhere *with him*, and Sinc refused to let that mean he didn't go anywhere either. But the boys were a different proposition altogether. I thought their relationship with their dad was just sad."

Gord had left home just before his nineteenth birthday in 1947, saying goodbye to further schooling to join a new radio station in Niagara Falls. His father had wanted him to get a journalism degree. "Out of one side of his mouth," said Gord, "he'd be declaiming that people had to stand on their own feet, but when I wanted to do that, oh, no!" Working in Niagara Falls, then Hamilton, then Oshawa, he was at home a good deal until his marriage in 1949 (his father was abroad, so did not attend). When he moved to Fredericton and then, in the early 1950s, to Montreal, the separation from home became more complete, but he never missed writing or—when he was making more money—phoning his mother every week.

While Gord was in the process of leaving the nest, Don, at university, spent one year in what he termed "the luxury" of being away from home, in residence. Otherwise he lived mostly at home. Sometimes he and his father went to hockey games together. But one story gives a general picture of their relationship: "I'd be dating at that time, and I'd say, 'Dad, can I have the car on Friday night?' Dad would say, 'Sure! Sure!' Then maybe on Thursday night we'd get into an argument at the table and when he couldn't win, he'd tell me I couldn't have the car." Don's memory of such picayune unfairness had not dimmed with time, but no longer rated more than a head-shake and a shrug.

The youngest son, Jack, was not as caught up as his brothers in the emotional battles, and says now that he rarely thinks of any specific incident unless he's reminded of it. "So I don't have many bad memories, but not many good ones either." Each summer he would go to Muskoka with his mother for the whole school holiday. His father would be there every weekend, as well as for a few weeks' vacation.

This was in general the home situation in 1948, with the exception of Doris Loach's increasing presence in Sinclair's life. They were frequent companions in Toronto. She was a regular summer guest at the cottage on weekends and for her vacation. When he was on a trip to somewhere interesting, Doris would join him there, if her work in the credit department of Simpson's Mail Order (and later Sears) permitted. Often she would be at CFRB to meet him after his late news, for dinner, a play, a movie, or some social event. Sinclair had press tickets to all the openings. Many of the others usually present at the same events had never met Gladys, but they met Doris.

Because they seemed open with each other, at that time Doris probably knew more than anyone about what pleased him and what bothered him. In her opinion, when he received a call from H. C. Hindmarsh in January 1949, a few days after New Year's, "he was completely comfortable in radio and gave no serious consideration to going back to a newspaper," but rather liked the idea oi the *Star*'s wanting him again.

Behind the call was the *Star*'s constant battle with the *Telegram* for circulation and advertising revenue, each trying to out-headline, out-write, out-sensation, the other. Hindmarsh asked if Sinclair would go around the world again for the *Star*, this time by air? He knew that would create reader interest, and had in mind comparisons: Sinclair's sensation-filled 1930s experience vs. whatever he found in the postwar world. The contract would be for twenty weeks.

The idea of being footloose again attracted Sinclair. His answer was yes. In February of 1949, after he'd told his CFRB audiences that he was off on a few months' leave, a *Star* headline read:

GORDON SINCLAIR ON HIS WAY, TRAVELS WORLD FOR STAR

His first leg was westward from Toronto. This was before commercial passenger jets were in use. Sinclair had flown a good deal, but rarely for much distance; the exception was the time he contracted malaria during his first visit to India and was flown to France in a twin-engined aircraft that had to land late each afternoon because it was not equipped to fly at night. Never before his 1949 trip had he been obliged to endure the vibrating roar of four piston engines and the confinement of being strapped in hour after hour (about ten hours then from Toronto to the Pacific coast).

It was inevitable that he'd find this kind of long-distance air travel a crashing bore. He'd been spoiled by his years of travel on leisurely ships, on which he drank and talked and played cards with interesting people, along the way changing, in effect, from a brash Cabbagetown kid to a worldly and knowing man. Ships and hotels and bars on solid ground were where he'd learned about fishing for lions, had met Charlie Chaplin, Richard Halliburton, and other globe-trotting adventurers, had flirted with many a woman—although he always said it didn't go any further.

That was a kind of travel in which he'd learned simply to stop when he liked the look of a place, whereupon story after story would beat down his doors begging to be written. Instead, now he landed first at Honolulu, to find it full of tourists visiting the sunken *Arizona*, a relic of Pearl Harbor. Nothing new in that. On to Tokyo "where Douglas MacArthur ruled like an emperor . . . [with] all those flunkies ahead and behind." In Yokohama he wrote:

The most pathetic sight in Japan today is not dead

buildings but living veterans. There are six million of these. They are the little brown men who over-ran Asia and fought with courage on a thousand fronts. . . . You'll see thousands of them here wearing their threadbare uniforms to work. That's the only clothes they have and since the war's been over for more than three years you can imagine the shape they're in.

Japanese civilians despised these bitter, cold, hungry men, Sinclair wrote. He said it with obvious sympathy, although he knew that many of his readers would be remembering the slaughter at Hong Kong and the horrors of the Japanese prisoner-of-war camps, and would be muttering, "Serves the bastards right." To Sinclair any underdog, however recently he had attained that status, was the inspiration he loved best.

Sinclair wasn't really happy with what he was getting as he moved along. Shanghai—he'd written it all before. Hong Kong—"far busier and more crowded than I'd ever seen it, but no stories. Maybe I'd lost my touch." Then it was on to Bangkok, in what was then Siam, and soon there must have been a distinct feeling of *déjà vu* for both Sinclair and his readers. Spring was there, 95 degrees F of it, and bodies stored for the winter just had to go. It was the classic 1930s Sinclair when he found a place where the winter's accumulation of bodies, "the well known . . . in jars filled with honey or a fragrant chemical," were being pulled to a cremation site by men yoked together, or by ponies, while small bodies in jars were carried in men's arms to where the funeral fires were being prepared "of charcoal, teak, sandalwood and various colored powders. . . . I wasn't able to tell how many of the winter's dead were released into the calm air of the spirit world this spring evening. . . ."

He kept writing what he saw, what he knew was there, what had worked before. But even with his usual staggering output, he felt uneasy. So much had the stamp of staleness, pre-warness, about it. Not what he was there for.

It was in Calcutta, finally, that he came alive almost by

accident. At the Great Eastern Hotel, where he'd stayed many times with the hired help bowing and scraping, he stepped up confidently to the registration desk and picked up a pen to write his name.

Without looking up, the clerk said, "No rooms."

Sinclair didn't twig. There were always rooms. He knew it, he'd benefited from it; rooms held in case someone arrived who was too important to turn away. He demanded to see the manager, and proceeded to raise a stink. He was a valued client, a this, a that, a journalist whose word was listened to by travellers, etc. The Indian manager, who had been educated, Sinclair thought, at Eton or Harrow, Oxford or Cambridge, was as polite as Sinclair was rambunctious, but the answer was the same, "No rooms."

About then Sinclair realized that this indeed was what he had travelled halfway around the world for: to find an India where a foreigner no longer could snap his fingers, or even just raise his eyebrows, and have what he wanted. "I felt like a minor edition of Colonel Blimp and a damned fool besides."

The manager offered to phone a nearby hotel that did have rooms, and reserve one for him. It would take a few minutes.

"Fine," Sinclair said. "I'll go and have a drink in the bar."

He was told that "since the coming of independence all bars are closed." However (the manager said this kindly) he *could* get a supply of booze by going to the appropriate ministry and declaring that he was an alcoholic and was therefore uncomfortable without the occasional transfusion of drink. But (gently) that would also mean he couldn't get a driver's licence.

He knew it would come out funny when he wrote it. He knew that the one thing the public liked better than a hero was a hero doing a pratfall. So he picked up his gear and staggered along, carrying it himself "for the first time in India" to the other hotel.

Also on that walk he let his readers know that India had not changed entirely. This was demonstrated in the person

161

of "one figure I'd come to know by sight 18 years earlier", a white woman who was a leper and whose pitch "was to approach white people asking for money and to stretch out a scabby wrist from which hung no hand."

For a while after that, however, Sinclair was afraid this recovery of his touch had been temporary. Bus trips, rail trips, visits to places he'd seen before and written colourfully about, didn't inspire him. "I kept feeling that this would make interesting stories for radio, but I'd done it all before in print."

It was only a matter of time. In New Delhi, an Irish hotel manageress named Mrs. Flanagan had no rooms and tongue-lashed him when he successfully used the similarity in names to register in a room being held for a Mr. Simpkins. But when Sinclair told her, "Well, look, lady, it was the middle of the night and I was tired and had no place to sleep and Simpkins wasn't here yet—what would you have done?" She apparently liked his style. She put a bed for him in a whitewashed former laundry room, far from the nearest toilet. He stayed for a while, he and Mrs. Flanagan lunching together almost daily in her quarters, she happily with a supply of cold ale. It wasn't quite like shooting man-eating tigers, but it had to do. When a real room came available, he still stayed in the laundry room.

In Karachi he roomed with a New York buyer of Persian-lamb skins "who rolled off Jewish jokes by the yard" and was castigated daily by telegrams from his office in New York along the lines of, "Was you drunk when you bought them skins, you fink?"

In Istanbul, where he'd never been before, he was put in a hotel that was about to be torn down. In preparation for demolition there was no power, no staff, no dining-room, but the rooms had beds and linen and he had three hundred of them to choose from.

He roamed out from there to eat at a restaurant from whose veranda overlooking the river customers could catch their own fish for lunch, and listened unbelievingly to a local legend that the birds flying restlessly over the river

162

did so because they were looking for Jesus. He argued that Jesus had never been in Turkey, and was told that there were years in the Bible when His whereabouts were unaccounted for and that one belief was He had drowned in this river. In Sinclair's world it was a story. "I don't know if it's true. What's difference? The birds are looking for a lost Jesus? It might be true. Who are we to say it ain't?"

Sinclair usually managed to ignore the big picture, that being part of his attraction, but when he reached Paris in May on the way home he made an exception. A major ongoing event of the time was the Soviet Union's land blockade of Berlin, part of a political showdown with its wartime allies, Britain, France, and the United States. Berlin was surrounded by, and a hundred miles inside of, Soviet-controlled East Germany. That made it geographically part of East Germany. But citizens in that part of the city called West Berlin (as later defined by the Berlin Wall) didn't agree. They wished almost unanimously to remain outside of Soviet control.

The Soviets didn't like that attitude. In June 1948 they had shut down all foreign road traffic from the west to Berlin. For eleven months U.S. and British aircraft shuttled back and forth, several flights per plane per day, in what was called the Berlin Airlift, to keep food and other essentials flowing to West Berlin. The airlift had captured world-wide attention from friend and foe alike.

Sinclair was enjoying the spring in Paris on May 9, 1949, when news came that the Soviets were lifting the blockade. The road from the west would be opened three days later and dozens of journalists would be racing to be first into Berlin. Sinclair cabled Hindmarsh asking if the paper wanted him to cover the reopening.

Two cables from Toronto arrived at Sinclair's hotel that afternoon. One was from Harry Sedgwick announcing the death of Jim Hunter, who had parlayed a strangely half-shouted delivery and the most comprehensive collection of widely held Toronto prejudices extant into the biggest news audiences in the city. Sedgwick was offering Sinclair

163

the news-broadcasting plum of the decade, Hunter's 8 a.m. and 6:30 news programs. The second cable was from Hindmarsh, saying, "Good idea. Proceed Berlin. File at take-off point."

Sinclair could have delayed replying to Sedgwick while he thought over the 'RB offer, but it was one of those things he didn't have to think over. More money? Who needed it? He cabled Sedgwick to say that getting up early enough to do news at 8 a.m. was not his idea of a good time, so thanks but no thanks. From Paris he caught a bus to Brussels and then on to Frankfurt, where he fired off a story to the *Star* about the media race about to take place. Then he managed to get on one of the airlift planes and wander around Berlin for a story before he flew back to Frankfurt to get ready.

The road was to be opened at 11 p.m. on May 11. Soviet rules were simple: any vehicle with the proper permits could use the road through Soviet-controlled German territory, but there must be no stopping, no turn-offs.

Sinclair's plan, of course, was to be the first western correspondent to reach Berlin by road. He hired a big black Cadillac with a siren, got the necessary permits, zoomed away on the stroke of 11, reached Berlin in an hour and fifty-three minutes—and finished fifth. "You know the one about nice guys finishing fifth. I'm a nice guy." He filed his "I'm in Berlin" story for the *Star* six hours and twenty minutes after leaving Frankfurt.

Then for a week he was billeted by press officers of the four-power administration in what had been a rich man's home in the Charlottenburg area. The house was now in the hands of two of the owner's daughters, whom he described as being about forty-five. He'd been in Berlin often and it was full of memories (even of seeing Marlene Dietrich's famous 1930 film *The Blue Angel*). As he toured the city in a yellow Volkswagen, there were never enough hours. He wrote about 3,000 words a day for the *Star* and felt good being in the midst of tension, uncertainly, danger, anger, and fear, all of which he could turn into human stories, his specialty.

What happened next he eventually told in two versions. Thirteen years later he told Nathan Cohen, then entertainment editor of the *Star*, that after a few hints from the sisters, he picked up ration coupons available to him but not to them. At their direction he bought what they wanted, including coffee. That night after the lights went out all over Berlin, Sinclair was nearly asleep when one of the women came to his room in her nightdress, carrying a candle. "I got the arrogant idea that she'd come on an amorous mission and I was about to be rewarded for the coffee." He doesn't tell us how he found out that this assumption was erroneous, but anyway, he told Cohen, the lady had come to tell him he was wanted on the phone. It was a call from Toronto. Hindmarsh was "saying he liked my stuff and asking if I'd like to quit radio and come back on the *Star*. I said sure, I was interested, and when should I come home? He said to take my time . . . ."

The other version came in his second volume of memoirs in 1975. In that one, the sisters had miraculously shed fifteen years. Now they were said to be about thirty, and one night

> the two young women, in nightgowns but together, came into my bedroom. All lights [in Berlin] were out at eleven so I could only make out the shadow of these women and could not understand them. The scene was more mysterious when they whispered. Observing that I didn't know what they were talking about, one of the women took me by the hand and led me out of my bedroom into another.
>
> I was then approaching fifty, these soft-voiced German women were about thirty. Somehow it didn't seem that I was being led into their bedroom for sex yet this leading by the hand in the dark of a postwar Berlin night, in a house where I was the only guest, didn't seem to offer any better explanation.
>
> The bedroom of the young women was beautifully furnished in comparison with the austerity of the one

assigned to me and carried a stimulating feminine fragrance. Not perfume but the fragrance of feminine secretions. There was a night table with a pen-sized flashlight and a telephone. The telephone receiver was off the hook and [when I picked it up] I was talking with Toronto. A sub-editor wanted me to go into East Berlin if that was possible. It was; no problem whatever.

Soon afterwards the two young women, always together, came to visit me with an interpreter to ask if . . . I could get for them, from the [American] PX, a badly needed item. They led up to this request with shy blushes that seemed real.

Could I please buy them some Kotex?

My book of ration coupons certainly included lots of Kotex and as a reward each of the girls gave me one of [their] Papa's bow ties and showed me how to tie it. I've been a bow tie addict ever since.

When he returned from Europe in that summer of 1949 he came through New York. Sometimes when he wrote a letter to Doris he would include a page for her eyes only, so that she could give the rest of the letter to Gladys to read. He also wrote to her directly. In one letter late in May he expressed some concern that Gladys suspected their relationship, and suggested that Doris "find a way" to bawl him out for something publicly to put others off the scent! A later letter to Doris giving his arrival time in New York added, "Sure hope you are there to meet me. Intentions strictly dishonorable; method of gratifying said intentions in doubt." She met him there.

Home in Toronto, he decided to stay at CFRB, but he also saw Hindmarsh and agreed that, starting September 1, he would write a weekly radio column. This soon roused howls of anguish from the targets of what he termed his "spite and spice", with everyone from Kate Aitken to the ever-popular Roy Ward Dickson objecting to Sinclair's insider-type shafts. Hindmarsh liked the controversy enough that one-a-week eventually became two, three, and finally six. Sinclair went into the 1950s stirring up constant waves of controversy in both the major media of the time, print and radio.

He had the best of both worlds. A sampling of seven hundred women by one of the early pollsters found him (by the numbers, at least) to be the best-known radio personality in the city. Often when there was a big story to be written, the *Star* asked him to do it. As it always tended to be something good for radio as well, no objections were heard from CFRB.

In April 1951 he was in the media throng at San Francisco to meet General MacArthur on his first return to the United States in many years. There were hundreds of reporters, but only one of them loaned his suitcase to General George C. Marshall to stand on so he could see better . . . Sinclair.

In October 1951, when Princess Elizabeth and her husband, the Duke of Edinburgh, made their first visit to Canada, Sinclair was on the royal train. Royal tours were plum assignments of the time, and this one had the added element that the health of King George VI was failing rapidly and it was clear that the young woman busy cutting ribbons and standing up bravely under tidal waves of mayors and aldermen would soon be queen. Actually, in his 1966 memoirs Sinclair promoted her prematurely to that office and a thoughtless editor (or no editor at all) let it slip by. Anyway, his chapter heading had a better ring to it as: Come at Once to Queen's Personal Car.

According to his telling of this anecdote, he was in his berth in the press car after the royal welcome to Quebec when he was roused by a man calling urgently, "I say, is there anyone here named Sinclair?"

When Sinclair owned up, the man said (Sinclair version) that he was wanted on "the Queen's telephone". He donned a robe and walked along the train to where the royal party was berthed. On the line was his brother George, saying that their father had walked the six-mile royal route in Toronto to see the decorations, then had come home and died. (Just after he had breathed his last, Bessie, in character, had shaken his body furiously and demanded that he wake up, he wasn't going to die on her.)

As Sinclair stepped away from the phone on the royal train, a woman introduced herself as one of the ladies-in-waiting, handed him a glass, and said, "This is Scotch whisky. Very sorry to learn of your loss." The train pulled out in an hour for Ottawa, and from there Sinclair flew home for his father's funeral.

A few months later Princess Elizabeth was called back to England from Kenya because of the death of her father, after which she did become queen.

Sinclair's connection with the *Star* persisted in such ways, besides his entertainment column, for several years. In 1952 he was on General Dwight Eisenhower's campaign train during his successful run against Adlai Stevenson for the U.S. presidency. In Toronto, Sinclair might broadcast an item he'd picked up from one of his dozens of unsolicited calls, and then do it at greater length as a *Star* exclusive. In the old days, Jocko Thomas remembered, a crowd of reporters would be getting nothing at all from police or firemen on some story, and then along would come Sinclair to have all the information whispered into his ear. Now he had become one of those media people, rare but not extinct, who even when they sit still have the news come to them.

When Edwin Boyd, leader of an infamous bank-robbing gang, was in the Don Jail in June 1952, Boyd, even in the lock-up a regular Sinclair listener, had a sudden brainstorm. Sinclair should write the story of his life! They'd split the take! The offer came in one of Sinclair's frequent phone calls from Boyd's wife, "an attractive soft-voiced woman with penetrating, almost hypnotic eyes". He didn't mention this on the air or in print at the time, but after Boyd had escaped from jail and was captured in a hideout on Toronto's fashionable Heath Street, Sinclair told all in a copyrighted *Star* front page story. The headline read:

GANG INTENDED TO HOLD UP FOUR BANKS AT SAME TIME, BOYD AIDES SAID—SINCLAIR

But the main body of the story covered his previously unpublished negotiations regarding the proposed book. At the time, he wrote, he had gone to the Don Jail's governor to ask permission to interview Boyd. Turned down, he had taken the request to the deputy minister of reform institutions. Turned down again, he'd finally discussed it with Major John W. Foote, the chaplain (as an honorary captain) at Dieppe whose story had helped launch Sinclair in radio. Foote, by then Ontario's Minister of Reform Institutions, told him any such book would be a form of aiding and abetting, making heroes out of hoodlums, etc., and how could he as a good citizen become privy to this man's crimes without telling the police? Sinclair extracted every ounce of interest from the situation, on air and in print, then let it drop.

By then the road north out of Toronto had become his major escape route. The love affair that so many Canadians have with cottage country had a firm advocate in Sinclair. Back in the old days when he'd helped his father fill a bag with suckers, he'd liked fishing, boats, tramping the woods, swimming the cool waters, loafing, and letting tensions drain away. Now he could do it all again. He would get up in the morning and open a cold beer and sit on the step of the cabin he'd had built so he could be private when he wanted privacy, watching the birds, the animals, and the fish jumping. His diary would mention the time he left the city, who left with him, their arrival time, the weather, At the cottage he kept a log-book detailing events there separately from his other diary. Every year, his log of life around the cottage provided him with on-air references, from a few lines on a newscast to whole editions of *Let's Be Personal* about animals, birds, how the trees were growing, how the fish were biting.

In these one finds a different Sinclair, as in:

> You've often heard the expression "crazy as a loon",
> and that may be because of his wild and lonely cry,
> but this summer in our little part of Muskoka there are

six loons and they are far from crazy.

If there is anything really stupid in these lakes, it's the deer. I was sitting on a dock one morning when a deer came swimming along just a few feet away. It headed for a rocky cliff and decided to climb out of the water at that spot where not even a daddy-long-legs type spider could have made it.

The deer clawed and slipped and clawed some more. It fell back into the water so many times it was exhausted. Yet all it had to do was swim in the direction of me and then walk out of there or swim around a corner and get out where there was footing.

I thought sure the deer would die of exhaustion, so got a paddle, walked into the water and almost pushed the thing around the bend.

Almost all his cottage items had that kind of observation, that homeyness, that sense of kindness to animals. He learned that a neighbour was shooting some beavers, so he went and asked why. These beavers had only been going about their normal pursuit of chewing down trees, eating as much bark as they wanted, then storing the rest for the winter. Except this time they had been storing the excess in the man's boathouse. They apparently considered this to be a real advance on first building a dam to make a good deep pond, and then building a beaver lodge in the pond. The man eventually got tired of clearing logs out of his boat-house, so he shot the beavers.

Sinclair related this pretty well deadpan, at the same time telling a good deal about beavers and transmitting unmistakably that the beavers had just been doing their job as they saw it. At any rate, he concluded, in any dispute he might have with beavers, if the only way to beat them was to shoot them, he still wouldn't.

He also told raccoon stories (garbage-can raiders) and porcupine stories ("happily the dogs left them alone"), and once noted, "We have one bald-headed eagle and six loons. One loon seems to have an affair going with the eagle." These sometimes tender and always observant little items became as familiar in their way as was his occasional use of four-letter words in other contexts. Anyone who owned, rented, or even visited an Ontario cottage could identify with the country part of Sinclair's persona.

Often he would mention friends in the area, people who sold bait or ran hotels or whatever. One of his best friends he first met in Bala, Gerry Dunn. Gerry had two claims on Sinclair's attention: Bala and show-biz. In the thirties, he'd been a pharmacy student and a semi-pro hockey player around Windsor and Detroit, getting together $11,000 to buy a store at Bala. Besides the pharmacy, he sold ice-cream and groceries and had a tiny outdoor pavilion where a few people would gather to dance. (One band included a young trumpet-player named Fred Davis, who later was to work with Sinclair on *Front Page Challenge*.)

By the time the Sinclairs began spending summers in the area, Gerry had expanded to meet the demand, until his famous Dunn's Pavilion was attracting customers from fifty miles around and could hold 2,000 for dancing to Duke Ellington, Cab Calloway, and other famous bands. The pavilion's record gate was 2,200 for Louis Armstrong.

Sinclair, to fuel his show-biz columns and broadcasts, would come over by car or boat at intermission time, often bringing Doris along. He would do his interviews in Gerry Dunn's office, with Gerry serving a drink or two.

At the time of one such interview, Duke Ellington was on the wagon. When drinks were offered he said he'd have ice cream instead. Gerry's son brought a brick of ice cream from the store. During that intermission, while Sinclair interviewed and helped Gerry polish off much of a bottle, Duke Ellington hung right in there—eating three bricks of ice cream.

In time, an easy, cottage-country ritual grew up. Gerry and his wife, Aurelie, would hear the phone ring on a Friday night. Sinclair would state simply, "I'm here." A few minutes later he and Gladys would arrive. Drinks would be poured. Gordon and Aurelie would play three games of cribbage at $2 a game, Aurelie putting her winnings on the mantel so that at the end of the season she could count up how much she'd taken Sinclair for. Gerry and Gladys would drink and talk. Sinclair's capacity for real friendship was often questioned by others, but for whatever reason, he and Gerry Dunn were easy-going cronies and Aurelie was one of the few he would listen to without fighting back.

In the late 1950's, affairs between Sinclair and Doris were, as Gerry Dunn put it gently at Gladys's funeral in 1987, "sort of getting out of hand". Something either had made Gladys see what was going on, or had made her decide to stop ignoring it. Whatever the reason, Gladys made the stand of her life. It was the one time, Gord said, "that my mother was tough." She ruled that Doris was no longer welcome in their home. Sinclair refused to give Doris up, and instead asked for a divorce, which in those days in Canada could be obtained only if the "wronged" spouse started the action and produced evidence of adultery. The court liked such evidence to come from a live witness, a service sometimes provided by shady private detectives. A receipted hotel bill made out to the lovers was also held in high esteem by some judges. It was a generally messy business, but it had no relevance here anyway, because Gladys flatly refused to give Sinclair a divorce.

Actually, for two years or so before this major battle, Doris had begun on her own to distance herself. The very openness of the relationship made her uncomfortable. She therefore arranged to travel more on her job. Besides this, she also began hunting for a place to build her own cottage. Gradually it became accepted, in appearance at least, that Doris was a separate part of Sinclair's life. Gerry Dunn believes that his wife, Aurelie, persuaded Sinclair to accept this compromise.

"So," Doris said later, "I never did have to decide whether to become Mrs. Gordon Sinclair. And while I would have married him in the forties, and probably would have in the fifties, I *would not have* in the sixties, due to our ages and the unlikelihood by then that we could ever have a family, which I wanted."

172

But there was also at least one sign that while the prospect of divorce seemed gone, it was not forgotten. A couple of years later, Doris was holidaying in the Caribbean when she had a call from Sinclair suggesting she meet him in Miami. He gave her the name of the hotel where he had reserved a room and told her to register as Mrs. Gordon Sinclair, which she did. When he arrived, he registered and indicated that he was joining his wife. They had some good days, including a leisurely drive to Key West, where they loafed around seeing the sights. When Sinclair paid the hotel bill back in Miami, covering the stay of "Mr. and Mrs. Gordon Sinclair", he handed Doris the receipted bill and said, "Keep this. We can use it if there ever is a divorce."

Linking known events to known outcomes, the most likely explanation of the final crisis over Doris came on a Sunday in the 1950s. Sinclair was due from New York by air that day and Jack, the youngest son, was home when Gladys suggested that she and Jack take the car and go to the airport to meet Gordon, as a surprise. It was truly a surprise.

In those days big windows in Toronto's old air terminal faced the area where all aircraft pulled up in full view. Portable steps were pushed into place, the door opened, and the passengers appeared. When Sinclair and Doris stepped out together, Gladys and Jack left and drove home without waiting to welcome good old Dad. When he arrived shortly thereafter, there was, Jack recalls, a furious argument "with a lot of shouting by him to the effect that Doris being on the plane had been a coincidence, that she'd been in New York on business as well."

It's not known whether this was the immediate reason for, or only a contributing factor to, the battle that caused Sinclair to ask for a divorce. Sinclair and Doris never did give up their relationship. Doris was never in the Sinclair cottage again, but soon had her own. As she didn't drive, she wanted to be close to public transportation, so she looked at lakefront places near Gravenhurst, made an offer to buy a beautiful rocky point, and built there the cottage that has been her summer home since. Gladys visited her there once, with Gordon. In later years Sinclair often would put a chilled bottle of champagne into his Greavette cruiser, the *Ten to Six*, and navigate to Doris's place, where they'd have their wine and cribbage as of old.

CHAPTER TWELVE

ATTACKING THE STUFFED SHIRTS

"You must control this man."
—Pierre Juneau, head of the CRTC, to CFRB.

Sinclair was not the first to prove it, but there is a deep well of hero-worship in any free country for anyone who can attain a position of power and still be accepted as a representative of "the little guy". He gets that acceptance because he dares to take runs at society's accepted values as well as at random targets of opportunity. The way lesser practitioners try to do it, a claim to being a fearless defender of the little guy may be built on nothing more than flogging targets so obvious that everyone else, including the little guy, is flogging them too. The Sinclair way was considerably more honest; the targets are often not obvious at all, except to someone with the God-given gift for letting fly with a passionate reaction to events large and small without allowing any foreign object, such as wisdom, thought, or fear of reprisals to block the way. That's the way cab drivers and beer-parlour habitués react; shooting from the hip, right or wrong, with no Marvin Mellowbell syndrome to deflect their aim. By the 1950s, where the little guy was God, Gordon Sinclair was his prophet—and naturally therefore was hyped as "outspoken, opinionated, prickly, not afraid to speak his mind, a man who tells it like it is," etc.

Something occasionally mentioned by friends as well as

by enemies, and really an occupational hazard of Sinclair's *modus operandi*, was that he sometimes carried inaccuracy to rare heights and managed to slough off any chagrin he felt when this was pointed out. Pierre Berton once said, "Gordon, I heard your broadcast last night and you were one-hundred-per-cent wrong." Sinclair just shrugged and said yeah, that was him all right, always getting it wrong. In not fighting back, he was probably feeling battered, unloved, self-pitying, over something else. Normally he would take on anybody, and normally, also, argue correctly that he might get some details wrong but he got the *story* right.

He certainly had volume on his side. He was writing and broadcasting four regular shows a day on CFRB: the news at ten to twelve (as he always said it, not "eleven-fifty"), preceded by the five-minute *Let's Be Personal*, and the news at 5:50, preceded by his five-minute *Show Business*. After Hindmarsh died in 1956, Sinclair no longer had as powerful an advocate at the *Star*, but he still had regular, although fewer, columns in the entertainment section.

Then came what was to be one of the major developments of his life. In May 1957 he was asked to audition with several dozen others for a CBC television show then intended to be a thirteen-week summer replacement. It was to be called *Front Page Challenge*. The idea had been suggested by John Aylesworth, a busy and successful television writer and performer in both the United States and Canada who based the concept on several popular U.S. shows of the time. The show's format was for a panel of four people with news connections or backgrounds to be challenged to identify major news stories by questioning guests who had been involved with the events. Then the panel would interview the guests for further details. Sinclair wasn't enthusiastic about auditioning. He'd professed coolness to television, perhaps because nobody had made him an offer. But he went to the audition.

There wasn't much of a budget, so early auditions were

held in the basement recreation room of CBC producer Harvey Hart. Sinclair thought later that luck had played a part in his selection for the panel.

After his first audition he mistakenly believed he had been asked to come again the following night. This was not the case. But when he turned up, they let him in anyway. He thought his performance on the second night got him the job. It might have had a connection, but it wasn't the main reason.

In Alex Barris's 1981 book *Front Page Challenge*, published by the CBC, he quoted Aylesworth: "Harvey [Hart] and I decided that the kind of panel we needed included 'the curmudgeon' and who could be better than Gordon Sinclair . . . and a pretty lady like Arlene Francis of 'What's My Line' [another popular U.S. show]. We tried a number of people [for the pretty-lady role] but Toby Robins was head and shoulders above everybody else." Dozens of others, prominent in either the news business or the pretty-lady business, were tried, but when the opening show was done live on June 24, 1957, Win Barron, a well-known newsreel voice, was moderator, and the panel regulars were Sinclair, Robins, and Alex Barris from the *Telegram*. Pierre Berton, then managing editor of *Maclean's*, had auditioned as moderator and didn't make it. Soon someone wisely tried him as a panelist, where he soon replaced Barris and has been a mainstay ever since.

The show was well received, except by newspaper critics, who ranged from the merely lukewarm to the openly mean-spirited. *Star* columnist Bill Drylie, for instance, was away in New York for *Front Page Challenge*'s debut, but that didn't prevent him from launching his torpedoes.

"Spies accuse us of sneaking off to New York to escape *Front Page Challenge* which opened Monday on Channel 6," Drylie wrote a few days later. "They also assure us the thing died, although the corpse will be kept around for weeks yet, perhaps for autopsy purposes."

Thirty years later, of those on camera for the opening

show, Win Barron, Sinclair, and Toby Robins—who had left the show in 1961 to resume her acting career—all were dead. So was Drylie. But *Front Page Challenge* rolled on and on.

By mid-December of 1962, perhaps as a result of his annual Christmas depression, Sinclair seems to have looked over his many commitments and decided to cut out one—the *Star*. He wrote his final *Star* column as a letter addressed to entertainment editor Nathan Cohen. He recalled the circumstances of his first column on September 1, 1949, how it had grown from one a week over the years to six a week, then back to five, in the middle 1950s to three, in 1959 to one again. "And now, Nathan, I'd like to drop the one remaining contribution. The *Star* and I have worked out disengagements five times since 1922. This is the sixth." And final. This column also introduced one more item of conflicting evidence into the debate over how many times he was fired by, or left, the *Star*.

From then on Sinclair's name was in the *Star* often, when the paper quoted listeners outraged at something he'd said on CFRB, or viewers outraged at something he'd done on *Front Page Challenge*. Because that show reached across Canada, Sinclair had become not so much Toronto's curmudgeon as the nation's curmudgeon. For years, everywhere the show's regulars went in Canada, together or singly, the first questions would be, "Where's Gordon?" and "How can you stand working with that bastard Sinclair?" One of the secrets of *Front Page Challenge*, Pierre Berton told Alex Barris in 1981, was definitely Sinclair, "because they wonder 'what is that son-of-a-bitch going to ask next?' "

At CFRB he had somewhat the same reputation through the years. At one point Harry Sedgwick was spending a lot of time in New York City on a government mission. One day Sinclair stopped at the switchboard, located just outside Sedgwick's office, and observed loudly, "I suppose this guy Sedgwick isn't around the goddam place again this week! This absentee president we have, no wonder the place is all going to shit!"

Hearing the uproar, Sedgwick's secretary, Lillian Cox, rushed out to exclaim, "Ssh, ssh, ssh! Mr. Sedgwick's in his office."

Sinclair, roaring: "I don't give a goddam if he is and you know why I don't care? I've got a million dollars and he hasn't!"

At this point Sedgwick, a man about the same size as Sinclair, came to his office door with a cigar in the corner of his mouth and said, "Sinclair! Come in here!" Sinclair stormed in and the door was slammed. The sound of voices gradually diminished in volume. When he came out, fascinated onlookers waiting for further explosions were disappointed: Sinclair strutted past them and out of the place. No one ever knew who said what to whom.

He had ways of treating friends that often were dictated by the passions of the moment, some fair and some foul. Once an announcer, Ross Millard, had left the station to go into business, which didn't work out, and so he was auditioning around trying to get back into radio. One of his auditions was as Canadian host on a U.S. program being carried by the CBC, Don McNeil's *Breakfast Club* from Chicago. Among those auditioning on air, a week each, were Ross Millard and the later well-known Elwood Glover.

One day when Sinclair mentioned this competition in passing, Jack Dawson said, "You know, it's really too bad, everybody at the ad agency is afraid to push Ross Millard because of the family connection."

"What family connection?"

"Well, the Canadian sponsor is Swift's and the president of Swift's is Ross Millard's brother-in-law. If he got it, everybody would cry favouritism."

Sinclair promptly made this an item in his *Star* column, naming the competitors for the job and adding, "Of course, the agency *won't* pick the best one. Why? Because the best one is Ross Millard, and Ross Millard is the brother-in-law of the sponsor's president! That's why they can't pick the best one!" Thus Sinclair deftly had converted potential favouritism into potential unfair prejudice. Millard got the job.

Dawson was involved in a somewhat opposite situation. For years he'd been hosting a fifteen-minute information show for Cities Service Oil Company on CFRB. After television arrived in Canada in 1952, Dawson auditioned at CBC for a live-TV commercial, the sponsor being Admiral. To his excitement and surprise he got the job and, as he tells it,

> I used to play a lot of cribbage with Sinclair and I guess this day I had just done one of the TV appearances. I was beating the ass off him at cribbage. He was the worst loser in the world and he was getting madder and madder and I guess at the same time I was just filled with the new TV thing, talking about how exciting it was and how I loved it, how it was just fabulous.
>
> Sinc finally paid me what he owed me and then he said, "You sure think a lot of that TV stuff."
>
> I said that I sure did.
>
> A few days later he saw me in the hall and said, "Have you read my column today?"
>
> I said, "No, Gordon, I very seldom read your column."
>
> He said, "You better read this one then, kid, it'll be interesting to you."
>
> I'd already read it, of course. Half a dozen people had made sure of that. He'd written that I was doing this TV thing, and that I thought radio, where I did this show for Cities Service, was going to go down the tubes, and he wondered why Cities Service kept me on the air when I had no use for the radio medium.
>
> I knew the Cities Service guy pretty well who hired me for the job. Later that day he phoned me and said, "Jack, how would you like to make $100,000?"
>
> I said, "What do you mean?"
>
> "How would it be if I wrote you and said that in view of Sinclair's comments in the *Star* today, you're

fired. Then you sue Sinclair for $100,000. I think
you'd get it—the show's good and it's got years to go.
If you like, I'll write you that letter."

I thought about it, but it was really just a joke.

Sinclair's old contretemps with Conn Smythe of the
Maple Leafs surfaced once again in the late 1950s. For the
1958–59 season he had a press pass good for all events,
from opera to wrestling. For hockey he had his own pair of
subscriber tickets, so he rarely used the pass or visited the
press room on hockey nights. But once he did, and was
standing at the free-lunch table eating a small bunch of
grapes when Smythe came into the room and looked
around to see what "crape-hangers" (as he customarily
called media people) were in attendance. Spotting Sinclair,
he rasped loudly, "Sinclair! Are you free-loading again?
Ever since you were a kid in Cabbagetown, as long as I've
known you, you've been free-loading!"

Sinclair had one grape left on his bunch. He carefully put
down the one grape and walked past Smythe and out of the
room, his very manner a silent insult.

The next morning at CFRB Sinclair was called to the
newsroom phone. A cheerful and friendly ex-soldier who'd
been in Smythe's Second World War battery, Spencer Gay-
lord (Spiff) Evans, was Gardens publicist at the time.

Jack Dawson heard Sinclair say, "Hi, Spiff! How are you?"
Then, "You're kidding!" Then, "No sense you coming
down. I'll put it in the mail." Pause for Evans to talk, then,
"Well, okay, I'll be here if you want to come in at two." The
news had been that the Gardens was lifting his pass. When
Sinclair hung up the phone he thought a minute, then
dialled his broker. "What's Maple Leaf Gardens trading at
right now? That high, eh? Well, buy me ten shares. Make
sure they're registered in my name."

When the broker called back that he'd got the shares, it
was almost news time for Sinclair. This was meat and drink
to him, the poor little Cabbagetown kid being pushed
around by a big mogul. And now he, the little guy, was

going to wipe the floor with the mogul.

"You know what, folks?" he barked into the microphone. "Today Conn Smythe lifted my press pass. I'm *persona non grata*, they call it, at the Gardens now." He went through the whole episode, including the one grape he'd left behind. "So now Conn Smythe thinks I can't go into the Gardens any more. Well, Conn, if you're listening, and I got a funny hunch that you are, you know there's no law in this country that says you can keep me out of the Gardens. And you know why, Conn? Because today I bought a piece of Maple Leaf Gardens, and the law says I can go in at any reasonable hour to view my investment." Two hours later Evans arrived, grinning, with his orders to pick up Sinclair's press pass in person. Sinclair persuaded him to write "Revoked" across it instead, so he could keep it as a souvenir.

A week or so later there was another hockey game. Sinclair was there, using his subscriber tickets. When he walked past Smythe's box, Smythe was entertaining guests—all in dinner jackets, not uncommon at the Gardens in Smythe's heyday. Sinclair, in his usual loud plaid jacket and louder bow tie, walked up the steps to Smythe's box and told Smythe, also loudly, in front of the startled guests, that this or that hockey player was no good and as a shareholder he expected a lot better show than he was getting, continuing to list shortcomings until the puck was dropped. Then he proceeded jauntily to his seat. Mission accomplished.

Sinclair's unpredictable outbursts in time developed almost as great a reputation around the radio station as they had at home. The advantage held by his radio colleagues was that if they were big enough in their own right they could stand up to him, as Dennett did occasionally, or kid him, as morning man Wally Crouter did, and make it stick. But nobody really wanted to take him on in a way that might escalate to the point that Sinclair stormed out of the station forever.

This was a definite consideration when CFRB hired Bob Hesketh in 1959. Hesketh had been a sports columnist at the *Telegram*, an individualist, observant, unafraid, one of the best in his field. But, not being paid on that level, he'd left journalism to work in public relations—at first with the world-champion Whitby Dunlops hockey team, a job right up his alley, but with a short life-span. That summer when Sinclair took his vacation in July, Hesketh and journalist Trent Frayne were invited to fill in. Frayne declined and Hesketh did so well that, on Sinclair's return, he was given a daily 5 p.m. spot of his own. But this was still on a free-lance basis, since the pay was not enough to make him give up his public-relations meal ticket.

Meanwhile, a debate was going on in station management about Sinclair. He was in his sixtieth year and, where earlier in life he seemed to have hidden any insecurity, now he let it out. When he was feeling low he would talk about quitting, causing his bosses to say that he was indispensable, they couldn't get along without him, etc.—as he no doubt hoped they would. All this while, however, they were very much aware of the hard fact that if he did quit, there was no one who could fill his time slot—that is, no one on staff. But there'd been a good reaction to Hesketh as a fill-in. In time, maybe, he would be another Sinclair. . . .

One day Hesketh and Jack Dawson, who had moved up the ladder to station manager, were sitting on stools at the Embassy bar across Bloor Street from CFRB. In this rather unlikely hiring-hall Dawson said to Hesketh, "Why don't you work for us, go on staff? The old bugger is quitting twice a week, and we want to be able to say, 'Look, if you're gonna quit, quit.'" More importantly, whether Sinclair quit or not, the station would have a back-up on hand.

When Hesketh took the job, the understanding was that he would be available any time, for whatever reason or time span, to take over for Sinclair. He couldn't have foreseen that this understudy role would continue for almost twenty-five years, or that some years the frustrations would loom considerably larger than even the substantial rewards.

Before CFRB's 1965 move from Bloor and Yonge to larger quarters on St. Clair Avenue, the newsroom was getting more crowded every year. Jack Dennett had inherited the

Jim Hunter news at 8 and 6:30. His desk and Sinclair's were jammed together in one small office, so that when both were in preparing their late newscasts (Sinclair's ending at 6 p.m., thirty minutes before Dennett's began), they typed opposite each other, head to head, a few feet apart.

Their mind-casts were also opposite. Dennett, who for some years had the largest single-station radio-news audience in Canada, represented a solid and traditional, small-c conservative, middle-class outlook. He was always for the right and against the wrong, and his news judgment and attitudes were honestly those of most of his listeners. Sinclair just as invariably was unpredictable, doing much of his shooting from the hip. Since their newscasts were so close together, naturally they had much of the same material from which to fashion their personal approaches. Jack Dawson recalls: "When Sinc would pick up his stuff and go in at ten to six to do the news, Jack would shut the door and turn up the speakers and listen to Gordon every single night, and often after that he would change his lead. On some stories, he would see what Sinc's approach was and if Jack was ambivalent in any way he'd take a lead from Sinclair. He learned an awful lot from Gordon."

But because of their diametrically different outlooks, sometimes they did have clashes. One such clash happened on December 16, 1960, when the newspapers were playing up the plight of a man named Alan Rose who'd been gravely injured in a Northern Ontario mine accident. He had been entombed underground for some time, then rescued and flown to hospital in Toronto, where doctors were trying to save his life. A prayer service on his behalf had been called that day for noon at the Anglican St. James Cathedral in downtown Toronto. Hundreds of people were gathering there when Sinclair went on the air. One must take into account that this happened at the time of year when, being near the anniversary of Jean's death, Sinclair's tolerance of the very idea of a beneficent God was at its lowest ebb.

In Dawson's recollection,

Sinc started with a brief round-up of the story, then said, "I see they're having a prayer service. It's going to start just as soon as I get off the air. As the clock strikes twelve, they'll be praying that God gives this guy a break, cures him. How could God be interested in this?" He went on to ridicule people who used the "he sees the little sparrow fall" syndrome for everything from getting rid of acne to winning prize fights, and ended the item with "The expected death of miner Rose causes some free-thinkers to quietly mention again that prayer is just a matter of superstition."

Well, Dennett came in to see me that afternoon. He was very annoyed. What an insensitive so-and-so Sinclair was, and so on.

I said, "Why the hell don't you do something about it, then? You've got a microphone—tell him!"

"I don't like to, particularly . . . " he began, then paused for a minute, thinking, and said, "God damn it, I will!"

A prominently displayed story in the next day's *Star* reported that Sinclair and Dennett "clashed verbally yesterday on CFRB broadcasts six and a half hours apart." Perhaps because Sinclair's phrase "the expected death of miner Rose" had come true despite the power of prayer, Sinclair was quoted only on his closing lines about prayer being "just a matter of superstition". Dennett for once got ten times as much space as Sinclair, his item being quoted in full.

He called Sinclair "my verbose and often controversial colleague", said they had shared an office for eleven years, so he knew what he was talking about, then blasted. People had a right to believe in the spiritual side of life. "Their religion is their own business, and the faith and hope placed by these people in their prayers and in their God is not something to be criticized or questioned.

"Mr. Sinclair may not believe—that's his privilege. But in

my view it is in extremely poor taste to take to the air to pooh-pooh religion."

Poor taste. Not exactly a dragon-slayer when applied to Sinclair. But he was furious that Dennett would attack him. The next afternoon in the newsroom, Sinclair went to the attack. He'd got a lot of phone calls and even mail (Canada had that kind of mail service then) condemning him and supporting Dennett; stung by both these turns of event, he called Dennett a bastard and a lot of other names, to which Dennett replied with a characteristically mild, "Gordon, now you know how a lot of people feel about things you've said about them." Then they sat down opposite one another to work out that night's newscasts.

At that time CFRB's president was Thornton Cran, a chartered accountant who had taken over in 1956. Cran greatly admired Sinclair and all the station's stars, was even said to hold them in awe. If so, that didn't include rolling over and playing dead every time Sinclair barked. One of the first of their confrontations came one day after Sinclair, in a black mood, had been staring out through the heavy plate-glass windows facing on Bloor Street. Suddenly, for some reason, the thought of fire occurred to him.

"God damn it!" he exclaimed, doing one of his instant-anger bits. "If this place ever caught on fire there's no fire door out of here, no nothing! We'd all roast in here like chickens!"

As if on cue, Cran came along. Sinclair button-holed him. Cran listened, and then said reasonably, "Look, Gordon, it's a plate-glass window, all right, but somebody could throw a chair through it and you could almost hang by your fingers and drop down to Bloor Street, we're only about twelve feet up. . . ." However, he didn't convince Sinclair, who stormed out muttering loudly about what the hell did big shots care, anyway?

Left alone, Cran looked thoughtfully at the windows. Then he called someone in building maintenance and ordered a steel ring inserted into the concrete wall near Sinclair's desk, with a stout rope attached to the ring and leading to a length of rope coiled near by. This was done. The next day when Sinclair came in, he stopped short at the coil of rope fastened to the ring on the wall. "What the hell is that?" he demanded.

He was told, as deadpan as possible, that it was his own personal fire escape. Everybody did manage to keep a straight face. Sinclair stared at the set-up for a moment or two, nodded, and soon was hammering his typewriter.

In Harry Sedgwick's reign, he'd had years to get used to Sinclair. Both spoke the same salty language. Cran came from a different background. He was English, and could display both a flair for what would bring publicity, and shock at some kinds of publicity that came unbidden. If he was in awe of the most famous of his staff—Sinclair, Dennett, Betty Kennedy, Wally Crouter—he wasn't above politely suggesting improvements.

Sinclair's clothes he wouldn't have wanted to do anything about even if he could have. But he did feel that Sinclair's choice of automobiles left much to be desired. "Gordon," he said, "you have great individuality in everything else, why do you drive such an ordinary car? It just isn't in character." He was the one who suggested that Sinclair should get a Rolls-Royce. Whether he also offered to have CFRB help pay the shot is not known.

A day or two later Sinclair showed up in the Rolls-Royce showrooms a few blocks from CFRB. Obviously he didn't look like your average Rolls buyer. The lofty salesman on duty wouldn't even unlock the car and let him sit in it, claiming that the man with the key was at lunch.

When Sinclair didn't admit defeat, the salesman also mentioned in passing that Rolls-Royces were not sold on credit. "Oh, yeah?" Sinclair said. "So what's the cash price of this one, then?"

The salesman told him.

"So if I wanted to buy one, could I drive it away right today?"

The salesman, amused, said that could be arranged.

Sinclair returned later that afternoon, laid the exact pur-

187

chase price in cash on the table, and said, "I'll take that one if you can have it ready for me to drive home at six o'clock." At six he strode in, got into the Rolls, and drove it home.

This was the car people would remember him by. And, one thing sure, Cran's instinct had been right: when a stately Rolls was being driven around Toronto by a small man in a pork-pie hat, bow tie, and plaid jacket, in short dressed like a Number 17 pizza, neither the car nor the man needed any further identification. Since this was in the early 1960s, the cost was a little less than $17,000. He drove the Rolls for eleven years, always bugged by the rigmarole he had to go through for repairs (few ordinary mechanics would touch it). Eventually he sold it for $8,000 to someone in Buffalo. Why Buffalo? So that his fans would not see it in Toronto and be disappointed that he'd got rid of it! He always pointed out that to drive what was supposed to be the best car in the world had cost him only $1,000 a year.

About the time of the Rolls purchase, CFRB was a client of Columbia Broadcasting System's news network from the United States. Part of the deal allowed CBS News to break into any program with bulletins that its editors considered to be of vital importance. So as soon as the designated number of bells rang, a U.S. voice cut in and went straight to air.

During the crisis of October 1962, when Soviet missiles were on ships headed for Cuba and President Kennedy agonized over whether stopping them would cause war, Dawson was driving home listening to Sinclair's ten-to-six news when it was cut off by a news bulletin on the missile crisis. This was followed instantly by Sinclair exploding into the open mike, "What the hell is going on? Yankee propaganda! If those bastards ever break in on me again I'm through. I'm through! I'll never come back! Goddam fools!" When Dawson got home, "the newspapers were calling, the CBC was calling, everybody was calling, and I was apologizing."

While Sinclair fancied himself as a cribbage player, it seems that Doris Loach was the only person he could beat consistently. The opponent who maddened him most was Wally Crouter, the station's long-time morning man. Crouter had spent many Second World War months in an army hospital in Italy with nothing to do but play cribbage. As a young man just out of the services, Crouter had played the first golf of his life with Sinclair, who introduced him to what was to become his favourite game when he lent him some clubs. He and Sinclair worked together, went to the races together, drank together, occasionally enjoyed the company of women together. But after a certain day in the 1960s, they never played cribbage together again.

This day at the Bloor Street studios, Crouter had stayed on for a bit of work after his 10 a.m. sign-off. When Sinclair finished at noon, they began playing. Crouter's playing techniques had been hard won in those long-ago dawn-to-dusk games in hospital.

> I took him for $55 inside of two hours, not that we were playing for such high stakes, but he kept doubling them, thinking he was going to win.
>
> After the last game he said, "Here's your fifty-five bucks, and you're going to buy lunch for me at the Pilot," which was a tavern near by.
>
> I said, "I'll do that," and he said, "And I'm never going to play another game of cards with you again as long as I live." Then he opened a window and threw the cards out onto Bloor Street. There were cards floating down all over the place. Not long after, we flew to France on an Air France promotion for seven days in Paris. When we were in the air I said, "Look, even if you don't want to play for money, it's something to while away the time." He said, "To hell with you, you demoralize me. I can play cards with anyone but you." And he never did play cards with me again.

Bill Baker, the old CFRB original, says that Sinclair's propensity for going into battle using language that was offensive even to people who agreed with his point came late in life "when he knew he had it made." One of the earliest incidents on record came after Prime Minister Lester Pearson had won his fight for a distinctive Canadian flag to replace the long-revered red ensign. Sinclair, a lifelong ardent Canadian nationalist, was all for the change. After the new flag became law, he was enraged one day over a speech made to a service club by a United Church minister from Port Hope. The Rev. Ross W. McKervil had said that to him the new flag's design looked like a beer label. Sinclair angrily reported what McKervil had said, finishing the item by practically shouting, "Any man who would liken the flag of his country—even if it is a new flag—to a beer label, would drink his own piss!"

Dawson got an immediate call from McKervil's lawyer demanding a copy of the tape. This could be delayed, as such requests routinely were. A day or two later, Sinclair got in the mail a patent-medicine bottle, full, with the original label soaked off and a typewritten label attached that read: "100% Grade A Canadian piss". It was signed, not necessarily authentically, with McKervil's name.

Sinclair went on the air at ten to twelve and said, "You know what I got in the mail today, folks? Do you remember Mr. McKervil? Well, I got this bottle today and the label says 100% Grade A Canadian . . . it's a four-letter word which I won't use on the air, but I'll use the word urine. Well, Mr. McKervil, if you're listening, at first I believed that the United Church should pay to have you visit a psychiatrist because I do think you need mental help, but meanwhile we've had the contents of this bottle analyzed and we also think you should see your medical doctor because you've got a kidney problem."

When McKervil filed suit, Cran had Dawson take the tape to lawyer Joe Sedgwick to see what should be done in the station's defence. "So I went down to Joe's office," Dawson said, "and played it for him. First thing he did was roar with laughter and say, 'Oh, Johnny, I just wish I were acting for McKervil!' I said, 'No, no, Joe, we're the client!' but he kept right on, 'Sinclair has held up a small-town minister of the gospel to absolute public ridicule! Defamed him! I could get you for half a million dollars if I got you for a cent!'

"I went back to Cran with that message, but in the end it just went away, never got to court."

There was one consequence, however: a letter from Pierre Juneau, then newly installed as head of the Canadian Radio-television and Telecommunications Commission; like Sinclair a Liberal, and a nationalist. After all, it seemed whatever outrage Sinclair had committed he'd been fighting for flag and country, both of which also meant Lester B. Pearson and the Liberal Party. Juneau's letter told CFRB that the station *must* exercise more control over Sinclair, but there had been stupidity on both sides. There the matter ended, quite mildly.

Even if Sinclair wasn't on hand when a big story broke, he'd usually find a way to play his form of catch-up. When Winston Churchill died in January 1965, Sinclair was on holiday in Florida. As soon as he returned, he said what in Florida he'd been seething to say:

> Why did people treat Churchill dying like the biggest news story since Napoleon? What do people expect? Churchill was ninety! When a man that age dies, where's the drama? Or even sorrow? I'll bet that right now Churchill is up there on that white cloud with the wings sticking out of his back, floating around with no trouble, and I betcha he has a bottle of brandy in one hand and a long Cuban cigar in the other.

General outrage. Switchboard alight.

But the most serious fracas with the law that Sinclair ever had at CFRB was caused by a broadcast in the early 1970s, just before a provincial election. The law at the time allowed newspapers to beat the drums right up to voting-day, while the broadcast media were prohibited from election comment within forty-eight hours of the voting. Sinclair thought the rule was unfair, and discussed the matter around the station. Don Hartford, who had become CFRB president in 1970 after Thornton Cran became chairman, agreed with Sinclair that the law was unjust and should be challenged. Go ahead, Gordon, was the message.

William Davis was premier of Ontario's Tory government at the time. Sinclair, although an avowed Liberal, said on the day before the election that Davis would win, and should win. He said that he knew he was breaching the Broadcasting Act in saying so. "So don't think I've done it through error. I've done it in full knowledge of what I'm doing. I am defying this stupid rule. I think the rule is absolutely nuts." He guffawed his way off the air, asking, "Are there any men with white coats and a long net in the control room yet to take me away?"

Sure enough, a writ was served on CFRB. Hartford and Dawson consulted lawyers Jack Coyne from Ottawa and Fraser Fell from Toronto's Faskin and Calvin law firm. Dawson's recollection is that Coyne thought CFRB didn't have a leg to stand on, saying, "You should go to court and say you're sorry, it won't happen again, get fined $500, and forget it."

This made Dawson mad. He asked Coyne if he had heard the broadcast. Coyne hadn't. Dawson got the tape broadcast and played it, then said, "We're the largest radio station in the country, proud of the people we've got, Sinclair and Dennett and the rest, and if, the first time one of these guys is threatened, we run for the hills, what does that do to them, and to us?" One thought in his mind as he spoke was that long ago Sinclair had told him he considered his CFRB press card more important than his *Star* card. "If you write something for the paper, maybe before its printed the editor or the brass in the front office get a call from somebody and when you read your story in the paper, something has been cut out of it. They can't do that to me on CFRB. I can say it and it's gone."

After Dawson's outburst, Hartford looked over at lawyer Fraser Fell and said, "Fraser, how do you feel?" Fell said, "It'll make me a lot of money, but I agree with Dawson."

192

The case did cost CFRB substantial amounts of money and time in court appearances over several years, all the way to the Supreme Court of Canada, which upheld a lower court's fine of $5,000 against CFRB. Commenting editorially on the Supreme Court decision, the *Globe and Mail* said that certainly the law had been broken, but it "is inconsistent and unfair and should be changed." It was changed; the Broadcasting Act was amended. Some people call it the Sinclair amendment.

CHAPTER THIRTEEN

THE LAST REAL SHOOTING STAR

*"Sinclair was the last real shooting star in the radio
business in this town. He had the formula for success.
I watched the guy for twenty-five years utilizing that
formula. When he put his news together it didn't
matter which was the major story. It did matter if
some guy in Tennessee shot his wife after catching
her in bed with another guy."*
—Bob Hesketh, CFRB commentator.

Once Hesketh was asked by a senior executive, "Can't you
be a bit more controversial, like Sinclair?" Hesketh replied
that if he felt strongly about something he'd say so, "but
don't ask me to be bombastic on Monday, Wednesday, and
Friday just to get the switchboard lighting up."

Sinclair's way sometimes was precisely that calculated.
He'd leave home most mornings around 9:45 with much of
his 11:50 news already typed, an amalgam of what he'd seen
on the early television news, what he'd read in the morning
papers, and his own views and prejudices. Marching along
CFRB's corridors, in what Betty Kennedy called his "cock-of-
the-walk" style, toes out, about 10:30 or so on what was
otherwise expected to be a slow news day, he'd turn into
the newsroom and announce, "Never fear, Sinclair's here!
Pretty dead this morning, but we'll light up the switchboard!"

At that, everyone in the newsroom would know that he was going to either offend people or polarize them, so that they'd phone in with reactions that normally would break down into roughly two categories: "That silly old bugger, what's he doing now?" or "I'm never going to listen to him again." But if there was any mass switch-off, it never showed.

The CFRB listening-area fanning out from Toronto has at least thirty available radio outlets, AM and FM. Some mornings at ten to twelve Sinclair commanded fifty per cent of the total audience. (Afternoons at ten to six he'd have a few points less.)

"In a market like this," said Don Hartford in a 1986 interview, "*one* person having fifty per cent of the total audience really shouldn't happen, but with Sinclair, it did." The cry of, "Hey, come and listen to what Sinclair's on about this time!" was what Sinclair always knew was out there for him, if he earned it. He didn't earn those ratings by mounting great crusades, riding waves of public opinion, or even clinging to certain heart's-core issues. Apart from his long-term scoffing at religion and his insistence that "adding rat poison to the water supply" in the form of fluoridation did more harm than good, he mainly ran his plays from the shotgun formation; that is, he just watched for targets of opportunity. He needled charities for spending too much on organization, consistently treated the Hospital for Sick Children as being unworthy of its high reputation, and took regular shots at the Block Parents system as being set up to make children fear old men (a couple of kids had refused his offer of a ride home one night). Sex in all its forms had high priority. As Pierre Berton put it, "He knew what was interesting."

In the years when he was showing up on radio and television, in magazines and subway advertising, on billboards—literally everywhere one looked, listened, or read—if he had any overall policy at all, it was that if most people were for it, he was against it. Or vice versa. On days

195

when opportunities to run against the flow were limited, he knew where to spot something else that would do, some way to get into sex, or religion, or both at the same time.

One day, for instance, there'd been a story that prostitutes were being banned from the ritzy Mayfair district of London. Sinclair read the story in brief, and then, in a comment on the situation from a rural vicar, he obviously found the follow-up he needed.

"It's all very well for our lawmakers to do this," Sinclair quoted the vicar as saying, "but what will happen to the poor things? I think it behooves every clergyman in England to search out one of these poor unfortunates and take her home and let her live for a few months at least in a godlike setting."

Sinclair let that sit there for a few seconds and then chuckled, "How about that, folks? Take a hooer home in the name of Jesus." Talk about lighting up the switchboard.

It's difficult to say which topic would have won Sinclair's Hall of Fame Award for Interesting Most People Most Often, if such an award had existed outside of his subconscious. Sex probably *should* have won, if only because he was often funny about sex, while he tended to be serious and didactic about religion. But to him, the church was a positive cornucopia of material. Some targets were less interesting than others, but not to Sinclair.

An example was a *Let's Be Personal* in 1967. As part of his omnivorous reading (several daily newspapers, many magazines, books of all kinds), he had come across a *Harper's Magazine* article entitled "God Is Rich". This described the Christian church in North America as "the least speculative but most spectacular growth industry ever". Naturally Sinclair climbed aboard immediately. He led off with,

> The wealth of the tax-free church is well known, that of the Christians alone adding up to the richest corporation in man's history. It's one of the amazing things of life that the organization which has the most

in assets is the very organization that is freed of the burden of taxes, and the very one created in the name of the man who told his followers to lay up no treasure on earth. . . . Look around you. See those large churches on the best corners. No tax.

Suggest that there should be a tax, just a small one, and they wring their hands: It would be putting a burden on God's work. The twin inconsistencies are that the richest of all the big, big rich is not taxed and that the big, big rich is named for Christ, who scorned money at every chance.

It's as easy for a camel to go through the eye of a needle as for a rich man to enter the Kingdom of Heaven, He said. But the church that stands in His name is richer than anybody. . . .

That did make some people angry, but any time he spoke about the church and money he was not so much Sinclair the Iconoclast as he was a Sinclair version of the *Report on Business*. On the other hand, when speaking on some theological aspects of religion he tended to *preach* as if he'd been ordained. But truly passionate Sinclair-on-religion virtuosity showed only when the subject was a personal God. He was pretty good on heaven and hell, too, but the personal-God subject was the broadest and most interesting. He blasted away on this subject many times in all the media open to him. The following example doesn't break new ground, but it is more comprehensive than other examples from his newscasts (which usually depended on news pegs that are of little interest now) or from *Let's Be Personal*.

In 1983 *Front Page Challenge* visited Regina. On the day Sinclair was to fly home, he spent an hour or two in his hotel room being interviewed by a *Leader-Post* reporter, Peter Edwards (whose salary of about $575 a week Sinclair quickly ascertained, with appropriate references to his own newspaper tops of $125). The following passage is reprinted, with thanks, from a tape Edwards made. Edwards asked, "Do you believe in God?" Sinclair, six months past his eighty-third birthday, but his voice strong:

> I don't believe there's any god who changes the weather or sends floods or drought. I don't believe there's any answer to prayer, either for or against, but I look at the skies over the Prairie here and see the stars on their courses all moving in the proper direction, directions that can be charted and marked down and predicted as for the future . . . there's got to be some force controlling that, whether you call it God or Allah, or whatever the Hindu gods are and all the rest.
>
> No, no, there's got to be something, but I don't believe in a personal god. I've heard boxers, knocked a guy out, knocked him senseless in the ring, thank God, think God helped him, Somebody up there loves him. That's a lot of bullshit.
>
> Who knows what God is? Some people say God watches the sparrow fall. Well, where was He when six million Jews were processed under Hitler? Was He indifferent? Was He out to lunch? Was He unable to tell what was going on, or didn't He care? Jesus Christ His son is supposed to be a Jew. Here's the Jews being processed like that, what did God do to help them? Did He maybe approve? Who knows? Any kind of war comes up, God is always on the side of everybody. They all pray to God. Which God?

Although raised a Methodist, he rarely zeroed in on any particular denomination in his criticism, and was demonstrably opposed to the pervasive Protestant anti-Catholic bigotry in which he'd grown up.

Thus he was anti-bigot (even though some found his anti-bigotry to be a bigotry of its own). One of his *Star* friends from the early days, Charles Lanphier, had left the paper to become a priest and head of what was called the Radio League of St. Michael's Cathedral. As early as 1934, Sinclair, on Father Lanphier's initiative, attended luncheons at what he called the "Priests' Palace"—probably the residence of the archbishop. "The first time this happened there was a bishop present and two monsignors and I felt a little out of place," he claimed, but in time he obviously didn't feel out of place at all. His friendly contact with Catholics was an often-mentioned part of his later life.

The first time he had publicly questioned commonly held Christian beliefs, it took place in about twenty seconds on CFRB, late in 1944. All he said was that he'd been in India and wondered why a *compassionate* God would tolerate the conditions he'd found there. He said the answer must be that this God could not cope, or was indifferent, or was too busy, but in any case was not concerned with human affairs; hence there was no answer to prayer.

From this he got hate mail, as he wrote later, "to a degree you can't imagine". His view was that he'd been critical of Christianity on only one radio station while every day across the country hundreds of stations were glorifying God or the church in various ways.

Naturally, since he was Sinclair, and having drawn this reaction, for the ensuing forty years of his life he never stopped saying his piece on religion. It must have amused him that in time the church embraced him in its own way. His name on the cover of a church publication, or in the index of a newspaper's religious page, was a guarantee of readership—if not always friendly readership.

Late in 1971 the religion editor of the *Toronto Star*, planning a full-page Christmas special, asked Sinclair and twenty-four others to answer the question "What does that man Jesus mean to me?" Sinclair obliged with about 150 words, saying that Jesus "had the guts" to stand up to Roman soldiers, and that the treason charge they got him on was a "bum rap", and, in somewhat of a *non sequitur*, he took a shot at the Kingdom of Heaven, with "From what I've heard of the place, who in his right mind would ever want to get into Heaven even for a short visit?"

In one *Let's Be Personal* he expanded this, saying, "The very idea of either heaven or hell is preposterous. Many people feel this but don't say so. . . ." After repeating his known sentiments on heaven, he took on hell. "This is too preposterous even to merit a line of consideration. It is no more real than hobgoblins, spooks, ghosts, perpetual motion, or everlasting happiness. . . . I know of no religion aside from Christianity which deludes itself in this primitive way." With these views well known, he was commissioned to write 1,200 words for a United Church of Canada in-church publication called *Mandate*, the request expressing the pious hope that his words would help "the Christian community learn to express strongly held opinions if they wish to influence the thinking of those who communicate to the public."

On *Front Page Challenge* Sinclair was the designated nun- and missionary-baiter. In his piece in *Mandate*, published in January 1977 with his photo on the cover, he told about one of these television encounters with a woman who was

> a missionary of some sect whose people go into far and dangerous places, and had seen her husband murdered [and] was expressing the oft-heard belief that God would take care of herself and children and her husband was safely in Heaven.
>
> Bluntly I asked, "Which God? They run all the way from A, B, C . . . Allah, Buddha, Christ . . . right to Zeus."
>
> She was non-plussed and I should have allowed the woman to regain her composure after she replied that there was only one God, but I plunged on:
>
> "And about your husband safely in Heaven . . . are you persuaded that when you reach there, you'll recognize this father of your children?"
>
> "Why, certainly."
>
> "Will he be at the age at which you last saw him? Will he be wearing clothes?"
>
> "Of course. Why ask such questions?"
>
> "I'm curious to know who makes the clothes, with

what material, and where they get it. I'm wondering how the clothes are kept clean. I am wondering if the goodly people in Heaven eat food, and if so, who produces it and arranges for sewage plants to carry away the excess."

What he *didn't* say about that encounter (which was with Ione MacMillan, whose husband had been murdered in the Congo) was interesting. The *Front Page Challenge* moderator, Fred Davis, remembers it well. A week earlier Sinclair had drawn huge criticism for something else he'd said, and apparently he wanted to lie low for once.

As Davis recalled:

> During the commercial, with the microphones off, Gordon leaned over to her and said, "I won't be talking to you on this interview, I'm in enough hot water." And she leaned over and said to him, "Don't worry, Gordon, I won't be too hard on you," practically throwing down the gauntlet.
>
> Pierre Berton was due to lead off the panel's questioning. He knew Sinclair had begged off, but after a few seconds, maybe he'd said all he wanted to. He quickly said, "Now I'll turn you over to the religious editor."
>
> So in effect Sinclair was set up. The other factor in what happened was something nobody knew: She was a strong person and was quite prepared to debate religion with Sinclair, but she had a rather quavery voice, on or off camera. Because of this, the audience thought she was going to break down and cry and perceived Gordon as an insensitive son-of-a-bitch, hammering her in her moment of grief.

Naturally, that form of shooting fish in a barrel brought demands that Sinclair be suppressed.

The same demands had arisen over a non-religious issue on *Front Page* in 1969 when he asked swimming champion Elaine Tanner if her menstrual period interfered with her training or her competitive performance. That time, only the less worldly or more opportunistic viewers, such as members of Parliament and the president of the CBC, who was persuaded by MPs to apologize to Miss Tanner by letter, were scandalized by Sinclair's question; not Tanner. At home in Vancouver she told a newspaper interviewer, "I didn't really think there was going to be such an uproar. It actually didn't bother me." Nevertheless, the question resulted in 2,500 letters to the CBC, 21 in favour of Sinclair.

All that was reported as part of a campaign to force him off the program. But little notice was given to information that defended him. Marge McGaman, a Young Women's Christian Association swim director in Saskatoon, wrote saying she admired his digging for facts. She also enclosed a reprint of an article entitled "Swimming During the Menstrual Period" that had been published in the March 1943 issue of the *Journal of Health and Physical Education* in the United States, stating generally that normal exercise during such periods had been found not harmful.

The reprint had been distributed by Tampax Incorporated. This apparently brought a warm glow to the person so many Canadians had been calling a dirty old man. Sinclair's letter of thanks to Marge McGaman noted in passing that he was one of the original stockholders of Tampax, and that his initial $4,400 investment would have made him a millionaire if he'd held it, instead of selling for a profit of $100,000 "when $100,000 was real money". No one mentioned conflict of interest. At any rate, Sinclair was not suppressed—or ever close to it. He was the show's meal ticket.

He didn't often become preachy about sex; he was more likely to try to joke. An item from California announcing two new nude beaches with unsegregated toilets caused him to laugh: "It's on the theory that if they can bathe nude together they can pee together." Or he'd take a complaint from the National Organization of Women (U.S.) about sexual harassment of women in offices and jeer, "Men in offices make passes at women in offices! Can you imagine! Another terrible injustice suffered no longer in silence!"

202

But sometimes he was serious. One such occasion was triggered by a June Callwood broadcast on CBC radio. He started his late newscast one afternoon (in his seventy-seventh year) with a few lines about a campaign to get sex-oriented magazines off the magazine stands in North Bay, then went on:

> Meantime on coast-to-coast CBC radio this morning [on the Judy LaMarsh version of the program now known as *Morningside*], there was explicit sex reporting beyond anything printed in such magazines. As I was driving here I was informed move by move about female masturbation, a subject in which I have limited interest.
> The woman who described this procedure was almost evangelical in her zeal for detailed presentation. There was also, on the national network of the publicly owned corporation, statements apparently comforting to some that the size and shape of the penis is of no lasting importance. . . .
> If you are irritated . . . don't call *me*, I'm a reporter reporting.

The next day Ross McLean, program director of CBC-Toronto's television station, wrote Sinclair a letter expressing disappointment, not officially (McLean was not connected with CBC radio), but as "someone who prefers to admire you and finds it impossible not to trust the taste and judgment of my friend June Callwood." He called her series "responsible and useful" and thought Sinclair's response "perverse and mischievous".

In Sinclair's reply to that letter he admitted that "it might take a psychiatrist to explain" his reaction to the program, and said that it wasn't an attack (which it was, of course), but

> here's where the psychiatrist angle comes in. I have probably used more sexy items on CFRB than all the other people here combined.
> I think it's an interesting subject that has definite

appeal but I seem to use it in the wrong or blunderbuss style and thus get frequent strong reaction. . . .

But the sexy items I have used have frequently been done in a humorous style and in no case, not once, were they so specific as the ones at CBC.

So I guess I was lashing out and saying, "For Christ sake why put the knock on Sinclair when the CBC stuff takes up where I left off!" That may be a weak explanation but it's the best one I have.

His argument denying that he'd ever been "so specific" no doubt was correct in his terms, but others wouldn't agree. One example is an exchange he had with a female listener over an item he'd done about Adam and Eve and their goings-on in the Garden of Eden. On his show he'd outlined their "sin" in his own terms ("screwing") and asked why a compassionate God would punish all mankind forever for the actions of this pair. The listener protested him being so "spicy". In his reply Sinclair ran through a few examples of how sex was treated elsewhere in the media, such as an article he'd seen in the *Star* on the colour of male sperm, and added: "I could give countless other examples of how the world is changing and because of these examples I don't think a casual mention of the word 'screwing' in regard to Adam and Eve is all that offensive."

Anyway, he never reformed. Some years later, when advertisements and commercials for condoms were being denounced as making sexual promiscuity even more prevalent than it already was, he said the arguments against using them were bunk.

Condoms had never been primarily for birth control, he declaimed, but always had been regarded as protection against venereal disease. In fact, he said, long ago when he'd been a seventeen-year-old private in the Canadian army, condoms were routinely provided free to recruits, "and the guy who gave them to me said if I didn't use them, my cock would drop off."

His friend Wally Crouter, who had been listening to the

radio, immediately called Sinclair and gasped, "Do you know what you said?"

"Sure I do," Sinclair said. "I got it written down right here in my script."

Sometimes when he had something figured out that he knew would cause a fuss, he would try out the idea on others in the newsroom, or even tip the news editor about what was coming. One Sinclair natural was a story that CFRB's news director, Don Johnston, recalled in 1986:

> A man in the United States had lost his penis in a surgical accident and was suing for damages. Gordon came in to me that day and said, "Well, Don, we're going to find out today what a penis is really worth."
>
> That was the point of his story, what a man's penis was worth in dollars and cents. Sometimes when he had something like that related to sex he would try to get some kind of a response from women here in the newsroom and that was one of those times. Pat Morse was his secretary then, and Millie Moriak—who became his secretary later—was an assistant in the newsroom. He tried it out on the two of them, or at least he staged a discussion so that they overheard, and then he went and did it on the air and came back into the newsroom, snapping his suspenders and saying, "Well, boys, have they started yet?" Meaning the phone calls.

For the insatiably curious, the outcome of the case does not exist in any available files.

Bill Hall, general manager of the station for nearly nine years until his departure in 1986, has at least two special memories of Sinclair. They had known one another since the 1950s, when Hall was a young broadcaster working for Hamilton's CHML radio, which was owned by a legendary broadcaster, Ken Soble. He and Sinclair met one night at the opening of Prud'homme's Niagara Barn Theatre, where Broadway stars often appeared in summer stock. Hall had been assigned to do a live half-hour, starting at eight, interviewing celebrities. The first celebrity to show up, about seven-thirty, was Gordon Sinclair, who, when asked, had said, "Sure, I'd be glad to come on your show."

He came back to Hall a little before eight and asked who else Hall had lined up. Hall said he didn't have anybody. Sinclair said, "Who's bird-dogging for you?" When Hall admitted he was it, a one-man crew, Sinclair said, "Son, you're in trouble, I'll give you a hand." Which he did, lining up a roster including Broadway's Billy Rose, the CBC's Andrew Allan, critic Walter Kerr of the *New York Times*, Wayne and Shuster, everybody who was anybody.

The next day at CHML Soble, not noted for compliments, congratulated Hall on his impressive array of guests and asked, "How did you manage to get them?" Hall replied that he had Gordon Sinclair working for him.

From then on, Sinclair was one of his heroes. They went their separate ways, rarely meeting, until Hall's first day as CFRB's general manager—February 1, 1978. Standard Broadcasting announced his appointment officially that day, then threw a big reception for customers, advertising agencies, and other broadcasting people at the nearby Ports of Call. All of CFRB's senior people were on hand, including Sinclair.

"That night," Hall said,

> Sinclair was doing ten-to-six news for one of the first times since he'd turned it over to Bob Hesketh. Hesketh had a commitment somewhere, and Gordon was helping him out.
>
> I left the office about quarter to six and had started down Avenue Road just as Gordon came on the newscast. It was pretty straightforward, nothing much happening that night, until about halfway through the newscast he had a story about President Carter having something of a gastric condition, a medical report from the White House saying that the president was very uncomfortable and couldn't sleep at night, pacing the floor and drinking soda water and so on.

When Gordon got to the end of it he paused and said, "Now, folks, what all that really means is that he farts a lot."

I'd never heard that word on the air before, and I started to laugh, and when he was signing off the newscast he said, "That's the news, the weather, the stock-market report, and the latest medical bulletin from the White House." And I knew exactly what the old bugger was doing. He'd been welcoming me, the new boy, and he's saying, okay, kid, here's what's on your plate. When I got home I tried to phone the station and couldn't get through for about an hour. When I did, the night operater told me, "Oh, yes, there were a couple of hundred calls." I said, "Were they complaining?" She said no, they were mostly men killing themselves laughing. That was Gordon.

CHAPTER FOURTEEN

"YES, MY AGE BOTHERS ME"

"Sinc's 70th birthday celebration was one of the worst things that ever happened to him because it made him realize how old he really is. His age bothers him."
—Jack Dawson, long-time friend and ex-station manager, in a *Toronto Life* article.

"Yes, my age bothers me. Look, a man gets old and it bothers him."
—Sinclair's rejoinder, in the same article.

When a group of his friends and business associates decided to celebrate Sinclair's seventieth birthday in public, who was going to fight it? Certainly not Sinclair, although it made him uneasy to go where he knew he was going to be praised. He knew all about the hoopla, both the heartfelt and the ersatz, that good organization, powerful sponsors, and enthusiastic friends can produce. Backing for the party and accompanying homage had come from the *Star*, CFRB, the CBC, and ACTRA, thus involving in the arrangements the *Star*'s president and publisher Beland H. Honderich, who'd been a young *Star* reporter when Sinclair was in his prime; CFRB's chairman, W. C. Thornton Cran, one-time provider of Sinclair's private fire escape; big wheels from the CBC taking time off from writing apologetic letters to viewers enraged by Sinclair's tactics on *Front*

Page Challenge; his closest friends from CFRB such as Wally Crouter, Jack Dawson, Bill Baker, and others; and a contingent of his acting and performing colleagues led by Pierre Berton, Betty Kennedy, and Fred Davis. With this line-up, it hadn't required any arm-twisting to have Mayor William Dennison declare June 3, 1970, to be Gordon Sinclair Day.

From the time he rose that morning, the phone rang and telegrams arrived—from Prime Minister Pierre Trudeau, former prime minister Lester B. Pearson, Ontario's premier John Robarts, industrialists and politicians of all stripes. But not all the acclaim was from brass hats. On his way to work in the Rolls, he stopped at a red light. The stranger in the car ahead ran back to wish him a happy birthday.

When he walked in to CFRB, there were more congratulations, cards, and gifts. His *Let's Be Personal* was entitled Gordon Sinclair Day. Gladys joined him for the drive to the city's official greeting-place, an outdoor platform in the square in front of City Hall. The crowd was estimated at 2,000, better than the national average for seventy-year-old broadcasters.

On the platform were what one might call the usual cast for such an occasion: aldermen, clergy, local politicos, and old friend Foster Hewitt. Various people spoke. Gladys was given a gold maple leaf. The mayor handed Sinclair the city's official cuff-links and claimed that every community needed the shafts of someone like Sinclair "to keep us from getting smug and self-righteous". Sinclair cut a birthday cake and shared it with the crowd. Then it was off to the Park Plaza for drinks, lunch, and tributes. Berton read the sheaf of telegrams. He also stated the Sinclair creed ("honest, outspoken, always ready to take the consequences"). As Sinclair's old colleague Gregory Clark, becoming frail, spoke, reporters noted that "the first trace of tears came to Sinclair's eyes." He wiped his eyes unabashedly when Juliette, who had her own warm relationship with her mother, sang Bessie Sinclair's favourite, "I'll Take You Home Again, Kathleen", and Berton led in singing "Happy Birthday" one more time.

But before that, as Sinclair was being piped in to lunch,

with Gladys also at the head table, there was a small but telling incident. At the family table, Don, sitting with Sinclair's brother George, Wayne and Shuster, secretary Pat Morse, and others, remarked when the pipes died away, "The one who should be piped in is not him, but my mother." This caused a startled look or two and annoyed the loyal Pat Morse. It was one of the rare times when Gladys attended a social event with her husband. A year later, in *Maclean's*, Barbara Frum, in an article about the wives of famous men, described Gladys as she could be seen from outside: "reticent and retiring, preferring to spend her days as she always has, visiting her daughters-in-law, crocheting, watching the afternoon TV dramas." The article quoted Gladys about her life—which included getting royal treatment at restaurants when she was with Gordon and being ignored, seated in far corners, when she was alone or with woman friends.

> When I married Gordon he was nothing, just a common reporter. I never had anything to do with his success. Except I kept the family together. . . . It was a lonely life in a way. I was busy enough with four children, but night times were lonely. I must have thought it was alright because I didn't complain . . . [but] if he hadn't become famous we would have had different types of friends. We would have been home playing bridge. . . . I wouldn't offer Gordon advice or ideas. I think he likes his own ideas better than mine. I'm quite sure he does. A lot of women try to have a say and it's caused a lot of trouble.

At the seventieth-birthday fête Don was remembering that, and as an outspoken representative of those in the family who knew the other side of Sinclair, was applauding his mother.

Many of Sinclair's outrages at home have faded from memory now, so let one stand as an example. Some years after the seventieth-birthday party, having dinner at home, Sinclair threw a full plate of spaghetti at Gladys. No one now remembers what his rage was about; rage needs very little to set it off, for those addicted. But the incident itself had a long aftermath. The spaghetti and its sauce missed Gladys and hit high on the dining-room wall on the kitchen side. The residue, some pasta and a splash of sauce, remained, because neither of the principals would relent and clean it up. When the matter was discussed around that same table after Sinclair's death, everyone in the room glanced instinctively at the place where the irrefutable evidence had been, then someone said, "I think the room has been replastered."

There is no specific evidence corroborating Jack Dawson's remark that the seventieth-birthday celebration made Sinclair begin to feel his age in a really spirit-troubling way. He didn't change his leisure habits or his working pace. He took his usual three weeks at the lake in July and the normal statutory holidays. At that time he hadn't yet made the arrangement that gave him a full week each time a statutory holiday occurred. But Doris Loach recalls that along in there somewhere—or perhaps a year or two later—their frequent custom of having a good dinner and then taking in the opening of a new play at the O'Keefe Centre or the Royal Alexandra Theatre changed almost imperceptibly to a good lunch and a matinee. She also remembers that 1970 was the last year Gordon drove his boat down the lake alone, or sometimes with Gerry Dunn, and climbed up the rocks to her cottage carrying a chilled bottle of champagne.

That autumn, around mid-November, he began to feel ill. Some thought it might be his usual pre-Christmas depression arriving early this year. He stayed away from his office for two weeks, but on the day he returned, a Friday early in December, work was a struggle. He felt well below par. But *Front Page Challenge* was scheduled to fly to Halifax that Sunday for a show on the following day, December 7, and he felt well enough to go.

On Monday in the Halifax hotel, he found he'd forgotten a nail-file, and walked to a nearby shop to buy one. On the way back uphill against "this terrible wind, I collapsed, bing, right in the slush." Two passersby picked him up and helped him to the hotel, where he felt all right.

The show was that night. The next morning he caught the airport bus for an early flight to Toronto. Fred Davis and Lorraine Thomson (later a member of the production staff, but then in charge of booking guests) were in the seat behind him.

"Suddenly," Fred Davis said, "my God, he stiffened out, I'd never seen anyone suffering like that, couldn't get his breath, went terribly white. I thought he was a goner. It lasted only a few dozen seconds but then, although he breathed normally again, he still was this awful colour, his face covered in sweat. 'Gordon,' I said, 'can we get you to a hospital, we can get the bus driver to forget the airport . . . ' He said, 'Oh, no, get me to the airport, I want to get home, but if I can get a drink I think I'll be all right.' "

They tried on the way to the airport, and when they got there, but at 6:30 a.m. couldn't get him a drink until (Sinclair said) they were aboard the plane. In Toronto Dr. Bruce Fenton had him taken into Queensway General Hospital for tests. These were continued the following day at Toronto Western Hospital. It is difficult at this stage to be sure what the tests showed; the *Star* quoted unnamed doctors as "suspecting" that Sinclair had suffered a heart spasm, a sudden contraction of heart muscles, causing interference with the heart's functions. When the newspapers checked, Sinclair, recuperating at home, said he was on probation and that "it wasn't a heart attack, that's for sure." However, four days after making that statement, he was back at Toronto Western for more tests; the hospital described his condition as "satisfactory". He wasn't able to work again for the rest of December.

Although Sinclair had complained about discomfort from a rapid and erratic heartbeat from the time in childhood when Bessie had taken him to the Hospital for Sick Children and had been turned away, this was the first time his heart had sent him to hospital. He didn't make much of it publicly; in fact he seemed to want to downplay the situation. But when he opened his cottage the following May, he was advised not to go alone in his boat for any length of time, the explanation being that he might not be able to handle an emergency, such as a sudden storm. In future, his visits to Doris's cottage were made by road, in the Rolls-Royce, and later in his other cars.

At CFRB the change in Sinclair after his heart spasms was noticed only in retrospect. He wanted more time off and Jack Dawson obliged, arranging a full week off around each statutory holiday without any loss of pay. A change also was noticed by at least one CFRB employee, Jill Loring, a copy-writer and editor who was with the station from 1960 until her retirement in 1986. She remembers that in the 1960s, "He often came in laughing and joking, sometimes making a remark in passing, such as 'New dress, eh' or 'Had your hair done?' and if he did speak, he called you by name, he knew everyone by name." As the years went by into the 1970s his manner changed; he "walked in slowly every day about 10:30, eyes downcast," and as he went about his work, "He always had his eyes down and his mouth down, too, never stopped to chat or ask anyone about themselves." Near the end she saw him simply as a "short, crabby-faced celebrity, totally self-absorbed". Yet she never stopped admiring him professionally for his writing. "He knew how to describe a scene, a person, or an event so that you could see it with him—in the minimum of words." Jill Loring didn't do badly herself when it came to describing a Sinclair scene in a minimum of words: "I was at a movie once and Gordon was some rows ahead. Suddenly he stood up and shouted loudly, 'That's it! I've had enough of this garbage! *Good*bye!' And stomped up the aisle and out, to great laughter from the audience, who recognized him, of course."

Sinclair's behaviour at opening nights was fairly well documented. Patrick Scott of the *Star*, who had once described Sinclair's broadcasting by saying that he "does not so much read the news, even his own colourful version of it, as read his own mind in public," sat in front of him at one opening.

In his own review, Scott noted, "At least old Gordon Sinclair let me know where he stood, largely because he happened to be sitting directly behind me, reviewing the show out loud between scenes."

And also, it seemed, in the waiting period before a curtain he could have other things on his mind. Robert Fulford in the 1960s was writing an art column for the *Star*. One night he was sitting one row in front of Sinclair at a Crest Theatre opening. As Fulford tells it,

> He leaned over:
>
> "Say, Bob, what do you think of Manly Macdonald's paintings? Any good?"
>
> "Well . . . " I searched my memory. I knew he was a Toronto artist of roughly Gordon's generation, hazy expressionist cityscapes, not so bad. "Well, he's all right, but I haven't seen anything of his that I thought was very impressive."
>
> "Okay. The reason I ask, I saw him on the street the other day and he didn't look so good. Terrible, in fact. I thought if he's good it might be worth buying some of his paintings."
>
> I must have looked blank. Gordon continued, "When an artist dies, you know, the paintings often shoot up in value."

Money often entered Sinclair's mind at odd occasions. Another story in this line is recalled by Don Hartford from 1975 after Thornton Cran died suddenly of a heart attack.

> At the funeral I sat with Gordon in about the third row. Ahead of us was Bud McDougald. The Crans were up front and Cran's body, you know, was there. McDougald turned back and asked, "Whatever happened to old so-and-so?" (I forget the name). Sinc

said, "I think he's doing all right." Then McDougald said, "How much money does he have?" And Sinc says, "About three million," and McDougald said, "No goddam way." And the voices, you know, could be heard and the family turned around and this got to be a serious argument about how much money somebody had, all during a funeral!

But, to return to Jill Loring's memory of Sinclair at the movie, while she couldn't warm to him as a person, except to be amused by such blow-topism, a lot of the promotional material used as spot announcements to plug his programs was her work.

To quote one: "Whatever is happening, an election or a blackout, a holiday or a change in the weather, may be the inspiration for another *Let's Be Personal* show with Gordon Sinclair. He's always timely, topical, and highly individual." Those words might well have been used to describe one program he dashed off on the morning of June 5, 1973. When his secretary, Pat Morse, was filing and indexing it later that day, she slugged it simply "Americans". He wrote it in nine, thirteen, fourteen or seventeen minutes (depending on whatever figure popped into his head on the hundreds of occasions later when he was asked about it). Anyway, it was written at speed—a few minutes of scruffy typing, and another few to improve it here and there in handwritten additions and subtractions that wandered into the margins. This done, he went to the studio at 11:45 and informed the world in ringing tones that it should be damn well ashamed of itself for incessantly dumping on Americans. To reread it now, quite apart from the all-out passion that made it famous, is to read great advocacy journalism.

He led off with news of the American dollar taking a pounding on the foreign-exchange market, hitting its lowest point ever in Germany, a 41-per-cent drop in two years. With that line he launched himself into the meat of his most famous single broadcast with the words "This

Canadian thinks it is time to speak up for the Americans as the most generous and possibly the least appreciated people in all the earth."

Then he was away in full flight about times all over the world when, in floods and earthquakes and wars and their aftermaths, the Americans rushed in to help. Germany, Japan, Britain, and Italy "were lifted out of the debris of war by the Americans who poured in billions of dollars and forgave other billions in debts."

In the late 1950s their reward for propping up the diving franc "was to be insulted and swindled on the streets of Paris." Now, when the Americans needed friends, newspapers all over the world were dumping on them instead.

> When the Americans get out of this bind, as they will, who could blame them if they said, "the hell with the rest of the world. Let someone *else* buy the Israel bonds. Let someone else build or repair foreign dams or design foreign buildings that won't shake apart in earthquakes. . . ." I can name to you 5,000 times when Americans raced to the help of other people in trouble. Can you name me one time when someone else raced to the Americans in trouble? . . .

> I'm one Canadian who is damned tired of hearing them kicked around. They will come out of this thing with their flag high. And when they do, they are entitled to thumb their nose at the lands that are gloating over their present troubles.

> I hope Canada is not one of these. But there are many smug, self-righteous Canadians. And finally, the American Red Cross was told at its annual meeting in New Orleans this morning that it was broke.

> This year's disasters, with the year less than half over, have taken it all and nobody, but *nobody*, has helped.

The broadcast went to his usual audience of about 350,000 in Toronto, southern Ontario, and neighbouring American states. Some who heard it laughed, remembering how he sometimes called U.S.-led unions "leeches, blood-suckers". They also recalled his exasperated reaction eleven years earlier during the Cuban missile crisis when his news was abruptly shoved off the air twice for CBS bulletins, and when he'd called the Americans "bastards" and decried "interrupting me for goddam American propaganda." Apart from that, there was little reaction at first. A few phone calls. It was not one of Sinclair's "let's light up the switchboard" triumphs.

But the spark was there for the later conflagration. His colleague Wally Crouter had judged it immediately as great Sinclair, and the next morning replayed it on his morning show. Then a radio station in Michigan phoned to ask for a repeat it could use. The answer was, "Sure." It hadn't been widely heard yet, but in the few places where it was heard, Americans were reacting with amazement, tears, and phone calls to say, "Play it again." His impassioned words had caught the United States when that nation's self-esteem was at one of its lowest points in history: Vietnam was seen as a global pesthole and Watergate as a national pesthole, American draft-dodgers were a political fact in many countries, and the energy shortage was hitting Americans in gas-pump line-ups. The original tape was eventually played for copying purposes so often that it wore out.

Lyman Potts, as president of Standard Broadcast Productions Limited, was the moving force behind CFRB's syndications in news and comment at that time. He had also established a couple of music-publishing companies. As the snowball began to roll, still slowly, in the summer months following the original broadcast, he began to handle the business side. "At first we made the program available on tape to a couple of stations in the States," he told *Rolling Stone* magazine a few months later, when the record was selling in the millions. "A station in Buffalo played it, and so on . . . they'd pass it around from station to station, newspapers would get the text and use it as the basis for editorials." Sinclair recorded it with background music, "Bridge Over Troubled Waters". It was all very unbusinesslike at that stage, but who could have foreseen what would happen?

In September a fan in Los Angeles sent the text, clipped from a Canadian newspaper, to a local disc jockey, Dick Whittinghill. He read it on KMPC and got thousands of requests for copies.

As the text spread on the air and in print, suddenly, as *Rolling Stone* noted, "a kind of middle-American underground" took over. AVCO Records got in touch with Lyman Potts early in December. Out of this came a 45-rpm single, with Sinclair reading his piece, now with a stirring rendition of "Battle Hymn of the Republic" as background.

About the same time, other versions were being recorded, some with and some without permission from either Sinclair or Lyman Potts. One that was done without approval was Byron MacGregor's reading on Windsor's CKLW, which drew 3,500 phone calls and a request from Detroit's Westbound Records to record it commercially a few days later. The original absence of permission to record was pointed out to MacGregor after the fact by Pat Morse. No action was taken, although Sinclair did rather put other recording artists on the spot by stating that all profits from his record would go to the American Red Cross. MacGregor soon followed that lead.

By Christmas of 1973, three versions were on sale—Sinclair's, MacGregor's, and one by Tex Ritter. Several radio stations had put together their own versions and were using give-away texts to raise money for charities. U.S. editorial writers, columnists, broadcasters, and ordinary citizens were talking Sinclair. Most of this was out-and-out laudatory, but writer and broadcaster Henry Morgan put it in his own perspective in his syndicated column early in 1974.

Six months earlier, Morgan wrote, Sinclair had been racking his brains for a broadcast idea and finally decided to say something nice about the United States.

At first he couldn't think of anything to say, but he was sure of one thing. The thought had never before occurred to a Canadian. It was worth a try.

Well, we all know what happened. The U.S. Congress immediately gave up all the palavering about Watergate; the two grations, inte- and segre-; who was paying Kissinger's carfare; and whether or not to go back to whale oil.

There's a bill up in the Senate to change the calendar to read April, May, Sinclair, July and August. . . .Apollo 43 is going to take off from Cape Sinclair; Passaic, New Jersey, is becoming Gordonville and McDonald's is offering a new $2 creation called Big Gordie. . . .

Morgan then launched a thanks-Canada column in return, acknowledging Canada's part in everything from the invention of basketball and the McIntosh apple to "giving people from Detroit somewhere to go without taking out life insurance," and for supporting Fort Lauderdale. "Thanks for helping to keep the peace, such as it is; thanks for going into wars when you were needed; thanks for being a wonderful country; and thanks for taking Marshall McLuhan back. This is unofficial. But sincere."

But for every piece that thanked Sinclair humorously, there were hundreds who never thought of kidding about something that had affected them so deeply. These were the writers of thousands of letters that poured in, bearing U.S. stamps and postmarks and addressed to Sinclair. These were·from ordinary Americans as well as the famous, ranging from state governors and congressmen to Senator Margaret Chase Smith and President Richard Nixon. At the rate of a hundred or more each day, these were being dumped on Pat Morse's desk. She couldn't keep pace, and they piled up unopened until the station's management provided help.

Travel agencies sent guided busloads of appreciative Americans to CFRB's front door. *U.S. News and World Report* printed excerpts. Its editor wrote his personal thanks to Sinclair. Newspaper editors wrote him to say they had been deluged with requests for reprints. The text was read into the U.S. Congressional Record seven times. Sinclair was named an honorary citizen of several states, and was cited by dozens of patriotic organizations. Many followed their awards with invitations for expense-paid trips so that he could appear in person. He turned everything down, except the annual convention of the Red Cross, whose financial troubles at the time of their previous convention had helped fuel his fire in the original "Americans".

Declining invitations to lead the Memorial Day parade in Chicago and the Kentucky Derby parade in Louisville, to read his piece at a Seattle concert backed by the Mormon Tabernacle Choir, and to speak before the Sons of the American Revolution and the Kentucky House of Representatives (to name only a few) was one thing; others do that too. But he really stunned some major TV producers, who customarily spend their time fending off would-be guests, rather than pleading for their attention. The man wouldn't even talk to them. Sinclair was not really well at the time the flood began. Well or not, some days he had Pat Morse handle the turndowns. This made for some rather funny conversations, if you can imagine people from the *Tonight Show* or the *Mike Douglas Show* or the *Today Show* trying to explain the inexplicable to the secretary of a man whose attitude was that he had his own work to do, and couldn't be bothered even to come to the phone.

Some of the impact was summed up by *Newsweek* in January 1974, under the heading: "The Good News—from Canada". Alongside a photo of Sinclair, the story began:

> In Boston, radio station WMEX gets 100 requests a day to play it again.
> In Milwaukee, a record store sold 5,000 copies in just two days—and took an order for a thousand more from one customer alone.
> In Atlanta, where it's already the Number One seller, WGST music director Jonathan Stone declares flatly: "In twelve years in radio I've never seen anything like it."

"It"...is a four-minute 40-second eulogy to America
called Americans, written by a salty, 73-year-old
Canadian newscaster named Gordon Sinclair. . . .
    To a nation bombarded by a year of unremitting bad
news, the message is plainly irresistible . . . record
companies are already planning . . . sequels.

No wonder. *Rolling Stone* reported in February that 3.5
million copies had been sold in five weeks. One version
"entered the Cashbox Top 100 at Number 81 December
29th and three weeks later had soared to Number 8. . . . The
records that people were buying so feverishly must have
answered a deep need in America's current demoraliza-
tion."

However, the anvil chorus of approval was not quite
unanimous. Some non-Americans didn't like the way they'd
been typed by Sinclair—Germans as only car-makers and
Japanese as camera-makers. Finland didn't like being
lumped in with nations who hadn't paid their war debts.
And then there was one dissident among the *Rolling Stone*
sources, disc jockey Don Imus at WNBC, New York, who
spoke in language Sinclair could understand: "That piece
of shit?" Imus exclaimed. "Oh, yeah, I play it. I play it at 78
a lot."

But he was no more than a loud minority. Besides the
three 45-rpm versions then on sale, all on the record charts
by late February, two more were due momentarily on LPs—
although *Rolling Stone* had been told the demand was
falling off. Owing to the number of sales and the lack of
information on what happened to some profits, it's difficult
to come up with a solid figure on how much went to the
American Red Cross. In 1984 one estimate was that more
than $400,000 had been donated from Sinclair's record. An
earlier estimate was that Byron MacGregor's would yield
about $280,000. That totalled somewhere close to a
$700,000 figure that Sinclair used in one interview.

But, after all, it wasn't done to make money, even for a
good cause, and the important impact was more person-to-
person. *Toronto Sun* columnist Paul Rimstead once hap-

pened across one of the people who was touched personally and deeply by the broadcast. This was the human result of Sinclair's few minutes of passion. Rimstead, at the time momentarily off the wagon, was in a bar in Kalamazoo, Michigan, in 1983, more than ten years after the original broadcast. Early in January 1984 he was one of those interviewed for a major feature story about Sinclair in the *Arizona Daily Star* of Tucson, Arizona. He'd got talking to another man in the bar, Rimstead said, and when the man found Rimstead was from Toronto, the man talked about Sinclair.

"I would have given everything to have Sinclair sitting in that bar so he could see how seriously his words affected one man," Rimstead told reporter Jim Fox. "I can't remember his name, but I will never forget his words. 'Every American my age, every veteran of Vietnam, is indebted to him,' the man told me. 'He said what had to be said at the time, when nobody else would say it—not even our president. He made us proud again. He told us to hold up our heads and walk tall. We were down and sliding even farther. Those words changed our lives.'"

It seems incredible, but at this time of his greatest international acclaim, when his recorded words were being played at home by millions (including, it turned out, Ronald Reagan), Sinclair was in one of the lowest of his low periods. From this distance, it seems to have been straight depression. The reasons were varied, and who can tell what relation the parts bore to the whole? He was being sued on two fronts. One was over a broadcast that was alleged to have been a slight to a Toronto woman who wanted her husband put in jail for non-support (Sinclair argued that any wife wanting to put her husband in jail was legitimate news). Another was for refusing to pay the last $250 on a $1,000 bet he'd made that the Dow index on the New York stock exchange would not fall below 800 in 1973 (which it had, twice)..

It was also income-tax time—an annual crisis during which Sinclair always became impossible. His state of mind may be read most accurately in two documents written in early January 1974, when he had been off work for about two weeks.

One was a note to secretary Pat Morse, accompanying a letter of resignation. The note read:

Dear Pat;
Here is a case where I rely on your personal discretion. Read this [resignation letter] and if it seems to you a reasonable note go to Dawson, please take it to him personally [not to his secretary]. If you think I disclose too much let me know and when I come in I'll think of some alternative.

I've just got, from my auditor, my income tax bill . . . $67,471.00 of which all but $2,210 has been paid. BUT!! The March instalment (about $16,000) has been less than 25% paid so I MUST find that.

Is it worth working?

(signed) G.S.

The resignation letter was two pages, double-spaced, beginning:

I'm sorry to be absent at this competitive time and unable to give solid assurance as to when I'll be back. This is likely to be the afternoon of Monday the 14th [of January]. You would be within your rights in deciding that you don't need an infirm broadcaster and if this is so just let me know.

When Gladys was in hospital for eye-surgery [a cataract operation early in December] in which there has been little improvement, our family physician was out of the country. Feeling down I asked the chief of medicine at Queensway if he could assign someone to look me over. Three physicians by direct test and a cardiologist by telephone did this. The first, who had never seen me before, urged that I stop work at once. All others agreed that I was suffering fatigue but should make a complete recovery. I therefore kept working but the Christmas period brought me down.

Since then our family physician has returned and his view is that my heart is weaker through fatigue but I'm free of disease. However, he does urge that I not return until he sees me again and suggests that someone at CFRB get in touch with him. . . .

This letter goes on to document all the calls made upon him. The mail and requests regarding the "Americans" had deluged Pat Morse. The latter task was left to her to handle "as secretary to the resident weirdo", when it should have been handled by the public-relations department. Much mail was not answered at all—or even opened.

He thought it probable "that these hassles would all end if I dropped out and on this point I'd like your advice. After all I'll begin my 75th year, 32nd at CFRB, before summer and I can't stay too much longer regardless."

If he did come back, he wrote, "Miss Morse will have to be relieved of some of the burden of zoo keeper to a celebrity. This sounds, and probably is, egotistical. Despite this vanity, it is true. But it is of real value to CFRB."

A hand-written note by Pat Morse in the margin of this letter reads: "Gordon tried to resign several times. I think I talked him out of this one."

He did return to work on January 15 with a *Let's Be Personal* on John A. Macdonald's 159th birthday on January 11, but was away again in April, stretching the Easter holiday to two weeks.

CHAPTER FIFTEEN

THE OTHER SIDE OF THE MOUNTAIN

"My heart is worse than last summer or the summer before so I've not been swimming. With me I think it's at least partly psychological."
—Letter from the cottage, July 16, 1974.

Sinclair frequently said that leisure bothered him, made him impatient to be doing something. But later in the letter quoted above he wrote, "Often I've been anxious to get back on the job after only a few days. This time I'm already wishing I had a longer vacation." One reason might have been that in the first weeks of that holiday he'd been working on the book to be published a year later as *Will the Real Gordon Sinclair Please Sit Down*. Even so, as the 1970s went on, a definite change was discernible. Publicly he was still firing both barrels at all targets of opportunity; privately he was insecure, uncertain, even fearful.

A bizarre example of this ambivalence had its beginnings one lunch-time in 1973 at La Scala restaurant in downtown Toronto. Some time earlier Sinclair on CFRB and Richard J. Needham in his *Globe and Mail* column had stated opposing views on the immediate future of the stock market, Sinclair optimistic, Needham not. They had bet a champagne lunch on the outcome. Sinclair won, so Needham was paying—and also had invited Dennis Barron, a mortgage broker. Barron's connection with the affair was that, in a letter to the *Globe*, he had supported Needham and opposed Sinclair.

At this lunch the argument was taken up again in a fairly light-hearted way—until Sinclair, flushed with this one success, bombastically offered to bet $1,000 that the authoritative Dow Jones index would not go below 800 between that point, in early August, and the end of the year. Barron immediately said, "You're on."

Putting the bet in writing a few days later, Sinclair rambled on rather pompously that his liquid worth at the moment (all in the stock market) was $1.5 million, that he was tired of "gloom howlers", and that he hoped Barron would accept his bet, ending with a patronizing, "Cheer up, son. You must be rather young."

The Dow did dip below 800 briefly, twice, before the end of the year, but when it came to paying the debt . . . oh, dear, the gloom-howling was coming from another source. One should take into account, again, that all this happened during the aftermath of his usual Christmas down-and-drinking period. Sinclair wrote Barron a letter on January 4, trying to settle for $500 plus another La Scala lunch. He pleaded "grievous financial losses" in the market. Also, he and Gladys had "suffered setbacks in health", and all in all he was unable to pay his income tax (the $16,000 quarterly instalment referred to in his aborted resignation that same month) without drawing on current income.

This might have been literally true, but he didn't mention actual figures—with good reason. Normally he'd have been the first to heap scorn on a man with an annual income close to $200,000 crying the blues. "Wish I had your foresight instead of my own buoyant optimism," he wrote, obviously not noticing the danger of giving buoyant optimism a bad name.

On receiving that letter, Barron phoned angrily to call Sinclair a piker, welsher, and cheapskate. Sinclair yelled back. But his next letter in mid-January, enclosing $500 and promising $250 in March and again in June, could have been accompanied by sobbing violins. Its burden of self-pity was combined with a more-in-sorrow-than-in-anger air, somewhat that of a poor-but-honest workman sturdily promising to meet his obligations however onerous they might be.

He mentioned that he had not yet been able to return to work, had no pension except the national old-age pension, and "being self-employed I'm not paid when absent." (He might have thought that was so, as it had been in his early contracts; but by then his absences did not mean docked pay.) As a result, "I am temporarily in money trouble. I went to the T-D bank to see if I could arrange to borrow what was needed to pay my just debt to you. They wanted 4-1 collateral plus 11 percent. I declined to pay." He also threw in that, had he won their bet, he would not have asked Barron for full payment; $500, or $750 at most, would have been fine.

Barron was unmoved. In March, Sinclair paid another $250, as forecast. But in May he wrote to Barron saying that was all, enough, finito, and he hoped Barron would take him to court over the other $250.

Barron did so. They turned up at Etobicoke Small Claims Court nine months later, in February 1975, where Barron and his lawyer, painting Sinclair as the "piker, welsher, cheapskate" that Barron had claimed, did their best to hold him up to ridicule.

Sinclair, representing himself, made no particular point except that he had decided not to pay. He probably had checked the law in advance. The judge ruled that the court could not enforce the terms of a wager. Naturally, Sinclair being news, the *Toronto Sun* covered the case with a full-page report headlined "'Welsher' Sinclair". This naturally pleased all Sinclair-haters, who did not hesitate to call him a fake, and worse. To one letter Sinclair replied: "I'm still the guy who gave about $250,000 to the Red Cross and for this I am not asking or getting an income tax allowance.

The professional money-lender who sued me gave nothing."

Yet the whole affair had meaning. Sinclair could have bitten the bullet, paid the final $250 quietly if grudgingly, and avoided the negative publicity. He chose not to. Friends simply shrugged and said, "That's Gordon."

Usually he was quite gentle in letters to listeners who disagreed with him. But there were exceptions. Early in 1973 he'd made merciless fun of the reported kidnapping of Marilyn Lastman, wife of North York's mayor (she had returned home alone and unharmed, apparently minus some valuable rings that were said to be part of a ransom but were later found in a drawer at home). One listener, in a letter to CFRB's president, ascribed Sinclair's attitude in the Lastman affair to his age, jealousy of the Lastmans for making so much money so young, and "Sinclair's opinion of Jews". Furious on all counts, Sinclair blasted back: "Because a man dares to speak his mind, you refer to senility, hardening of the arteries, jealousy," he wrote. "Your letter was bigoted . . . despicable . . . and in my view that makes you a despicable person."

Once he got past the Christmas of 1973, the despondent resignation, the lost bet to Barron, his annual income-tax depression, and the tendency even in business letters to mention his and Gladys's poor health, Sinclair seemed in better shape. He still poked away a bit about fluoridation of the water supply being a cancer threat—but only when he had new ammunition, such as a 1975 U.S. study showing that cities with fluoridated water had higher cancer rates than the national average. His ratings were holding steady at around 335,000 listeners at ten to twelve and a few thousand less at ten to six. He seemed to be taking family and health pressures more in his stride. A letter to Pat Morse from Muskoka on May 20, 1975, sending along a couple of Let's Be Personals for typing, sounded quite upbeat.

He'd been opening the cottage. "None of my sons or nephews came to help this time and Gladys can't help so I've been surprised at my own ability to get things together.

I even launched the boat myself when an expert who had faithfully promised to be here last Friday didn't come and hasn't come yet." The weather was great. That afternoon he was going to plant flowers, "a job previously done by daughters-in-law". The old attitude of "I'm okay, I'm not through yet" shone through.

A couple of weeks later CFRB threw a party at the station for his seventy-fifth birthday. It was a custom in the newsroom to have a party for every birthday—usually a bottle of wine, a little food, and a few minutes off. Soon after Don Johnston had arrived as news director years earlier, he'd banned the first such party of his regime on the grounds that a newsroom was no place for booze. Sinclair had come in to Johnston's office, closed the door, gently argued that it was a unity-building custom worth preserving, and won the day.

The Sinclair seventy-fifth, of course, was not the standard smallish bash. Among telegraphed greetings were those from Prime Minister Pierre Trudeau and Ontario's premier William Davis. More surprising was a phone call "to wish you the best" from one of the most indomitable of Sinclair's long-time sparring partners, the Rev. J. R. Mutchmor, who had been thundering from pulpits for about as long as Sinclair had been in long pants, and indeed was considered by some as an ecclesiastical version of Sinclair.

As long ago as 1965, Sinclair had worried to writer Alexander Ross that he seemed to be in danger of being tolerated, even liked, and that being ignored could not be far behind. Here was thought-provoking evidence. Was such a doughty adversary as Mutchmor tiring of the fight? Could this be a sneaky trick by the forces of religion? No matter: Sinclair's reflections at the party on his career and its longevity included the profoundly self-explanatory line, "You must be what you are."

In August he was invited to open the Canadian National Exhibition and did so with a ringing, "I was born in this city. I was raised in this city. I went from this city to see nearly all of the world, and this is the place I want to live and die."

At work over the next few years, however, there was a change. He seemed more dependent on others, especially in his *Let's Be Personal*s. Secretary Pat Morse would clip items from the *Wall Street Journal* or other publications and he would use them freely, with a minimum of personal input. She and Millie Moriak, the newsroom assistant, would turn in bits about everything from stray dogs to night-club acts, and he'd read them verbatim.

Once CFRB's Jill Loring wrote for him what she intended as background for a broadcast about her father's antique business, then about to close down. In it she made an offhand remark that her father had not been just any second-hand-furniture dealer. She was surprised when her memo was typed and returned for her to check, word for word with her handwritten draft, except that Sinclair didn't like the line about her father's not being just a second-hand dealer. He'd taken that as a slight to his father, who'd been in the second-hand line briefly, and he had written in a sharp line about class-consciousness. Jill Loring, asked to check the item before use, had meant no slight, so cut both references, her original and Sinclair's rejoinder. Sinclair could have restored the cuts, but he didn't. Instead, he told Jill Loring in person that he didn't like what he'd read as an anti-little-guy crack—and did not speak to her again.

When he had others write some of his *Let's Be Personal*s he always gave credit—unless it would embarrass the originator. One example of this kind of consideration, dating back to the 1960s, was recalled in 1986 by E. Paul Zimmerman, a senior executive of Torstar Corporation.

Just before his parents' fiftieth wedding anniversary, Zimmerman had been delighted to hear Sinclair devote much of one broadcast to his father, Dr. G. F. Zimmerman, "with emphasis on [my father's] exceptional athletic prowess". The younger Zimmerman, grateful, called Sinclair and asked for a copy of his notes to use at his parents' anniversary party. Sinclair replied, "You can easily get a copy from your father—he wrote them and passed them along." Paul Zimmerman, much taken aback, thanked him and kept his father's secret.

As the 1970s wore on, there were also some changes in Sinclair's life that only he and Doris Loach could know. Because of his continuing trouble with painful angina attacks, his doctor suggested that he be extremely careful not to get over-excited. One outcome was that the sexual side of their relationship came to an end, after thirty-six years. As well, they decided that they should no longer travel out of the country together because of the complications that would ensue if he fell seriously ill, or even died, and their presence together on a foreign trip might be made public.

Their discretion in public for so many years had been exemplary. Betty Kennedy said that in all the time she'd known Doris, she had thought her frequent presence with Sinclair at plays, receptions, and other functions had been simply that of a good friend—"Just the fact that if you're going someplace, it's more enjoyable to have a companion, and Gladys usually wouldn't go." Pierre Berton thought the same. Some other Sinclair friends, notably Alan Savage in the earliest days of the relationship and Wally Crouter later, were better informed, having made trips with Sinclair and Doris. Nobody except Sinclair and Doris knew, however, that at one point during the 1960s Doris had tried to break off the relationship by not answering phone calls, and refusing to see him—an estrangement that apparently ended with a note saying he'd like to take her to lunch "if you'll promise not to bitch."

After that, their long and mutually satisfying relationship was resumed, Doris often being there by prearrangement to meet him when he finished at CFRB or *Front Page Challenge*.

As he grew older, when he cut down on his workload it was mainly CFRB that suffered. Elsewhere he was as busy as ever. He wrote a submission to the Ontario Royal Commission on Violence in the Communications Industry, arguing that "no book in any language is as violent as the Bible" and that "violence is an essential part of human nature, essential to survival . . . and without it everyone would become pitty-pat cream puffs." (This drew a letter which read, in full, "You jackass, if you love violence, one of these days I will lay my knife on your throat—see how you will love it.")

Also, he rarely refused free-lance work, writing introductions to books that dealt with times he knew about first-hand—including one on the lake steamers of his younger days—as well as magazine articles for *Chatelaine*, *TV Guide*, and others. He apparently didn't argue about fees. *Maclean's* paid him $300 for one article. For another he received $1,200 from the much less well-known *Front Row Centre*, a cable-TV magazine.

The $300 piece for *Maclean's*, written in mid-1977, was Sinclair's celebration of Quebec's place in Canada, a passionate piece of advocacy journalism which began:

> French is the most beautiful language in all the world and must, even if the cost is high, be preserved.... It *must not* disappear from Quebec but it could perish if efforts are not made to preserve it. To the credit of Robert Bourassa and René Lévesque, the French tongue will be preserved and to the credit of Pierre Trudeau it will expand and grow until at some future time Canadians—and the Québécois will be Canadian—will speak French as naturally as they drink water.

It would have been natural for the Prime Minister to have sent him official thanks for expressing such sentiments, but the problem was that he was not always so officially applaudable.

Three weeks after the supportive piece in *Maclean's*, he blasted the government for admitting refugees from Southeast Asia, attributing the policy to "do-gooders screaming that we must save the boat people, just as they have howled about baby seals, polar bears and desert scorpions." He called the boat people "unhappy drifters" who belonged in Asia. "There are millions of acres of empty land in Manchuria where the rice diet is familiar," and refugees should go there instead of becoming dependants in Canada, he said.

In light of that, there must have been some debate in the

Prime Minister's Office about thanking Sinclair for what he had said about the French and Quebec. But Prime Minister Pierre Trudeau was equal to the task, applauding the praise, ignoring the criticism.

> Dear Gordon:
> In recent months I have been greatly impressed by the eloquence with which you have promoted the continuing unity of Canada. Your fair-minded appeals for tolerance, understanding and compassion point clearly to the only lasting solutions to our current national difficulties. Much of the battle to see our country beyond the current challenges will depend upon the courage and wisdom of respected commentators such as you.

The letter closed with "my very warmest personal regards".

As a footnote, Sinclair's sentiments on preserving French drew supporting letters to *Maclean's*, and his outburst to his huge noontime audience about the boat people also was widely approved. A compilation of telephone calls from the station's listeners agreed 20-1 with Sinclair.

He didn't do nearly as well with an attack on the Block Parents association, which he considered "a despicable import from the American black and white slums of the south Bronx".

"It teaches our Canadian children to distrust all strangers, to fear all strangers, to be insulated against the natural intercourse between people, and I despise it." When another CFRB commentator, Art Cole, took the opposite tack more than a year later, Sinclair protested to management about being undercut.

But although he was described as "dyspeptic broadcaster Gordon Sinclair" in some news reports of such outbursts, he was so good at switching from the ridiculous to the sublime and back again that people always had some new Sinclairism to talk about.

One of his items was greeted so fondly that a tape of it

was played as comic relief at a service club. It concerned a woman toll-collector on the Pennsylvania turnpike. She'd been having an affair with a truck-driver, and when the two of them were caught at it in the toll booth during working hours, she was fired. She was off work for ten months while the firing was appealed. She was finally reinstated, but without back pay for the time she'd been off work. Sinclair's summing up on the reinstatement was, "So the lady won't get paid for the time she was laid"—long pause—"off."

Although he was very willing to write for other publications, he habitually turned down speeches, even those with high fees attached. His attitude was that writing could be done on time he could control, while speeches required turning up somewhere at a specific time—a form of restriction that he'd rarely accepted, except for his radio and television work. When *Front Page Challenge* was on the road, he was expected to appear at various functions with the rest of the panel for promotion purposes. He would meet such obligations, even if it were simply showing up, chatting briefly, then leaving. "People understood that he needed his rest, and appreciated that at least he'd come along to say hello," Betty Kennedy said.

But sometimes on such occasions he'd be the old Sinclair. One such occasion was recalled by Pierre Berton:

> We were in Calgary and the Women's Canadian Club asked us to lunch. At the end of the lunch each of us was asked to say a few words to these ladies, mostly being of a certain age. Freddy [Davis] got up to say what a great pleasure it was to enjoy Western hospitality, etc., etc. Betty got up and said, "You know, I partly come from Calgary, I worked here, I love it, it's a beautiful city." I got up and said I was here during the war for two years and Calgary has changed but it's always great to be out West, blah, blah. Then Gordon got up. I'll give you the full Gordon Sinclair speech. He said, "Oh, sitting at the bar last

night with Lorraine Thomson, we were talking about the economy and there's this girl next door and she was talking to this guy who was a furniture dealer and the furniture dealer said, god, the economy is terrible, I'm in the furniture business and I'm losing my ass. And the girl said, that's nothing, I'm in the ass business and I'm losing my furniture."

And then he sat down. And there was this silence. And then a little titter. And then everybody laughed. And I said, "Gordon, you're the only guy who could do that and get away with it."

Of course, his national reputation had been built on *Front Page*. Everyone in the show's regular audience, panel and staff, had memories of outrageous things he'd said on this or that occasion, how he'd said them, how Fred Davis would smoothly extricate the combatants and go on to the next segment. Many of these are detailed in Alex Barris's excellent book, titled *Front Page Challenge*, published on the show's twenty-fifth anniversary, but were personal memories as well of his unpredictability. "Something would come up and it would trigger something in Gordon that could only happen with Gordon, because nobody else had his kind of experience," Betty Kennedy said. Pierre Berton's view was that "you never quite knew when he was going to break out, or about what. You'd get a guy on, some s.o.b. of a racist or something, and we'd all be going at him about that, and Gordon would instantly take the other side."

One guest was an English-born mercenary who had been fighting in Africa. All the other panelists had demanded, in various ways, how he could possibly take money for killing people. It was all very one-sided, with a high moral tone, and the mercenary, young and without much education, just didn't have any answers. Then it came to Sinclair. Everyone expected he'd continue the pounding, but he asked mildly, "What kind of pay do mercenaries get these days?" That was something the young man could talk about.

As he and Sinclair talked money, the air of self-righteous bullying evaporated. "Gordon didn't care so much about his own personality on the show; he wanted to make a *show* of it," Pierre Berton said. "When things were going mildly or quietly or predictably, Gordon would jump in and quite often save the show."

Berton felt that he learned a lot from Sinclair about how to phrase a question, and how to emphasize a surprising answer.

> He would ask the question, and if the answer was surprising, to make sure the answer wasn't missed by the viewer, he'd repeat the *answer*. That was important, because in TV stuff does go by. The guy would say something outrageous and Gordon would say, "You mean to say that . . . " and he'd say the whole thing over again. Now that he's no longer with us, I try to do that kind of thing, and he taught me how to do it.

People who were angered by what Sinclair said sometimes imagined that after the show there'd be discussions among the panelists, with the others saying to him, "You shouldn't have said that." According to Betty Kennedy, that simply didn't happen. "Everyone on the panel respected the others as professionals. People would say to me, 'Doesn't Gordon Sinclair make you cringe?' I'd say, 'No, I have no need to apologize for Gordon. He doesn't embarrass me, he's a big boy, responsible for himself.'"

It was tempting sometimes for Fred Davis, having watched somebody being dismembered by Sinclair, to say something that would take the edge off. Once, in the show's first year, he did apologize for something Sinclair had said. Sinclair let it go that night, but a week later in the make-up room he blasted Davis, who fought back, and they had a major row, even though, as Davis said later, "I knew I was wrong. It wasn't my role to apologize for anyone."

They patched it up quickly. From then on Davis would defuse any touchy situations in his own way, such as by thanking some thoroughly battered guest for being such a good sport. One guest needing such ministrations was the Rev. Rolf McPherson, Aimee Semple McPherson's son. Sinclair set him up by asking whether his mother ever drank.

Rolf said, "No, never."

"Well, I've got news for you," Sinclair snapped. "Over the years, your mum and I split many a jar together."

Aimee's loyal son was so angry that, as Sinclair wrote, "He wanted to throw a punch at me after the show." Davis smooth-talked him out of it. A later protest from a lawyer engaged by Aimee's son came to nothing.

And sometimes Sinclair could bring a laugh out of a very unpromising situation, such as he did when one guest, a churchman, was going on about the difficulty of discussing the ethics of sex when the only way to talk to many people was to use their own four-letter words. To this Sinclair interjected blandly, "How about a three-letter word, then? Lay."

His drinking, which had been behind many Sinclair family stresses, he never allowed to impinge on the show's effectiveness.

"Quite often Gordon would arrive having consumed a bottle of champagne," Pierre Berton said.

> But it didn't hurt his performance. I think it even helped—it made him a little zesty. The one time I saw him in bad shape, it wasn't a *Front Page* thing. We were in Vancouver for the ACTRA awards, and Gordon was supposed to present the Gordon Sinclair trophy. A couple of guys got to him, "Come on and have a drink, Gordon," and he went. He came to rehearsal [for the awards show] and he was really out of it. I took him by the arm, he didn't know where the hotel was, and I took him there and got him to bed and I said, "Now, Gordon, are you going to turn up?"
>
> "Yeah," he said. "I'll be there."
>
> But he never turned up. I knew he wouldn't. Somebody else presented the award.

237

Late in the 1970s he often turned down invitations of a purely social nature, pleading difficulties at home that were very real.

For some years, by then, he and Gladys had had no live-in help, although her eyesight and ability to move around were severely restricted. After he turned over his ten-to-six newscast to Bob Hesketh in 1976, he felt he had to go home around four or so to handle any shopping required and to serve the evening meal. The actual preparation of the meal would have been done in advance by a long-time family employee, Gladys Chamberlain. She came each morning to handle housework and do some food preparation before leaving in mid-afternoon. A woman Sinclair had brought from Germany as live-in help in the early 1930s, Frieda Schweizer, had left to be married, becoming Frieda York. Late in Sinclair's life, by then a widow, she returned to the Sinclair home for a few years, nominally as a companion but also in effect as help. She died in the early 1980s.

At CFRB, Sinclair's news-making eruptions became less frequent. But while the fire was sometimes missing, his normal working habits were largely unchanged. He would arrive in mid-morning with his news partly done. He was usually ahead in *Let's Be Personal*s. These sometimes would be updates of items he'd used years earlier—such prospects were kept in a file labelled "Possible repeats". Sometimes he'd write a fresh one, if it was on a particularly topical issue.

On mornings when he felt unable to work, he'd call in, sometimes with very little notice, and Bob Hesketh would receive a call at 9 a.m. or later that he was needed right away to do the noon news. But most days Sinclair would function as usual, writing and delivering his two morning shows, going for lunch and a drink or two, leaving his secretary to field the phone calls that always followed controversial items. In mid-afternoon he'd record his *Show Business* piece, which would precede the late-afternoon news, and then he would drive home about 4 p.m. He was always a very organized worker. At the end of a day he'd either have handled everything or thrown it away, and his desk would be clear.

For a man with such a reputation for chasing the buck, he had a surprisingly mild way of negotiating contracts. Don Hartford, CFRB general manager and later president, recalled that this was always an amicable discussion. Of course, Sinclair being Sinclair, he didn't use an agent. It would have gone against the grain on two counts: first, he didn't want anyone else taking a cut of his pay; second, his pride in handling finances precluded his asking for help.

As a result, he wasn't the highest-paid radio news personality in the city, getting about $100,000 a year at his peak. At one time Berton, doing daily three-minute stints for radio station CKEY, got more than Sinclair did for his whole day's work at CFRB. "In retrospect," Don Hartford said in a 1986 interview, "we never paid him enough."

Bill Hall, who became general manager in 1978, recalled similarly friendly negotiations.

> Each time we talked contract, at the start he'd say that he didn't know how much longer we'd want him to work, that maybe he was losing his touch and maybe he should quit. I'd say we wanted him, for sure, and he'd say something like, "If you think I'm slipping any time, I want you to tell me. I don't want to be the last to know," and I'd say okay. Then he'd say, well, if he was staying he thought he should get more money and I'd agree. I'd ask what he had in mind and he'd say he'd like to hear what I thought. When I'd tell him he'd say, "Gee, you really want to pay me that?" and I'd say sure, and that would be it. I'd put it in writing a day or two later and when the first pay arrived with the raise in it, he'd call and thank me.

However, he was partly responsible for getting the pay up for *Front Page* regulars in the middle 1970s. Berton, as he put it himself,

> formed a little union of Gordon and Betty and Freddy

and me, but actually it started because of Gordon. He was always interested in ratings and everything else about the show. One time he found out what the CBC was charging for the commercials. We found that the CBC was making a million or more a year from *Front Page*, so I talked to the others and said, "Let's get some more money." We got it up a little year by year. At the end he was making about $2,000 a show.

In the show's first thirteen-week summer run, the pay per show had been $60.

By 1979, a "grand old man" atmosphere began to grow up around Sinclair. He reported that letters calling him a son-of-a-bitch had dropped 19¾ per cent. The City of Toronto gave him its Award of Merit. At CFRB they were planning a big party for his eightieth birthday, a year away. Suddenly someone thought, Will he still be here? The plans were switched to his seventy-ninth.

For this event the station promoted, with all the means at its disposal—which were plenty—a June 3 birthday party to be held on the street outside the radio station at the corner of Yonge and St. Clair. The mayor, the Metro-chairman, and other biggies were on hand, along with the police pipe band. The street signs were changed to read "Young and Sinclair", and a crowd estimated at 5,000 gathered for the kickoff at 12 noon, as soon as Sinclair was off the air. Besides the usual speeches, the station management presented their very emotional birthday boy with a new contract, which didn't specify salary, but guaranteed him employment for another six years, until he was eighty-five.

A few weeks later a letter arrived from Esmond Butler at Government House in Ottawa saying, "As of today, you have been appointed an Officer of the Order of Canada." Invited to bring along a guest to the investiture a few months later, he chose his grandson, Jim, Don's son, who was to drive to Ottawa from Queen's University in Kingston, where he was studying. When the time came for the investiture in early November, Sinclair was unwell, recovering from an illness, so Don Johnston also accompanied him. A photo of Sinclair in his grandfather's kilt in the Sinclair clan tartan, receiving his Order of Canada from Governor General Ed Schreyer, was carried in many newspapers. To Sinclair, his Order of Canada was the greatest honour of his life.

Two weeks after that investiture, with the United States in an uproar over American hostages being held in its embassy in Iran, he wrote another piece praising the Americans and sympathizing with their new ordeal. It was recorded, and in a few weeks came out on the flip side of the original (which, after selling many millions, had been out of stock for years). The new one also was sold commercially, orders being filled for U.S. radio stations that were again faced with a need for national reassurance. Over the years Sinclair had said that if he'd known the original "Americans" piece was going to make so much money, he would have worked out some kind of a split, such as 25 per cent to the Red Cross and the rest for him. Live and learn. This time Sinclair would get his own royalties.

In a 1979 letter to his son Gord there was, among other things, an acknowledgement of his mellowed attitude to Gord, who, as Sinclair had confessed to one interviewer, "now makes more money than I do."

The letter made a joking play on the fact that, back in 1900, his father, Sandy Sinclair, had registered his name as Allan Gordon Sinclair, making Allan his legal first name. The Alfie mentioned in the letter was the Sinclair dog of the time. Even though the letter's general tone is cheerful enough, the last line is more purely Sinclair.

The letter ran:

> Dear Gord;
> I went over to London [Ontario] to see a play because the play was supposed to present full front female nudity and I wondered if London would be ready for that. Turned out there was no nudity, male or female, front or side.

Misleading publicity.

My expenses were $75.50 but since this cheque is made out to Gordon Sinclair and I'm Allan Sinclair you use it for a dinner with Linda on your birthday.

If $75.50 doesn't cover it, bill me.

We—your mother, Alfie and me—are slowly falling apart due to age.

Alfie is the only one, so far, who shits on the floor.

Salut;

(signed) Dad.

CHAPTER SIXTEEN

THE LAST THREE YEARS

"It's corny, but true, to say I'm glad to be back. I don't have the temperament for idleness."
—On returning to work after a heart attack, September 1, 1981.

Sinclair started his usual summer vacation on July 10, 1981, early in his eighty-second year. Nineteen days later he recorded in his cabin's log-book that for all that time the weather had been gorgeous but the fishing bad; he'd caught only one "decent" bass. Another Muskoka note was that old friend Eddie Mortimer at Gravenhurst had died in his eighty-fifth year. Sinclair missed him. Gerry Dunn had a bad leg and couldn't get in his usual golf. There'd been a fire on Sinclair's boat, the *Ten to Twelve*, but the five passengers ("who didn't include me") put it out with water. Sinclair was grateful that they'd managed without using the fire extinguishers, which tend to damage a motor, or so he thought. Inevitably, when the topic was his beloved *Ten to Twelve*, someone recalled the time that Don, attempting to repair its steering mechanism, hooked things up backwards. Although Don and his father had their deep differences, this was commonly believed to have been a mistake. Taking a guest for a run, Sinclair zoomed out from the boathouse in great style, until he spun the wheel to the right and the boat turned left.

After the nineteen beautiful days, he was due back at

work. Gladys, in her eighty-fourth year, crippled, nearly blind, her hearing impaired, and with a mastectomy not many months behind her, was helped into the car and, with Sinclair driving, they headed for the city in a downpour. The rain made him tense. "When heavy trucks passed I couldn't see and was afraid to stop." He was tense for another reason as well. Pat Morse had been his secretary since the late 1960s. Now, in a dispute with management over pay and duties that had boiled up while he was on holiday, she had told him she was quitting.

He had been home a short time when severe chest pains began. He did nothing until the second wave of pain hit, then phoned an ambulance. Firemen with oxygen arrived as well. At Queensway Hospital he was hurried into intensive care, where Dr. Arvi Perl's diagnosis was that there'd been no coronary, Sinclair's greatest fear, but that there had been was heart failure because of excessive fluid in the heart area. Dr. Bruce Fenton, who had arrived from his own vacation in Muskoka, concurred. At CFRB, fill-in arrangements were made for the indefinite future, while at the hospital the switchboard was busy telling callers how he was.

He was kept in intensive care for five days, during which time the fluid was drained away. As Sinclair said, "During lonely nights when I was wired to a wavering heart-beat, trying to tuck a cold urinal between my legs, trying to roll over without entangling coloured wires, I realized I was a pretty old guy." He found those days a bore, except for the ever-changing guard of nurses, one with "gorgeous green eyes", whom he said he embarrassed in some way, and another "a merry black girl who bathed me, all of me." But much of the time he was filled with gloomy thoughts that this might be the end of his working life.

Family and friends had been hearing such prophecies for many years, but "the doctors would hear none of this pessimism." Less than three weeks later he was home, and there, for the thirty-ninth anniversary of his first CFRB broadcast, he taped a *Let's Be Personal* for August 20. He told his audience he had lost weight but had a strong appetite and was doing a spot of walking each day. He wasn't ready to go back to work but "wanted to get this broadcast in because it marks the beginning of my fortieth year at CFRB."

In another week he felt well enough to travel to Muskoka for the wedding of his granddaughter Connie, Gord's daughter, who worked in radio. Sinclair, head of the clan, was happy that Connie, who had been in love with Muskoka since childhood, had chosen the little church at Bannockburn for her wedding to Sudbury-born Michel Fortin. Michel was with an advertising agency—"both being fluently bilingual and Michel handy with tools, a good lad to have around." The wedding brought a good deal of family palavering, comfort, and joy, not to mention some wry memories of not so long ago (in terms of long lifetimes) when the "old man", as the family called him now, furiously ordered the father of the bride, the mother of the bride, and the pretty little girl who was to become the bride, to be gone, right now, to get out of the cottage, over one of the multitude of picayune disagreements that had scarred Sinclair's relationship with his oldest son.

Three days after the wedding Sinclair was back at work full-time. Again proposals were made by news director Don Johnston and others who wished to lighten his load.

Why not let us organize a setup that'll let you do your broadcasts from home?

No!

But jeez, Sinc, that drive to work and back every day through all that traffic on St. Clair, stockyards and all! If you don't want to tape at home, we could have someone drive you here and back, the company driver or a limousine service.

When the day comes that I can't drive my own car, get myself to work, then I'm not fit to come to work and should quit.

CFRB concern about his driving remained very real. One morning in the building's underground garage, he scratched the whole side of a new Thunderbird on a post. It would be embarrassing all round if he got into an accident, especially a serious one. Beginning at the age of eighty, he'd had to take a driving test every year and had always passed, but that didn't entirely reassure the worriers..

Nevertheless, the daily routine he resumed, including driving himself to work, was exactly as usual. He started by listening to the 7 a.m. radio news and making notes as he went along; then he'd watch the U.S. news on television, read the Toronto morning papers and the *New York Times*, and eat breakfast. By about 8:30 he'd walk into his smallish den off the main entrance hall, next to his own bathroom, and start transforming his notes and observations into news items. He might also write *Show Business* or *Let's Be Personal*. His typing was fast and two-fingered, featuring careless spelling and bizarre spacing. The spaces looked as if he idly tapped the spacebar a few times any time he had to stop and think. When an item was finished, he'd scribble amendments in ballpoint. When he had finished what he could do at home, he'd clean up, make a final bathroom stop to avoid being caught in traffic with his prostate condition that had plagued him in later years flashing flood warnings, walk outside, maybe check the flower beds, maybe give the dogs a little run, and head for work.

His natural newsman's attention to U.S. news sometimes had a personal cast. Ronald Reagan's first foreign trip after his inauguration in January 1981 had been to Ottawa. On his arrival he mentioned Sinclair's 1973 "Americans" broadcast, saying he had the record at his ranch and would very much like to meet the man who had written it. The Prime Minister's Office immediately called Sinclair.

In the recollection of Don Hartford,

> He came down the hall and said, "Don, I just got this telephone call from Ottawa", told me what it was about, and asked, "What do you think?" I said, "Well, if the President of the United States and the Prime Minister of Canada want you to go to Ottawa, I'll tell

you what I think you should do—go to Ottawa." We had a jet we could use, so we phoned to get it rolled out and Sinclair, Don Johnston, and I, just the three of us, flew to Ottawa.

It was treated as really something, a human-interest footnote to the main story, the President wanting to meet this old guy that sometimes Canadians just took for granted as part of the scenery. There were television crews at the airport, people being moved out of hotel rooms to make space for us. Sinc was in his element.

After he and Reagan were introduced, they chatted a couple of times, including a bit of kidding about ages, "he the oldest president at inauguration, me the oldest broadcaster in Canada."

At the state dinner most of those present were in couples, but among the singles were Sinclair and Jim Brady, the President's press secretary. The two of them "sat at a table where the other guests were French-speaking. So Brady and I got along well, talking about things that were more personal than official, little knowing that in a few months Brady would be shot down in an assassination attempt on the President."

Jim Brady's life, and his chances of ever returning to normal, hung in the balance long after the President was out of danger. And when Sinclair came on the air with the story, he had that something extra, something personal, from the time he'd spent with Jim Brady.

After his summer heart attack, Sinclair showed in various ways, some of them quite minor, a growing concern about his own mortality.

In November he wrote to his sons saying that with Christmas coming up, he and Gladys didn't want Christmas gifts of any permanence. The possessions they had accumulated over fifty-five years of marriage, forty-seven years in the same house, were enough, even too much. Soap, shaving lotions, wine, handkerchiefs, or candy would do fine for him, he wrote; cosmetics and shortbreads or fancy biscuits for Gladys. "But nothing useful, or to be stored in a cupboard. Pass it on to the grandchildren."

There was also the larger question about what was to become of the house and the cottage. He had said to friends, "Sometimes I wonder who'll live in the house." He put out hints. In many families, applications for consideration as future owners of such attractive real estate would have come quickly. But not among the Sinclairs.

So when Sinclair intimated that he would like to know what his heirs had in mind about those properties, which he treasured as the tangible parts of his legacy, there was no sign that the question had even been heard. There was certainly no answer.

This could have been due to wariness, memories of incidents from the past in which an expressed preference suddenly became a bargaining chip (such as Don's disagreement with his father at dinner Thursday causing withdrawal of permission to use the car Friday).

"I think he really would have been pleased if somebody had told him what they wanted," Don said later. "As far as I know, nobody did."

The disruption at the office had been settled by then. Pat Morse, who, over the years, had shown a real talent for organizing Sinclair's output and handling letters and calls that would have snowed him under, was gone. Millie Moriak, who had worked in the CFRB newsroom since the middle 1970s after considerable experience at radio stations CHUM and CKEY, had filled in as Sinclair's secretary earlier when Pat Morse had been away ill. During that fill-in period there had been stresses. This was caused partly by one Sinclair characteristic that had withstood the test of time—his habit of baiting women. Through long practice, Pat Morse had worked out ways of handling his more extravagant sallies with equanimity. But a combination of Millie Moriak's personality (volatile), and the fact that during Pat Morse's absence she had taken on the extra workload of the Sinclair secretaryship while keeping up her regular newsroom work, built up to a flash-point.

One trouble, she recalled, was that "I was over-awed by Gordon, I had admired him for so long. But there I would be among all those men and he would come over to my desk and say something really raw that everybody could hear and would just leave me dumbfounded and speechless. I would go home [to the nearby apartment where she lived with her teen-aged son] in a fury. I thought, 'This just can't go on.' But I still found him too formidable to discuss it with him face to face. . . ."

What she did instead was write a memo, in Gordon's own language. Before giving it to him she had copies made for the station manager, the news director, and others. Don Johnston called her in "and pleaded with me not to send it to Gordon, that he would be very hurt, that he was a vulnerable man, very sensitive. I said I was vulnerable too, and sensitive, and had to have it in writing to set the record straight, what I was putting up with."

When Sinclair read the memo, he didn't say a word to anyone but put it on the bulletin board with the note "We get letters." The following day he didn't come to work or call in, and Millie stewed that maybe Don Johnston had been right, she had knocked the ground out from under him.

On the second day she put a rose on his desk, along with a note saying she wasn't apologizing, but that the friction between them was perhaps an unfortunate misunderstanding that she hoped could be cleared up. He accepted the rose, read the note, and invited her out for a drink. They talked, and "we were just fast friends for ever more after that. And I was so ashamed of myself after I really got to know Gordon. He had a barnyard edge to his humour. I came to find he was often that way with women. It might have been his way of flirting."

After that outburst, during which the Moriak memo was photo-copied by others and circulated among radio people from Montreal to Vancouver (no copy is known to exist now), Pat Morse came back to work for a short time before

Sinclair's 1981 heart attack, but felt adamantly that she should be getting more money. The crisis might have been smoothed out if Sinclair had been around to do it, but by the time he returned from his vacation and his heart attack it was irrevocable. Sinclair wrote Pat Morse a fulsome recommendation a few months later. Attached to it was a note that read, in part, "Hope it helps. No finger-wagging, but you should not have quit on impulse."

Meanwhile, fireworks over, Millie Moriak got on with the job. Many memos exchanged between them in the next few years established a sound working relationship, which included his recognition that she had a mind of her own.

Once he gave her an item to retype about the possibility that at least some of many rape charges that came to court were trumped up, for spite or other reasons. The subject had been discussed between them. Along with his piece was a note: "MM. I rewrote this item a couple of times to try and make it acceptable and may have failed. When you are typing it don't do your thing as a feminist, but as mother of a lad who could be falsely accused of rape."

During the few years they worked together, Millie Moriak came full circle from the angry outburst she had put on paper. Her realization of how emotional he was, how important it was to try to shield him from sudden shocks, came when long-time Toronto radio personality Joe Morgan died. Sinclair was out to lunch. As he was coming in, another broadcaster, Bob McAdorey, phoned to speak to him about Joe Morgan's death. He immediately took the phone, so Millie didn't have a chance to prepare him. When he found that he'd been called to answer a question about a friend's death that he hadn't known about until that instant, the shock was so great that he could scarely speak for weeping. She realized then, as others had discovered before her, that "he was very, very open about his feelings, whether it was anger or sadness or whatever."

And open he was, about everything, in spades. About that time he confided to Don Hartford rather despondently that he "couldn't get it up any more," didn't have any sex life at all. But one day, when he was eighty-three, he went out for his usual walk after his noon news, and when he returned he was cheerful, grinning, exuding bonhomie.

"Well!" Millie Moriak said. "You look as if you've been having a good time!"

He spread his arms wide. "I really did! I got laid!" He bustled away, chuckling.

Approximately the same jubilance was seen, for the same reason, on another occasion. Early one evening, Pierre Berton was driving away from the Westbury Hotel. As he pulled into the street, there was a tapping at his side window. He looked up, saw who was tapping, and wound down the window to hear Sinclair burst out with the glad tidings that he obviously couldn't bear to keep to himself. Laughingly, Berton congratulated him. In neither case did Sinclair elaborate.

By now, the situation at home was causing increased concern among his colleagues at CFRB. He enjoyed going out, but because of his home duties he rarely could accept any of the many invitations he received. Even when someone was living in, they naturally wanted days off, and on weekends, when he and Gladys usually were alone, he cooked the meals. Being so homebound contributed to his depressions. When he didn't feel well enough to come to work, he would stay home, and, in Don Johnston's opinion, this made the situation worse, because when he stayed home, it was with an invalid wife and the regular help—not only "a houseful of women", but a house in which he had little stimulation that might bring him out of his despondency.

"The longer he was home, the more depressed and frustrated he would get, so that when Betty Kennedy went out, or Millie and I went out, our main aim would be to get him to set a date to come back, and then he'd say, 'Do you really want me to come back?'"

Apparently Gladys thought his state of mind was related to job insecurity which she felt might be real. During one visit, when Don Johnston and Millie Moriak were leaving,

Gladys asked them anxiously, "You think the station will have him back?" Another time she asked Don Johnston, "Has he been a bad boy again? He's been acting up like he's going to be fired, like you're going to fire him." Johnston reassured her, but obviously there was little or no reassurance available in the Sinclair household, his gloom so intense and misunderstood that it infected everybody in the house. As visitors mentioned later, one major trouble was that there was no one always around to say, "Don't be silly, he isn't just some guy who can be laid off, or a kid in trouble because he's acting up."

For the twenty-four years that Bob Hesketh had functioned as Sinclair's main understudy, his contract (until Bill Hall changed it to make Hesketh more his own man) specified that he was to be on hand when Sinclair was absent. They had been in regular contact at the office but not outside of it. Sinclair had been in Hesketh's home once; Hesketh had never been in his, although sometimes they would sit in Sinclair's office and talk.

Hesketh never thought that Sinclair felt threatened by him as a stand-in.

> His ego would overcome that, most of the time, but in the last few years sometimes he'd get quite emotional, I guess because of his tough home situation, Gladys's condition and all the rest. One day he cried—he cried quite easily in those days—and said, "I hear you want me out of here."
>
> And I said, "Not particularly. I gave up wanting you out of here ten years ago. If you're not gonna quit, you're not gonna quit." And he said, "You know, if I quit here I'm gonna die." And that seemed true, because that was what he was doing. CFRB and *Front Page Challenge* were what kept him alive. And yet for a long time my life was predicated on what Sinclair wanted to do, and in the long run it didn't matter anyway.

His lack of really close friends all through his life left him with very few who could help when his spirits needed a boost. Still, there were some, although not close friends, who figured prominently enough that he was always "on" in their presence. Occasionally he would meet Ruth Atkinson Hindmarsh, the widow of his original guru at the *Star*. In her nineties, Mrs. Hindmarsh was still going regularly to her office in the *Toronto Star* building as head of the Atkinson Foundation. "I always had a radio near by for his broadcast when Gordon was alive," she said in a 1986 interview, not long before her ninety-fourth birthday, "I didn't want to miss it." At her ninetieth birthday party at a daughter's home, he turned up carrying one long-stemmed rose for her.

Ontario Lieutenant-Governor Pauline McGibbon was another favourite; he called her "Governor", kept his listeners informed on her travels (not many in the news media did), and attended many of her receptions and her dinners for holders of the Order of Canada. Her successor, John Black Aird, made a habit of dropping in on Sinclair at CFRB every few weeks. Aird credited Sinclair with helping him be effective in many speeches he had to make representing the Queen. "At first I wasn't really used to speaking to people I didn't know, and I told him that. He's the one who taught me to bone up in advance for every audience, find out what they stood for, not to say anything if I didn't know the subject. He gave me a real lesson in communicating, how to read an audience and find a rapport."

Sinclair always attended the Lieutenant-Governor's annual New Year's Day levees. Aird noted, as did others, that "he didn't ever mix and join in groups the way others did, but stood alone all evening, and observed."

Occasionally he went to the races with Doris for major events at Woodbine racetrack, fending off friends who were always trying to get him to bet more than two dollars per race. Other days he might go with Wally Crouter for merry lunches in the Woodbine dining-room, usually in company with Bruce Walker, publicity director for the Jockey Club. This resulted in one incident that became a standing joke among Sinclair, Crouter, and Walker.

Sinclair's prostate trouble usually didn't bother him as

long as he was sitting down. Near the end of one cheerful occasion, in which there had been much champagne and laughter, he got up to go to the bathroom but didn't quite make it.

"When he came back, he had his jacket off and was carrying it in front of him, sort of hiding the front of his pants," Crouter said. "I said, 'What the hell, Sinc, it's not so hot in here that you have to take your jacket off.'

"He was laughing, but he said, 'Wally, I peed my pants!'"

He held his jacket up to show the damage, and Crouter said instantly, "So okay, we'll wait until they dry!" Which they did, with the conversation becoming even merrier as a result.

Late in 1982, a capable full-time housekeeper, Olive Nugent, was found. This helped as he was bothered by arthritis in both knees, which caused unsteadiness at times. At Christmas all the family gathered, sons and wives and grandchildren. In his annual *Let's Be Personal* review of the year just past, one item was that his dog Maybelle, "black as the inside of a bruised crow", was overweight and on a diet, but "continues her daily routine of nosing her way into my bedroom at dawn, drinking from the toilet bowl, then licking my face until I waken."

In the summer of 1983, a man telephoned Sinclair at the cottage to say, "Uncle Archie is celebrating his seventy-seventh birthday today and he wonders if you'd like to go to mass with him?" Sinclair replied that he didn't have an Uncle Archie, but the call turned out to be on the level. To some people, Archbishop Philip Pocock, once head of the Toronto Roman Catholic diocese, was always Uncle Archie. Sinclair had known him for many years. Sometimes they had gone fishing together—as unlikely a pair as one could imagine. "I've had my reward in getting to know a good man," Sinclair would claim. So he said okay, he'd go to mass.

The caller picked him up by boat. It was, Sinclair said, his first mass, except for funerals, and it was celebrated at the little white church of St. Anne's at Whiteside on the mainland. The church was packed, with some standing in the doorways, and the mass was "one of those serene occasions of tranquillity that come only now and again. In my mind I'd associated the mass with solemnity and dark colours but the vestments on this occasion were apple green and the congregation in brilliant summer cottons gave the appearance of a picnic."

Later in 1983 he worked steadily until the end of November, his *Let's Be Personals* covering such disparate topics as the poem "In Flanders Fields" by Colonel John McCrae; the career of Louis "Satchmo" Armstrong, whom he'd listened to and interviewed at Gerry Dunn's Pavilion in Bala; questions of money and God; mystery writer John LeCarré; grizzly bears; the difficulty of making money by investing in Broadway shows; the time he had tried to run away with a circus when he was a boy; and the thorny question of garbage pick-ups in Etobicoke, where he lived—recalling that when he and Gladys first had the house there'd been no garbage pick-up, so they'd burned it or thrown it in ditches.

His last working day in 1983 was December 5. He was home ill for the rest of the month, much of it spent in bed. One day just before Christmas, when Doris Loach had realized from a phone conversation that he was feeling very down, she visited him there. Gladys's long ban on her presence in the Sinclair home had ended more or less by default. In 1981, on retiring from her nearly fifty years in the business world, much of that as a credit executive, Doris had contracted to work part-time for another three years. Her working days were Monday, Tuesday, and Wednesday. From then on, she and Sinclair met at least once a week for lunch on her free days. One day in 1981 he'd asked her to come home with him to straighten out some of his papers. When she walked in, Gladys did not recognize her. Sinclair said, "Come on, Gladys, you remember Doris Loach."

Early in 1983, with income-tax time looming, he'd sent the CFRB car for Doris and they spent a long weekend in a suite at the Sheraton Centre in downtown Toronto. By day

Doris sorted through dozens of unopened envelopes, some containing cheques, getting his financial statements organized. In the evenings they would wine and dine in good restaurants, usually on seafood, which they both loved.

When she arrived to see Gordon during his down period just before Christmas of 1983, she hung up her coat and said she was going upstairs to see him. Gladys came with her to his bedroom, gamely negotiating the steps with her walker, perhaps still wanting to keep an eye on them.

Sinclair's December 1983 depression-cum-illness lasted, as usual, through Christmas and the New Year's holiday. On January 3 he was back at work. A few of his *Let's Be Personal*s through January, February, and March were repeats, with a few update sentences, but almost all were new, including one about spending an hour or two in a Yonge Street bar, where he sat in a corner and simply watched the apparent aimlessness of those who came and went; a keenly observed low-key piece, as good as any he could have done, ever. He took a week off near the end of March, prolonged it another week because of illness, returned for two days, then missed nineteen days, mostly bedridden, depressed, and worrying about his failing strength. That period ended soon after the visit from Betty Kennedy mentioned earlier.

By Good Friday, April 20, he was planning his return to work for the following Tuesday. On that day, he produced a *Let's Be Personal* on the subject of finding himself short of cash, then trying to find a bank that was open on the Easter holiday weekend.

On each of the following three weekends he took Mondays off to cut down his workload. On Thursday, May 10, he had lunch with Doris for what turned out to be the last time they saw one another. They had a cheerful time. On Mother's Day, May 13, some of the family dropped in to see the old people. Grandson Michael Sinclair, Jack and Pat's son, who works in films, was among those present. To Michael, his grandfather was different on that day than he had been on other such visits.

256

"You know, you'd come in and be there for five minutes and he'd say, 'Don't feel obliged to stay long.' In other words he was trying to get rid of you. But when we came down this Mother's Day, he wanted us to stay for a long time."

In retrospect, Michael's insight was part of a *feeling* compounded by several unrelated impressions. Many people had noticed changes in him. His handwriting had suddenly gone shaky, tending to trail off a page. He had stopped writing in the log-book at the cabin, his last entry being: "I hope someone will keep this up." And he had actually had friendly talks with his sons.

In addition, he had also seemed much more considerate—one relative even used the word "kindly"—towards Gladys, whose memory by now was a sometime thing, and who had confided to her son Jack not long before that one of her regrets in life was that she hadn't become a milliner, which had been her ambition before meeting Gordon.

The day after Mother's Day, Sinclair decided to go for his 1984 driving test. He passed, and the next noon told his listeners engagingly about how polite and considerate the examiners had been "to an old man in scruffy clothes with no appointment".

That was his *Let's Be Personal* for Tuesday, May 15. He followed it with his ten-to-twelve news and the chat with Betty Kennedy about taping two *Front Page Challenge*s the next day.

Millie Moriak gave him a note saying he was invited to a Meals on Wheels luncheon at City Hall on June 5. He'd once been chairman of the organization. "They want to present you with a plaque," her note said, and he scribbled on bottom, "Why not? First date of my 85th year."

Another note asked, "Could you do a *Let's Discuss It* with Larry Grossman [then Ontario treasurer] Thursday, 12 noon?" He wrote on the bottom, "OK."

Then he went out for lunch and a drink, and came back to tape his *Show Business*, which was to be aired at 5:45. He liked that show especially. It took him back to his days as

257

Variety's Toronto stringer. Almost forever, it seemed, he'd been extolling the merits and exposing the weak spots of actors and actresses, other critics, films, plays, concerts, night-club acts—the whole showbiz ball of wax.

After the taping, somewhere between three and four, he left the office for home.

CHAPTER SEVENTEEN

THE END

"I shall miss you"
—Letter from a listener.

At 5:45 p.m. on May 15, 1984, CFRB played the opening bars of "There's No Business Like Show Business", to introduce Sinclair's show. This was followed by the sponsor's message and then Sinclair's familiar voice in the show he'd taped early in the afternoon, the latest edition of his jaunty five-a-week programs about show business. At that moment, the owner of the voice was far from jaunty, but could not have known how desperately deep was the trouble he was in. Arriving home, he'd found there was shopping to be done. He and Olive Nugent, the housekeeper, were heading for the supermarket when it suddenly became urgent for him to find a bathroom. He wheeled into the parking-lot of a restaurant he knew, left the car, and hurried inside. On the stairs to the washroom he lived the last conscious seconds of his life.

When restaurant staff saw he had fallen and was lying motionless, they ran to help. Getting no response and finding no heartbeat, they made an immediate call to Metro's emergency number, which was linked to fire departments, ambulance services, and the police. After a few minutes, the housekeeper, waiting outside, thought of his poor health. Hadn't he been gone uncommonly long? Hadn't she better check? She entered the restaurant to find Sinclair unconscious, with no signs of life, and she was there when an ambulance arrived, along with an emergency vehicle from the Etobicoke fire department. The firemen, carrying an inhalator and oxygen, got his heart started again, and the oxygen was continued as the ambulance, sirens wailing, sped away.

A few minutes later, two telephone calls arrived almost simultaneously in Don Johnston's office at CFRB. One was from Bill Walker, another CFRB man. Walker's son, who worked at radio station CJCL, had heard from a friend in the ambulance service about a call involving Gordon Sinclair. The other caller, name unknown, said the Etobicoke fire department had had an inhalator call for Gordon Sinclair. This caller gave the name of the restaurant. Johnston grabbed the phone book, found the restaurant number, and was told, yes, Sinclair had collapsed there and had been taken to Queensway Hospital.

During Sinclair's 1981 bout with heart congestion, he'd been in Queensway. Johnston knew a member of the hospital administration, Hilda Maguire, because she had worked closely with CFRB then on reporting Sinclair's condition to people who called. Now she was able to confirm that he was there, had suffered cardiac arrest, was still unconscious, and that his condition was serious.

Johnston wrote a brief bulletin and sent it to air, then got on the phone to others in the station's management and to the two Sinclair sons, Don and Jack, who lived in the Toronto area. As Gord in Montreal had made a habit of calling one of his brothers every week, they knew he was in Europe on vacation. They would get in touch with him.

Johnston worked rapidly to organize everything that he could possibly anticipate for the night to come, "knowing by then from what the hospital told me that it would be sort of a death watch." Then he went to the hospital. Don and Jack, their wives, and some other members of the family were there. In France, Gord was working on catching the first flight back.

Johnston found that family members on hand were already giving thought to a grim possibility. Sinclair was being kept alive through life-support systems. He had told them in the past, specifically in a letter to Don ten years earlier, that if he ever fell into a condition that offered no hope, they were not to keep him living by artificial means.

It was the following day before Doris Loach knew. A friend phoned first that he had had a heart attack, then Millie Moriak with news of how grave his condition was. That day newspapers were giving front-page coverage to his collapse, and broadcasters monitored his condition every few hours. The hospital's bulletins held out little or no hope. With death seemingly imminent, at CFRB many of his old tapes were being played and portions were selected to be linked by Torben Wittrup's commentary into a tribute that would be the station's obituary. These warm reminiscences and segments from past broadcasts combined to emphasize in the best way possible, by the echo of his own former vigour with words and ideas, that never again would this cocky, opinionated, totally unquiet Canadian strut into the newsroom on otherwise dull mornings and crow, "Never fear, Sinclair's here!" The tape, running more than thirty minutes, was to be held for the final word.

Around noon on May 17, about forty-two hours after the attack, Don Sinclair called Johnston. As he spoke, he was so broken up that, Johnston said, "I knew it was him, but that's all." The call was to say that, in consultation with the hospital's specialists, the family had made the decision that the leader of the clan had instructed them to make.

A CFRB news bulletin minutes later reported that Sinclair was deeply comatose, having suffered "severe and irreversible damage to the central nervous system", and that the family, in consultation with Dr. L. E. Gotham Clements, a specialist in internal medicine, had decided to discontinue life support.

That support was withdrawn at 2 p.m. Four hours later, precisely at the usual sign-off time for the ten-to-six evening newscast that Sinclair had given for so many years, he died.

Two days earlier, at the time of the first attack, Jack and

Pat Sinclair, who lived with their family north of the city at King, Ontario, had moved into the Sinclair home to be closer to the hospital. The rest of the family were there with Gladys as well when death came. Gladys, then five weeks away from her eighty-sixth birthday, had been told, but it was not certain that she fully understood. Lists were made of people who should be notified and invited to the funeral, which, ten years earlier in a letter to Don, Sinclair had directed should be private.

One name on the call-list was Doris Loach. Pat Sinclair, using the phone in the study, phoned Doris's number "by the hour" she said later, but could get no answer. The reason was that as soon as Doris heard of his death, she left for Gravenhurst and her cottage, which has no telephone. "I didn't want to be around that weekend," she said two years later. "I guess maybe I should have contacted the family, but I didn't. I just didn't. To me it was the end of an era, a large part of my life, and I thought, 'That's it, that's it.'"

It was a week later before she knew that the family had tried to reach her. Gladys Chamberlain phoned her to say that people at the funeral had been asking for her, that she had been on the list to be called, and that when one of the younger generation asked, "Who's Doris Loach?" someone had said she was the girl-friend.

News coverage of Sinclair's death was unparalleled in living memory for anyone short of a prime minister. The *Star*, naturally, did it best, a major front-page photo and story, as well as two full pages inside on his remarkable life and times.

One photo showed him as a young man in a dashing fedora at a typewriter in 1939. Another was taken at the Kashmir-Tibet border post in 1935 at the time he had joined the Yale-Cambridge expedition and showed Sinclair in pith helmet. He appeared in his kilt, receiving his Order of Canada from Governor General Ed Schreyer in 1979, and in a violently checked jacket, leaning out of his new Thunderbird in 1983 (the caption included a quote from a colleague who claimed that once Sinclair had been seen wearing fawn trousers, a purple sports jacket, a pink shirt, a yellow tie, and a green pork-pie hat with a red feather).

The *Star* printed his final *Let's Be Personal* in full, below a reproduction of a Sinclair story from India that had been printed on May 17, 1932, exactly fifty-two years earlier. The story, datelined Delhi, began:

> A hundred thousand Hindu hoodlums ran riot
> through the bazaars and boulevards of India's capital
> today squirting red ink, purple dye and green acid on
> every moving thing to pass their way from Brahmanee
> bulls to camel caravans or ruling rajahs....
>   What's the big idea, you ask. Well, if I were to
> outline the Hindu mythology behind this frenzied
> behavior you'd be disgusted and I'd be jailed.... It
> just proves that anything can happen where women
> wear rings in their noses and cows bed down in hotel
> lobbies....

It was purest Sinclair, complete with children losing their sight because of coloured acid squirted into their eyes from water-pistols, the whole festival of the goddess Vishnu being explained to Sinclair later in the story by the beautiful Maharani of Cooch Behar—who had given Sinclair an elephant that day as a token of her esteem.

He didn't explain then or ever what happened to the elephant, but many years later he had a lively discussion of the events of that day on *Front Page Challenge* with that maharani's grandson.

The *Star* also carried a half-page headed:

TRIBUTES TO SINCLAIR POUR IN FROM FRIENDS AROUND WORLD.

One lengthy message was from the congressman who had first read the text of the "Americans" broadcast into the U.S. Congressional Record. But chief among the others, and representing them all in one way or another, was one from Prime Minister Trudeau that included such words and phrases as true pioneer, irreverence, bluntness, offbeat, enthusiasm for life, not always easy to agree with, never difficult to admire, and, near the end, "I join all Canadians in lamenting the loss of a well-loved citizen who enriched our days and enlivened our evenings. . . ."

The *Globe and Mail*'s national edition included an editorial and devoted more than half a page to an obituary, including a recent picture of Sinclair smiling as if he'd just made a million, the caption reading, "Gordon Allan Sinclair: 'I don't want to hurt anyone's feelings and I never have.'" An arguable point. It also included a line about his scorn for the very idea of heaven or hell: "Asked once what his reaction would be if he found there was an afterlife, he replied, 'I'll say, Sinclair, you're in one hell of a mess.'"

A few days later, under the heading "Farewell to a Cherished Curmudgeon", *Maclean's* chimed in with a full-page assessment, including one of his quotes: "I am not consistent. People in their coffins are consistent."

But if any of the dozens of farewells printed or broadcast across the country could be chosen as most definitive, it was Robert Fulford's carefully considered article in *Saturday Night* in August of that year. It was personal, anecdotal, and warm. Fulford somehow resisted telling his story of Sinclair's interest in Manly Macdonald's standing in the art world. Of everything written about him in death, Sinclair's favourite line probably would have been Fulford's, "On his good days his writing had a rushing sense of wonder that few journalists ever achieve."

For the final goodbyes in Butler's Funeral Chapel on Dundas Street West, only family and friends were present; the only media people were from CFRB and the *Star*. The appropriate and sometimes funny farewell was delivered by tall and spare Dr. Stewart B. East, the retired minister who had founded Islington United Church but had also been chaplain of the 48th Highlanders and knew what a kilt could mean to a man. Mentioning Sinclair's professional scepticisim and professed agnosticism, Dr. East suggested that by then he had probably arrived at the place he thought didn't exist and was saying something like, "Well, Sinclair's here. What are you going to do about it?" Later everyone adjourned to the golf club that had been the Sinclairs' neighbour for fifty years, and over a good bar and food, with Gord Sinclair as host, held an old-fashioned wake with everybody having a drink and remembering the good times.

A few days later in City Hall Square, there was a public service of remembrance with Betty Kennedy, Toronto mayor Art Eggleton, Pierre Berton, Bob Hesketh, Wally Crouter, Lieutenant-Governor John Aird, Ontario premier William Davis, Metro chairman Paul Godfrey, Gord Sinclair, and the Metro Toronto Police Pipe Band. A 48th Highlanders of Canada corporal, Ian Steingazner, piped the "Lament".

Near the end of May a letter of condolence arrived for Gladys, headed The White House, Washington, and signed by Ronald Reagan. The President extended his and Nancy's "heartfelt sympathy", recalled what Sinclair had said about Americans in 1973, and gave the opinion that Sinclair

> really deserves to be considered almost like a citizen of our country because of the depth of his devotion to the ideals of liberty and justice which belong not to the United States alone but to free people everywhere.
>
> Those ideals have lost a valiant champion, but your husband's memory will continue to inspire me and countless others for many years to come. Nancy and I, along with many other Americans, are keeping you and your family in our prayers. God bless you.

Years earlier, on one of Sinclair's birthdays in the 1970s, he had designated his son Don to be executor of his will. A letter setting this out went to Don, with copies to his two brothers and their mother. When Don's son Jim was called to the bar at the end of the 1970s, the will had been rewritten, Sinclair directing that Jim join his father as joint executor. These choices could have been seen as an oblique bow to Sinclair's long-ago, and loudly delivered, advocacy of university educations for his offspring, and for their offspring. Both wills were basically the same, providing that Gladys would have the use of the family properties and estate income for as long as she lived, and that after her death the capital (stocks, bonds, treasury bills, and the appraised value of the cottage and the home) would be split equally among the three sons. There were no bequests to others. The estate thus would not be settled totally as long as Gladys lived. She stayed for a while at home, but because she required twenty-four-hour care, she spent part of the rest of her life in a nursing home.

In her last years she suffered from Alzheimer's disease and sometimes would not recognize her family. She died on February 1, 1987, by which time the estate to be split equally among the three brothers totalled about $3.5 million.

On the first meeting of the brothers after their father's death in 1984, Jack said, with the agreement of the other two, that he and his family would like to have the family home and to buy it from the estate. They sold their home in King and moved on October 1, 1984. Two years later, having made only a few changes, they still had not completely gone through the papers and records and books in Sinclair's study, although they had found one amusing item.

This was a fairly new tape-recorder, containing a tape in which Sinclair was heard from time to time telling Gladys, "I'm going to test this thing now." Then he could be heard saying a few words, followed, after a stretch of blank tape, by an explosive, "I can't make this goddam thing work!" He apparently never did. Jack figured out that after each test message, his father would press Fast Forward instead of Rewind, so would hear nothing but blank tape. He finally gave up.

Use of the cottage on Lake Muskoka also had to be settled. Don and his wife Louise already had their own cottage three miles down the island. Both Jack and Gord expressed interest in the home cottage. During a temporary

266

impasse, they once discussed, briefly, tearing down the existing cottage and building a duplex on the site to accommodate both their families, but no one liked that idea very much. If it had come to a crunch, probably Gord would have had first call on the cottage, but he settled it in his own way.

He and his wife Linda came from Montreal, researched nearby properties for a few days, and bought a well-treed island, complete with a two-storey cottage and boathouse, only a few hundred metres across a channel from where the Sinclairs and in-laws and families had spent so many summers. From Gord and Linda's island they can see the home cottage and Sinclair's old cabin. In summer they drive from Montreal with their family. Connie Sinclair-Fortin and her husband Michel and their family drive there easily from Toronto. Jack and Pat and their part of the clan are just across the passage, while Don and Louise and their family are a five-minute boat ride along the shore.

Connie was the one who took up her grandfather's logbook in accordance with his wish that someone keep making the entries after he was gone. Gord has the gracious old boat that his father enjoyed so much and used at will, no matter what plans had been made by others. It is still called the *Ten to Twelve*, and always will be.

Even for the most uncommon of men, it is sometimes difficult to decide upon an epitaph—or in this case something to serve as an epitaph, even though not carved in stone. While readers will recognize now that with Sinclair what you saw was not precisely what you got, his *persona* to the end was that of Toronto's Cabbagetown: a street-wise guy whose native rough-and-tumble came out in words and ideas. Big house, big cars, a few million bucks—"So what?" the cabbies and barbers and beer-parlour debating societies would ask. "He's still one of us."

Therefore, in Sinclair's case one hesitates to bid him farewell in the well-honed words of some professional, and that categorization fits not only most of his media contemporaries but also, without offence intended, the correspondence secretaries of Prime Minister Trudeau and President Ronald Reagan.

So try this. Not long before Sinclair's death, a Torontonian named George Walling was leaving the area for Victoria, B.C. He made a list of people he felt deserved proper goodbyes, formal and informal. Sinclair was one of them.

"I spent my life within the sound of your voice," he wrote in a letter to Sinclair. "I shall miss that. Acerbic, angry, passionate or sentimental depending on what set you off, you were *always* there, a constant, comfortable reminder that the world was still okay as long as you were popping off at someone or something. More than once I have pounded the steering wheel of my car in disagreement or slowed down because of laughter. I shall miss you."

INDEX

A NOTE ON THE AUTHOR

Scott Young has successfully pursued careers as a writer, broadcaster, and journalist. He won his first National Newspaper Award in 1959, which was followed by other national and international awards. At the same time, he was writing short stories and novels, three of which were translated into Russian. Altogether, Young has written over 35 books. In 1984, he published *Neil and Me*, the biography of his son, one of Canda's most famous rock musicians. His biography of Foster Hewitt entitled *Hello Canada*! (1985) was welcomed by Canadians from coast to coast.

Mr. Young and his wife, writer and editor Margaret Hogan, live on an acreage north of Toronto, where they are often visited by the sons and daughters of their extended and extensive family.